THE PRESENTING PAST

THE CORE OF PSYCHODYNAMIC COUNSELLING AND THERAPY

Second edition

MICHAEL JACOBS

OPEN UNIVERSITY PRESS
Buckingham · Philadelphia

Open University Press
Celtic Court
22 Ballmoor
Buckingham
MK18 1XW

email: enquiries@openup.co.uk
world wide web: http://www.openup.co.uk

and
325 Chestnut Street
Philadelphia, PA 19106, USA

First edition published 1985
Reprinted 1988, 1989, 1990, 1991, 1992 (twice), 1993, 1994 (twice), 1995, 1996

First published in this second edition 1998

A catalogue record of this book is available from the British Library

ISBN 0 335 20196 2 (pb)   0 335 20197 0 (hb)

Library of Congress Cataloging-in-Publication Data
Jacobs, Michael, 1941–
    The presenting past: the core of psychodynamic counselling and therapy/Michael Jacobs. – 2nd ed.
        p.   cm.
    Includes bibliographical references and index.
    ISBN 0-335-20197-0 (hardcover). – ISBN 0-335-20196-2 (pbk.)
    1. Psychodynamic psychotherapy.   I. Title.
RC489.P72J34   1998
616.89'14–dc21   98-18440
                                                                            CIP

Typeset by Type Study, Scarborough
Printed in Great Britain by Biddles Limited, Guildford and Kings Lynn

'It's in vain, Trot, to recall the past,
unless it works some influence upon the present.'
Charles Dickens *David Copperfield*

Time present and time past
Are both perhaps present in time future,
And time future contained in time past
T. S. Eliot 'Burnt Norton', in *Four Quartets*

CONTENTS

PREFACE TO THE
SECOND EDITION

Writing about the past and the present, in the course of a major revision of the first edition of this book, I am very conscious of the significance of time. In the first place, there has been quite a passage of time since I wrote the manuscript for the original edition, and the present – some thirteen years on. I am amazed at how much the world has moved on since then, not only with topical references to the Thatcher years being thankfully obsolete, but also in the changes in attitudes, which is reflected in a comparison of some of the issues referred to in each edition. The way relationships are described has changed ('fiancé' is now an outdated term); and there are welcome shifts in values, which this new text reflects. But even more so I realize how much my own thinking has developed in such a relatively short time. Any text becomes fixed in print when it is published, and I am aware, reading the first edition in detail, how it reflects a particular stage of my own development as a therapist and counsellor. I was less questioning then than I am now of my psychoanalytic roots. Nevertheless I am more in touch with those roots, and the passing of years has seen more thorough application on my own part of the ideas of a wide variety of psychoanalytic writers. I and this book are still steeped in the fertile waters of that particular form of theory and practice, but perhaps more freely floating than I was before.

I am aware too that the term 'psychodynamic' has developed a meaning that has given psychodynamic counsellors and therapists an identity of their own outside the narrower psychoanalytic community. I find, still somewhat to my surprise, that my writing has contributed to the ever-growing interest in and fascination with psychodynamic counselling – much better represented now both in the literature of counselling, and in its practice. This too is a significant change in the counselling world, in a relatively short time, although the psychodynamic has always been better represented amongst psychotherapists.

Time also shows me how in the first edition I hovered on the edge of stage theory and lifelong themes. I could not let Erikson's ages go, and so took them as chapter headings; yet I was already playing seriously with the idea of themes and variations. This new edition takes a decisive leap out of stage theory and developmental models into the timelessness of themes, something which always was recognized in the principle of the past being played out in the present.

As I write I am conscious also of the future. It is doubtful whether I will revise this book so radically again. Since the time of its revision has in its own way become frozen in print, I recognize that in time some parts of this edition will become outdated. If this second edition continues to have the success of the first, the reader in a few years time must remember that ideas develop, theoretical positions change, values shift, and research throws up new information. I cannot anticipate those changes, however much I wonder what they may be. I have stressed throughout this edition how prone psychological and psychodynamic thinking is to cultural and social construction. By all means let the reader question my assumptions, and challenge my mistakes; but consider too that it is possible that I may also be doing the same, wondering in years to come what can have possessed me to write such-and-such, however much what I write at present is the latest in my own thinking.

It is difficult to believe, given a first edition of over 25,000 copies, that there was some doubt about accepting this book back in 1984, when Harper and Row were first considering it. I have John Skelton and the Open University Press to thank for finding the book amongst a package bought from Harper and Row, and for giving it the promotion that has enabled its success. I was fortunate in writing the right book at the right time. In more recent years Jacinta Evans has encouraged and facilitated my work with the Open University Press, and I thank her and all the staff, with whom I also currently work as an editorial consultant, for their hard work on producing this edition. I also thank my wife Moira, who constantly supports my writing and my other work; and who, like me, will no doubt be pleased that now this major revision is over, we shall have just a little more time for ourselves.

Staying on a family note, a new edition and a new preface gives me the chance to mention a new generation, who were not even a twinkle in an eye in the first preface. In their own way they take my past and that of my forebears into the future. This book is then particularly dedicated to my grandchildren, for the moment Laura and Joshua, and without imposing pressure on my children, perhaps others yet to come. While we hope to change the present by what we learn from the past, only future generations will know whether or not we were successful. Some day, sooner than we think, they will be our keenest critics.

Michael Jacobs
Leicester 1997

PREFACE TO THE
FIRST EDITION

Without two groups of people this book would not have been possible. The first consists of those clients with whom I have worked over twelve years, who have provided confirmation (at times) and the necessity of refinement (at other times) of analytic theory. Should any of them, despite my disguises, recognize themselves, or parts of themselves which today are hopefully less troublesome than once they were, let me reassure them that their identity remains known only to me. And I can only thank them for all they have taught and given me.

The second group consists of the students at Vaughan College Leicester, who by their questions, their confusions, and their wish for material to be relevant to their helping work, have forced me to clarify what I mean when I use terms used in analytic theory. So often in teaching it is the teacher who learns most. Apart from the lecture material which my colleague Alan Lilley and I have given, our classes have studied Lowe's *Growth of Personality* and Rayner's *Human Development*. The influence of both will be obvious (and I hope acknowledged) in various places in the text. Since Eric Rayner was at one time my own therapist, his influence will no doubt be more extensive than even I have realized. Yet Lowe lacks illustrations of counselling situations, and Rayner's ideas, although thought provoking, are frequently so terse that their relevance to counselling can easily be missed. I hope I have been able to provide a ready-reference for counsellors which draws together, and supplements, longer and more detailed texts recommended in counselling training, and that in doing so I may help establish the relevance of analytic theory for those who are tempted to rely on the here-and-now alone.

Others, past and present, have been important in my own development: different generations of my own family have helped mould me, and present friends, especially Denis Rice, and Simon and Mary Phipps, have positively encouraged my teaching and writing. All these people illustrate for me the significance of my theme, and my hope is that they will share in anything of merit found in these pages.

Michael Jacobs
Leicester 1985

THEMES AND STAGES

Psychodynamic counselling and therapy involves a number of important elements, which perhaps is what makes the psychodynamic approach more and more interesting to those who go on developing in their work. While in no sense wishing to undervalue the importance of basic listening and responding skills, nor the centrality of a positive therapeutic relationship (which the counsellor or therapist is largely responsible for ensuring can be created), the ongoing experience of working with people leads to more and more thirst for understanding of how different personalities function, why people think, feel and behave the way they do, and how to respond best as a therapist to a variety of situations.

A psychodynamic approach engages the therapist in three key areas. The first is the practical application of a number of ways of enabling, containing and understanding the therapeutic relationship, which I have described more fully in *Still Small Voice* (1982, 1993b) and in *Psychodynamic Counselling in Action* (1988). Many of the features of this practical aspect can now be found in other therapeutic approaches, but it is perhaps to the psychoanalytic origins of psychodynamic work that we would look for the value of regular, time-boundaried sessions, free association and free floating attention on the part of client and counsellor alike. These allow unconscious processes more freedom. Psychodynamic method also involves the importance of working through defences and resistance, as well as the use of transference and counter-transference, probably the best known of all psychoanalytic concepts. Sometimes these aspects of psychodynamic work have been labelled 'techniques', often by critics who do not know this approach from personal experience. It is an unfortunate term which does not do justice to the depth of personal involvement of the therapist with the client's struggles to articulate and share her or his experiences. Nevertheless there *are* these technical aspects to psychodynamic counselling and therapy, knowledge of which enhances the therapeutic relationship and allows the possibility of greater understanding, over and above the empathy and other core conditions that are identified as central in other counselling approaches. As long as such technical aspects are not used punitively or manipulatively by therapists, they have much to contribute to the work.

The second element: human development

The second key element in psychodynamic counselling and therapy is the development of a model of how people develop from childhood and through adolescence into adult life; and what this process imparts to them along the way. That is the emphasis of this book, and this chapter explains why it is so relevant to counselling and therapy. Indeed the question 'why?' is particularly relevant here. Generally it is taught in most counselling approaches (although not in cognitive–behavioural therapy) that the question 'why?' is an unhelpful one to ask the client. If people knew the answers to such questions as 'Why do you feel this way?' or 'Why has this happened?', they would probably have less need of the skills of the therapist. Yet the question 'why?' is not invalid: it is rather that it is a difficult question to answer, even if it is one to which many people would like an answer. So, like the cognitive therapist, the psychodynamic therapist also asks 'why?', but rather more silently, waiting for the opportunity to find where the client's own answers help piece together the all-too-often complex reasons behind the question. When clients also ask 'Why? . . . do I feel this way? . . . do I always seem to . . . ?' the therapist can seldom provide a quick answer. Indeed often the answer is for the time being put to one side, awaiting the point when some tentative answers may be tested. The answer may lie in the past, and in earlier relationships, protected now by the veil of forgotten memory. Answers to the question 'why?' *are* found through counselling and therapy, but seldom in the early sessions. When glimpses of those answers are seen they often help people to understand their situation, and to set their present troubles in a wider context, sometimes preparing them to meet future instances of similar feelings. Answers do not always take away pain, but they can bring relief.

The type of questions which clients often ask, and indeed the explanations that they themselves try to find, may come because we live in a post-Freudian era. In other words, Freud's own search for the origins of mental (or what we might call emotional) suffering lay in looking at a person's history. His case studies provide examples of uncovering, layer by layer, as if in an archaeological dig (to use his own metaphor), layers of the mind (or of consciousness) until early trauma can be found. My picture, particularly true of Freud's early studies, remains a powerful image in the mind of those who without prompting start to talk about their past – past relationships, childhood and adolescence, even about family history a generation or two ago. Novels and films (witness the frequency of the flashback as a cinematic technique) support such a view of human nature. So the second dimension of psychodynamic work is that which looks at the past, at human development in general and at the personal history of the client in particular.

There is nothing contradictory about the necessity for good personal qualities in the counsellor and therapist, and the quest for knowledge, whether of technical aspects of the therapeutic endeavour, or of psychological processes. Developmental psychology – the study of the growth of the person from birth to death – has particular relevance for the counsellor and therapist, although it is for them a specialized kind of developmental psychology, concentrating upon personal relationships, and the growth of the personality, and paying less attention than perhaps most developmental psychologists to intellectual or cognitive development, to biological and physical development and to social and cultural learning. Psychoanalytic and psychodynamic explanations of personal development tend to focus upon feelings, fantasies and families. This book carries that emphasis, although it also tries not to neglect these other dimensions, especially where they are significant in understanding the different facets that contribute to making people who they are.

The significance of understanding developmental processes needs to be rooted in an example, the first of many therapy or counselling vignettes in this book that will relate the study of personal development to the practice of counselling and therapy:

Ann came to see a counsellor in her first year at university. She had deferred her place for twelve months because her father had died two months before she was first due to go to university. She thought she had worked through her grief, during a year in which she had first nursed her dying father, and then had to look after her younger sister and help console her mother (who had left Ann's father and the family some years earlier). She was frightened when, soon after coming away to college, she found herself crying at what felt to her like the slightest provocation. She thought she should have grown through all that.

Ann's counsellor was an experienced Cruse bereavement counsellor, as well as working in a university counselling service. She not surprisingly recognized (as the reader will have done, since the grieving process has become common knowledge) that for Ann to experience such grief 15 months after a death was not unusual, especially when she had spent so much time looking after the interests of others in her family. The counsellor was able to reassure Ann that her feelings were natural; and early in the first session said, 'You've been so preoccupied looking after everyone else that you haven't had the chance to look after yourself.' A little later in the session, when Ann said she thought she could cope on her own now, the counsellor suggested that Ann might be wondering whether she could rely on her counsellor to cope with the distress she felt about her father's death. They in fact met for six months, once weekly, providing space for Ann to express feelings that she had up to that point been unable to share. Eventually there came a point when it was obvious that Ann thought it right to end her counselling, having had the chance to express many of her feelings.

By contrast, an older woman, Beth, who had also nursed her father when he was dying, still could not bring herself to use the room in her father's house (which she had inherited) for herself, even though her father had died ten years ago. Her mother also had left the home and family years before, and (like Ann) Beth had been deeply attached to her father. But her complete inability to contemplate even entering the room, except for the briefest time, made it obvious that hers was a grieving process which had gone beyond the normal bounds. It was as if the room stood for some part of her own mental processes that were locked away. The process of therapy was a longer one, in which more complex family relationships had to be unravelled and in one sense 'exorcized' (Beth at one stage talked of bringing in a priest), before first she was able to contemplate entering the room, and in the end felt it was right to use the room as her own.

These two examples show different aspects of the experience of bereavement. There are many good studies of the process of grief that can enrich the counsellor's sensitivity and expertise and that demonstrate how valuable a psychological model can be in this work (e.g. Worden 1991; Lendrum and Syme 1992). In the first edition of this book I set out in the concluding chapter a straightforward summary of the stages of grief, as they appear in Collick (1986). This is now set out in Figure 1.1. These stages are probable (and indeed common) reactions to different types of loss, although they are not all necessarily felt by everyone, nor do they always appear in this order.

shock:	'I just went cold.'
numbness and unreality:	'This isn't me.'
disbelief:	'It can't be true.'
yearning:	'Come back.'
emptiness:	'An aching void.'
searching:	'He must be somewhere.'
anxiety:	'Must I sell the house?'
anger:	'He had no right to leave me like this.'
guilt:	'If only . . .'
remembering:	'I'm afraid of forgetting.'
depression:	'I'm too tired to bother.'
loss of identity and status:	'Who am I?'
stigma:	'I'm an embarrassment to others.'
sexual deprivation:	'To have someone's arms round me.'
loss of faith:	'Why?'
loneliness:	'I just dread weekends.'
acceptance:	'He'd have laughed about it.'
healing:	'The loved object is not gone, for now I carry it within myself and can never lose it' (Abraham 1927).

Figure 1.1 An example of stages of bereavement

Knowing the different experiences that can occur in the course of bereavement a counsellor or therapist is better equipped to recognize the different aspects of the grieving process in the client. Freud (1917) was one of the first to identify the similarity between some cases of depression (or melancholia, as he called it) and aspects of the process of mourning. In both instances identification takes place within the personality with an object (or person) who has in some sense been lost, and whose characteristics may be said to contribute to the formation of the personality or 'character' of the one who has experienced the loss (see also Freud 1923: 367–8). This process of incorporation, internalization, identification or introjection (all these terms are used almost synonymously in psychoanalytic literature) also leads partially in Freud's view to the formation of the conscience, or super-ego: this is formed from internalization of the parent. The critical or warning 'voice' which many people are aware of in themselves is often capable of being identified, upon closer questioning, with one or both parents at least as they were perceived by the client when a child.

The third element: personality structure

Freud's paper on mourning and melancholia, and his later papers that develop the ideas of incorporation, are the first signs of what has come to be known as 'object relations theory', the term 'objects' standing generally for 'persons'. Object relations theory is an example of the third element of a psychodynamic approach to counselling and therapy, which is more difficult to study or to demonstrate objectively than are many features of human development. This third area concerns models of how the mind works, or of how the personality might be structured. This has always been an area of speculation which Freud aptly called 'meta-psychology', since it bears the same relationship to empirical psychology as 'meta-physics' (a type of philosophical reasoning about the spiritual or the immaterial) has to the way empirical science deals with matter. When using the terms 'mind' and 'structure' in this context we need to remember how loose this type of thinking is, since 'mind' means something different to a therapist and counsellor, unrelated generally to the way the brain or intellect may be understood by a neurologist or a psychologist.

Similarly, to describe 'personality' as having a 'structure' is to use a metaphor that appears to give it a definite form. The reader will be familiar with Freud's description of the mind as constituted of id, ego and super-ego (1923). As Freud himself recognized, by classifying such ideas as meta-psychology, this is a speculative picture of how the personality might function, not a definitive map of topographical areas of the human brain. I do not wish to engage here in a more detailed description of these familiar if somewhat outmoded terms; but it is important for a fuller understanding of psychodynamic theory, and its application to practice, to remember that very often psychodynamic psychotherapists are using images and metaphors in their attempts to describe different dimensions of human experience. Just as the poet Gerard Manley Hopkins could write that '. . . the mind, the mind has mountains; cliffs of fall,/ Frightful, sheer no-man-fathomed . . .', so the language used by psychoanalysts to describe the mind has the same symbolic quality, in an attempt to portray an area which is in many ways unfathomable.

This third element of psychodynamic thought draws then not so much upon external observation as upon introspection – the therapist's own internal monitoring, as well as the therapist's attempts to reach inside the mind of those clients who engage in such therapeutic exploration. Psychoanalytic thinking has moved beyond Freud's id, ego and super-ego, even though these terms sometimes still remain useful pointers to the basic conflict that can exist between our desires and our needs (the id) on the one hand, and our internalized sense of what is right and wrong (the super-ego) on the other, in which the ego ('me' or perhaps the central self) often feels to be acting as the arbiter, while trying simultaneously to relate to the demands of the external world.

Psychoanalytic thinking about the structure of the personality is by no means uniform, although the different models all start from Freud's observation that in the process of mourning the object (or the person) that is lost is replaced through the grief process by an inner representation of the same object. This process of internalizing is one which those who have worked through grief may be familiar with. The person they have lost in some sense now lives on inside them. This internal presence is more than a memory of what the lost person was like, or what they said; it is more like experiencing them in some sense as still part of the present, sometimes with a conscious or unconscious dialogue taking place with them.

Starting with this insight into the process of mourning, psychoanalytic thinking has come to see how all kinds of significant external relationships are internalized in the process of human growth and development. This internalization process starts as early as life itself, when early separations involve both some kind of loss, and the need to replace that which is lost. Many potent experiences contribute to the way in which we develop, not only in guiding us one way or another, but in building up our inner life and character.

In the generations that have followed Freud's pioneering work the human personality has been described in a variety of ways, many of which appear to contain elements of 'truth' – or at least images which we might recognize in ourselves or in our clients. This has led to a whole school of psychoanalytic theory known as 'object relations', which takes different forms, but shares common ground in the hypothesis that we internalize not just people, but also our experience of them, and the two-way relationships we have with them; and furthermore that we also internalize fragmented and imbalanced aspects of those relationships. Psychoanalytic writers like Melanie Klein (see Segal 1992) therefore believe that we have within us 'good objects' and 'bad objects' (a different type of conflictual model to that between id and super-ego). The good objects provide us with a sense of nurturing and comfort (even when we are on our own), the bad objects are experienced as attacking and persecuting us (even when there is no external threat).

Other analysts put forward different 'divisions' of the personality. Winnicott, for example, refers to the 'true self' and the 'false self' (Winnicott 1965b: 140–52), an apt description for the way we can experience ourselves as acting a part, rather than in touch with a more genuine expression of ourselves. Jung elaborates a multi-dimensional model of human personality, including a structure consisting of the ego, the persona (a social self rather than the more pervasive false self in Winnicott), the shadow and the self. Jung describes character in terms that have become common parlance: 'extrovert' and 'introvert', and he distinguishes between feeling, sensing, thinking and intuitive character types.

A different structure again is put forward by the Scottish analyst Fairbairn –

in many ways a difficult writer to grasp – using different terms to identify aspects of the ego. Fairbairn abandons Freud's concept of the id altogether, instead suggesting that a baby is born with a 'unitary ego'. He continues to use the word 'libido' (desire) but he sees libido as primarily seeking an object (a person) to relate to, rather than an object to provide relief of tension. This primary ego is differentiated in the early weeks after birth, as a result of the experience of both the satisfaction and the frustration of object (or personal) relationships. This fragmentation leads to an unconscious libidinal ego (an ego which seeks the promise of relatedness); an unconscious anti-libidinal ego (that is hostile to such contact or gratification); and a conscious central ego which is 'the self of everyday life' (Guntrip 1961: 330). The relevance of such thinking can be seen in an example quoted by Guntrip, of a man who has relationships with three women: one with his critical and rejecting wife; one with a sexually exciting but inaccessible mistress; and one in his fantasy with an ideal woman (Guntrip 1961: 325). Guntrip provides one of the most accessible descriptions of Fairbairn's ideas, as well as a helpful history of the development of psychoanalytic models of personality structure up to the 1950s.

Some of these ways of describing personality structure are referred to later in this book, as ways of finding a language that identifies (although does not necessarily explain) a client's personal experience; or that provides the counsellor and therapist with pointers to understanding possible internalized dynamic interactions. My own sense of working with many clients in person, and hearing about many other clients in supervising therapists, is that the ability to draw upon these different sets of metaphors can be advantageous. A counsellor or therapist does not have to adhere rigidly to one psychodynamic model of personality structure. There are occasions when the simple tripartite model of id, ego and super-ego (and indeed straight Freudian oedipal theory) appears to fit the picture which a particular client presents. There are other occasions when only Melanie Klein's stark picture of infancy and childhood seems adequately to describe the client's and therapist's experience of each other. Chapter 3 contains examples of how apt her concepts can be, even if at first sight her writing often seems fantastic and 'over the top', with its images of 'biting', 'tearing apart' and 'destroying the good object'. We can therefore think of the extensive library of psychoanalytic literature as providing in its own way as rich a variety of human character and relationships in the reading of the therapist and counsellor as a library of novels, poetry and drama does in our reading at leisure.

These three elements – the therapeutic relationship, theories of development, and theories of personality structure – therefore constitute the psychodynamic approach. This can more formally be defined as referring principally to the theories of Freud and post-Freudians, in which there is perceived to be a constantly moving set of relationships (dynamics) between different aspects of the personality, formed of past and present relationships between the growing individual and significant others, and thereafter consciously and unconsciously influencing relationships within the internal world of the individual, as well as with the external world of persons and objects. This external world includes the relationship with the therapist or counsellor, who is able to use her or his perceptions of the client, and the client's perception of the therapist to construct possible ways of understanding the client's relationships with aspects of himself or herself (his or her internal world), and with others.

Models of development

The differences in psychoanalytic literature in identifying aspects of the human personality are also true of models of human development. Similarly any of the maps that have been drawn of human growth are only approximations, always flawed, but setting out potentially valuable observations and hypotheses in a clearly defined form. Such models, like the process of grief summarized above, are often portrayed as a series of stages. Two such models are Freud's psycho-sexual stages (1905), or Erikson's psycho-social stages (1965) which I explain further below.

A key text on developmental psychology emphasizes that 'the term *stage*, used simply to describe observations, as is often done in everyday language, has no scientific or explanatory value' (Mussen *et al.* 1969: 23). What the authors mean here is that stages do not explain behaviour; although they do have some value in the sense of making distinctions clearer. Stages are generally distinct periods of development, where certain aspects of behaviour, thought or expression (that often occur together and are therefore clustered) are obviously present in a way that was not evident earlier. Although stage theory has descriptive value (which is why I wish to introduce some examples here) it is essentially artificial, a construct of the theorist rather than an endemic feature in human nature. Such theories have their weaknesses, particularly the tendency to put people into boxes, and label them normal or abnormal depending upon whether or not they appear to have successfully negotiated the sequence of stages expected of them by age or life position. This is not necessarily the intention of the theorist, but it is a consequence of such writing, as I caution more fully in Chapter 2. Measuring development by stage or age is something which many parents are aware of as they observe their children's growth; for some this is a natural concern to see their child take new steps; for others it becomes an ambitious anxiety which frequently has a deleterious effect upon the child, who always feels the obligation to achieve. Erikson called this 'a projection on child development of that success ideology which can so dangerously pervade our private and public daydreams' (1965: 265). Other reservations about using developmental models I explain further in the next chapter.

When Freud put forward his theory of infantile sexuality, he outlined three stages of development, each of which focuses upon a part of the child's body, which is the source of satisfaction or 'pleasure'. There is therefore a three-stage theory consisting of oral, anal and genital phases where first the mouth, then the anus, and then the genitals are the centre of the child's concern. It is a very physical, or body-centred theory, although in the course of time psychodynamic theory has got too divorced from the 'soma' or the body, and tends to dwell overmuch on the 'psyche' or mind. The first stage, the oral, centres upon feeding, with the mouth the means of 'incorporation' of the breast (Freud's term, 1905: 117); the second stage, the anal, shifts attention to 'mastery through the agency of somatic musculature' (1905: 117). Although the focus of this stage sometimes appears to concentrate upon defecation, Freud includes the pleasure of muscular exercise generally and wonders whether this has 'any connection with sexuality' (1905: 122). The third stage is the genital, where questions of sexual differences and the origin of babies form a focus of the child's interest. Later Freud was to call this the phallic stage, reserving the genital stage for its fuller expression in adolescence.

This appears to be a three-stage model, although Freud adds another phase, that of latency, which I describe more fully below. By implication there is also the stage of adolescence, making five stages in all. Adulthood is not delineated as having any particular stages, although Freud may imply that much of adult life consists of working through the legacy of the stages of childhood. Indeed we shall see that, for all its weaknesses, this model (together with the Oedipus complex which is an integral part of it) can throw light on some of the ways in which adult clients present themselves and their relationships in therapy and counselling.

The weaknesses in the model are obvious. It focuses so much upon the erotic pleasure of various parts of the body, and on the satisfaction of the child's needs, that it appears to neglect relationships with others, except inasmuch as they provide or frustrate satisfaction for the child. My own over-simplification of course neglects the vast corpus of Freud's writing in which can be found qualifications to what appears to be a completely egocentric picture of a child's needs or drives. Another difficulty is the way in which the term 'sexual' is used, as if it is to be equated with genital sexuality. Sexuality as we commonly understand it is of course much more the subject of the third stage of development, or, even in its full expression, it is reserved for adolescence onwards.

Nevertheless the prevalence and pleasure of oral and anal foreplay in sexual play are recognized by Freud, as they must be by all therapists, as part of a fuller picture of sexual behaviour, so that it is perhaps not far-fetched to suggest the presence of eroticism in the first two stages of orality and anality. Yet, again thinking about sexual relations and their link to other forms of human relating, the model is insufficient when it appears to suggest that relationships are largely about the need to discharge tension (erotic or otherwise), however true this may be of some situations and of some people.

A model which is more complete, but which takes a clear lead from Freud's psycho-sexual stages, is the psycho-social theory of the Eight Ages of Man. It is called 'psycho-social' rather than 'psycho-sexual' because sexuality occupies a less central place in Erikson's scheme, while societal aspects assume a larger dimension. Although Erikson gave a title to his model largely before gender consciousness made the word 'man' less acceptable in intellectual discourse about humankind generally, he does in fact show a male bias in his work, which feminist psychologists and therapists have criticized (e.g. Gilligan 1982), and indeed which the reader needs to be conscious of in relation to all developmental studies, since so many are written by male psychologists or psychotherapists.

Nevertheless his scheme has much to be said for it still, especially if it is adapted and applied in a less definitive way than the model is drawn, that is, as a series of clear steps. Used more loosely, his apparently straightforward model helps provide ways of describing and identifying features of personal development which run through the successive chronological ages of an individual's life.

Erikson extends Freud's three (or five) stages into adult life, making eight in all; and he frames the issues of each age as being much more than erotic pleasure, and about much more than the satisfaction of bodily desires. The differences can be seen by placing the two sets of stages alongside each other, as in Figure 1.2. Set alongside the description of the stages are the tasks which Erikson suggests are key issues in each age, together with my own version (in an over-simplified summary) of what might be considered the aims of each stage in Freud's scheme.

Freud	*Aims*	**Erikson**	*Tasks*
oral stage	feeding	oral	basic trust vs mistrust
anal stage	muscular pleasure	muscular–anal	autonomy vs shame and doubt
phallic stage	oedipal resolution	locomotor–genital	initiative vs guilt
latency	learning	latency	industry vs inferiority
adolescence	genital expression	adolescence	identity vs role confusion
(adulthood)	love and work	early adulthood mid-adulthood late adulthood	intimacy vs isolation generativity vs stagnation integrity vs despair

Figure 1.2 Erikson's extension of Freud's stage model

There are other stage models used in developmental psychology and in psychoanalytic theories – such as Piaget's (1950) model of intellectual functioning, with four stages, the final one of which (that of being able to think conceptually) begins at around the age of eleven. Using Piaget, but building further upon it to examine the development of moral thinking, is Kohlberg's research (1981) into how we make moral judgements, refined to take account of gender differences by his colleague Carol Gilligan (1982). Fowler (1981), using the stage theories of Piaget, Kohlberg and Erikson as the main resources for his own research, has mapped out the development of stages of faith or belief, which I have myself used critically in my own study of the psychology of belief (Jacobs 1993a). Other developmental studies can be found in the work of Havighurst or in the observations of psychologists who have concentrated upon adulthood, such as Levinson *et al.* (1978) and Golan (1981). These and other theories are well documented by Sugarman (1986). It is interesting to note how many of those referred to in this paragraph were published as major pieces of research at around the same time, as though stage theory had then its greatest popularity.

How might such stage theories be useful in therapy and counselling? They suggest, of course, tasks and attitudes – whether physical or intellectual, or stages of emotional development – which a therapist might expect to find at different ages, and which generally can be said to constitute adult maturity. Older psychoanalytic models of what happens when people break down suggest that where there is a crisis or a conflict for an individual he or she will tend to regress back to a position of relative safety or security. Technically known as 'regression', this psychological self-defence was likened by Freud, using militaristic terms, to an army needing to retreat to its first secure base before facing the enemy again. Pursuing this metaphor, a person can then regroup, or in psychological terms renegotiate earlier issues which were not favourably dealt with earlier. Another possibility is that people can become in some respects 'fixed' or stuck at a particular stage of development, and demonstrate, for example, a dependent, obsessional, or competitive character, depending upon whether their developmental block is located in oral, anal or genital stages (to use the Freudian psycho-sexual model). This similarly is a defence, known as 'fixation'.

The Erikson model is also progressive, and can be used as a template to locate possible sources of personal difficulty. His eight ages have some resemblance to a staircase, in which one tread rests upon the other; or even to a tower of children's wooden building bricks. As long as each brick is placed squarely upon the one below, and the first one has a firm foundation, the tower remains stable as it grows upward. Using Erikson's terms, where sufficient trust is achieved in the first age, through its foundation in a reliable relationship with the nurturing parent, this forms a strong base upon which to achieve autonomy in the second age. Upon autonomy is then built the capacity for initiative, and so on. Staying with this image, if the bricks are not set squarely upon each other, the tower grows but has inbuilt structural weaknesses. There comes a point at which either the stress of external circumstances (in the analogy, a heavy footstep nearby), or the internal pressures (the structural stresses of its construction) causes the tower to collapse. This especially occurs when one of the lower bricks has not been placed squarely, in other words, where there is some form of developmental 'weakness' or incompleteness, due to the prevailing circumstances of that period of a person's life.

When such a tower falls, it normally falls only as far as the first badly placed brick. It seldom takes the lower, stable bricks with it. So it is in a human crisis. Where the weight of later stresses in adult life, external or internal, impose impossible strain, collapse or breakdown frequently goes back as far as the stage at which developmental issues were not satisfactorily resolved. It is therefore possible that a counsellor or therapist, learning more about a person's history, especially of their childhood and adolescence, will be able to locate points at which obvious trauma occurred, which has left a 'fault' (Freud indeed compared it to a *geological* fault, not a *moral* one) in the personality structure.

Chris had been delivered prematurely by caesarean section shortly before his mother's death. After a short period with his father, he was moved to his father's parents' home, where he spent the first two years of his life.

When his father married again, Chris (who had seen little of his father in the intervening years) was moved back to his father's family, where the rest of his childhood was relatively untroubled, although his relationship with his father was always strained.

In his adult life Chris found himself attracted emotionally and physically to women a good deal older than himself. His own sense of this was that he was continually searching for the mother (and the grandmother) whom he had lost so young. Through his therapy he was able to return (in imagination and in actuality) to places associated with his mother. In his therapy particular attention focused upon the breaks (for holidays) and eventually upon the termination of the therapy, which itself had to be premature. The links to his separation from key maternal figures assisted him in understanding why his feelings about these aspects of the therapeutic relationship were so strong.

Where there have been particular traumatic events earlier in life, it is not surprising that they should have influenced a person's attitude to certain situations thereafter. Freud's original work focused particularly on the precipitating trauma which had led to the patient's symptoms, although in the earliest days of his practice he did not always seek this trauma in early childhood, but in more recent history. It is however a caricature of psychoanalytic work to imagine that every therapist is looking for a particular traumatic incident as the sole explanation of current difficulties. The idea that 'I must have been dropped on my head when I was a baby' is as far-fetched as the myth of instantaneous cure following the dramatic uncovering of a long-repressed incident. Nevertheless the sentiment behind such imaginative approaches to therapy contains a sufficient germ of the truth, that the past does influence the present.

Therapists and counsellors can accumulate considerable information about a client's past from the stories which their clients tell them, and from the questions which clients themselves ask about their own history. But the past does not only influence the present: it can also be seen actively working in the present. The difficulties which the client brings frequently represent a repetition, if sometimes in a different form, of former conflicts. This is what Freud meant by the phrase 'the return of the repressed'. Past relationships can also be reflected in the relationship style(s) which the client adopts towards the counsellor or therapist, a phenomenon known as transference that can occur in all human relationships. Experience suggests, and some of the examples in this book will confirm it, that knowledge and re-experiencing of their past history helps both client and therapist to make sense of where they find themselves now.

The view of development that can therefore be taken from stage theory or a model based on distinct ages is that unfinished business and unresolved issues from the past often have a powerful effect on living in the present. By implication satisfactory resolution of present issues in the therapeutic relationship can help the past (and indeed the future) to be faced, renegotiated and in some respects even relived 'but with a new ending' (Alexander and French 1946).

An alternative approach

Such models of progressive stages, as I have already suggested, have serious weaknesses, as indeed does developmental psychology as a whole (see Chapter 2). The first is that they are somewhat arbitrary in their divisions of human growth and development into definite ages. Stage theories can differ considerably as to the number of stages there are, and where the beginning and end of each stage is located in time. One of the virtues of Levinson's model (1978) is that he has incorporated periods of transition between the major life stages, periods which are long enough (five years) to make it unwise to look to a particular age (such as thirteen years old) as the start of a particular developmental stage (such as adolescence). Furthermore a linear model not only suggests that development goes in a straight line, but also appears to imply that once a stage has been negotiated satisfactorily the basic tasks have been accomplished; or, using Erikson's Eight Ages, that the basic strengths have been acquired once and for all. This is plainly not so: trust, the issue which Erikson identifies as central to the first age, appears in different forms throughout life, and changes its object at different stages. The blind trust of the baby is not helpful in the second age, where increased mobility means learning *not to trust* situations and objects which are potentially dangerous – fires, stairs, etc. Parents of the second-stage child themselves have to learn a new kind of trust which is careful but not over-cautious. This in turn represents a type of trust which could be said to be part of Erikson's sixth age of generativity (which includes parenthood). The basic strengths or 'virtues' (Erikson's term) which form the major part of each stage continue to develop throughout life, in the new circumstances that constantly present themselves. Erikson himself recognized this, and (extending the same quotation used above) included a footnote: 'The assumption that at each stage a goodness is achieved which is impervious to new inner conflicts and to changing conditions is, I believe, a projection on child development of that success ideology which can so dangerously pervade our private and public daydreams' (1965: 265).

One way of overcoming this particular weakness in the Erikson model is not to picture a straight staircase, but to combine the images I have used of staircase and tower. Introducing a cyclical element into progression instead of the linear model, personal development might be seen as more like a spiral staircase. In effect we might then say that each of the eight 'treads' which Erikson calls the Eight Ages are repeated in each complete turn of the circular staircase: in each of the chronological ages therefore all the issues (of trust, autonomy, initiative, industry, identity, intimacy, generativity and integrity) are repeated. This metaphor may increase the stresses in the model, but that is true to life. Using this image, the issues of childhood are thereby reintroduced in the normal process of living, particularly in those crises of adult life through which nearly every person has to pass – but the issues identified as being part of adult life (such as intimacy, creativity and integrity) are also part of early experience.

Erikson perhaps allows for such a cyclical element in his famous remark about the final stage: 'Where adults have integrity enough not to fear death their children will not fear life' (1965: 261), although his reference here is to the connections between generations, like a series of cog wheels, where, as in family systems theory, change in one individual affects others in close proximity. There are however other reasons to support this particular view of developmental theory, as a cyclical rather than a linear process. Two can be seen in particular developments of the Freud/Erikson model and a third support comes from Melanie Klein's theory of 'positions'.

The watershed of adolescence

In adolescence, issues from early childhood are thrown into the melting pot. If adolescence is a definite stage, it is also clearly a major transitional time between childhood and adulthood. A number of issues become more real than ever before, because the adolescent now has the strength, the will and the status to enact what in childhood years could only be fantasies. Using Erikson's Eight Ages, the first three major themes of early childhood are taken up in adolescence and reworked, with greater opportunity of realizing them fully. In addition adolescents in Western society are in education until at least their mid-teens, so that issues from the latency period struggle for a place amongst the strong reawakened emotions of earlier stages, which now in adolescence all too often threaten and interfere with educational tasks.

I have already cautioned against being too precise when mapping out human development, and this applies equally to the period of adolescence, which is a time of rapid change in moods and aspirations. Nevertheless, adolescence can be seen as a watershed in Erikson's model, especially if we follow the division of adolescence into three periods – early, middle and late – as suggested by Laufer (1974) and others. Figure 1.3 shows how each of these successive periods in turn can be seen to take up themes from the first three ages. Thus early adolescence, with sexual development pushed more obviously into consciousness by physical changes at puberty, picks up the themes of sexuality from the third age. At the same time this set of issues points forward, preparing the sexual identity of a young person for the sixth age of intimacy. This is why it can be said that each period of adolescence looks backwards and forwards, like a true watershed.

Middle adolescence could be described as being particularly concerned with issues of independence from parental influence, and moving towards autonomy and self-direction. Dynamic issues of the second age are thereby picked up with considerable force – battles of will are even harder, with physical strength and determination making young people formidable fighters for themselves. This middle period of adolescence is also the time when there is the desire for economic independence, by moving into the area of work, whether in paid employment, or in the self-motivated attitudes to work required for study through further and higher education. Looking forward, this period of middle adolescence lays the foundation for middle adulthood (Erikson's seventh age) where generativity is singled out as a major task, as a parent and as a worker. The late period of adolescence, where there can be intense concerns about the state of society and the world, and experimentation to find a sense of belief and purpose (including one's own identity), has

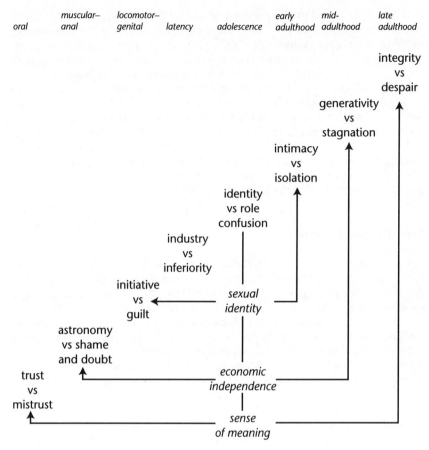

Figure 1.3 Adolescence as a watershed

obvious links with the first age, where Erikson has identified issues of trust and the emergence of the rudimentary 'self'. Yet this later period of adolescence also prefigures the final stage of the Eight Ages, that of ego integrity, where confidence in a person's overall handling of his or her life is a necessary step towards the acceptance of death.

These issues are described in more detail in later chapters. The point I wish to emphasize here is that it is artificial to demarcate issues and confine them to certain ages. As in adolescence, issues that appear to be particularly pertinent to each period can surface at any time. They are never resolved by passing through one age alone. Issues about sexuality, about authority, and about issues about faith, hope and integrity, all central to the period of adolescence, have appeared before in childhood, and will remain concerns throughout life.

This is not just true of the age of adolescence. The key issues of adult life – intimacy, generativity and integrity – are just as obvious in early childhood. The quality of intimacy of mother and baby, or of father and child, lays the foundations for good or bad personal–sexual relations in adult life. Winnicott and others recognize the generativity and creativity of the child in the creative illusions of infancy (Winnicott 1965b: 180), or in the production of stools (something the child can produce and give to a parent), or in play (Winnicott 1971: 65–85). It is also part of latency, where Erikson identifies 'industry' as the virtue of that age. Creativity and generativity are not confined to middle adulthood where Erikson chooses to locate these achievements. Integrity, or wholeness, is as much an issue in overcoming the splitting of early experience in Klein's view of the infant, as it is in Erikson's identification of this issue as central to negotiating old age and death. Indeed it is because these issues run throughout life that in this edition I no longer split off (as I did in the first edition) variations of the major themes into the phases in adult life, but integrate adult life fully into the themes themselves.

The theme of latency

Latency seems to have been excluded from the backward and forward directional arrows I have worked into Erikson's model in Figure 1.3. Perhaps it is a distinct period, bearing no relation to the others, although a former colleague supports the argument for seeing all eight sets of issues as present in this stage as well. Hunter (1983) has described latency as a 'mini-cycle of development', and the task of the teacher as building up in a child a sense of *hope* so that learning can take place, and the *willpower* to see the task through, especially in the early stages when the task seems too difficult. The teacher needs to point towards a direction for learning that indicates its *purpose*, and to build on an appropriate method so that the child gains *competence*. This will lead to *independence* in learning, and a stage of *ego integrity* that generates reliability (*fidelity*), and *love* of learning and its potential for life, a *caring* attitude, and *wisdom*. The words in italics are the 'virtues' of each developmental age that appear in some versions of Erikson's Eight Ages.

Nevertheless I want to make a distinctly different point about latency, since the term used to describe the fourth stage of development in Freud and Erikson is a curious one. Freud suggests that in the latency period (ages approximately six to twelve) developmental drives and aims diminish in intensity (particularly oedipal issues, which should have been sufficiently resolved), and re-emerge forcefully again at puberty. It is clear to any casual observer that children of this age do not cease being interested in sex; they use plenty of terms associated with genital and anal images in their jokes. They may have a 'girlfriend' or 'boyfriend' at school, even if the relationship is very different from an adolescent relationship. They may treat their teachers as substitute parents, with intense loving feelings. There will probably be authority struggles at home and perhaps at school. The intensity of all these emotions may be less strong than they are during adolescence, but it is difficult to see a child in the latency stage as other than continuing to experience the emotions and interests from the previous stages. This, as I have already suggested, is to be expected if each age involves *each* of the issues that Erikson identifies as significant for personal development.

The stress in the latency stage is on learning, and learning there certainly is. Latency traditionally refers to a stage of development where these tasks of learning basic intellectual, manual and physical skills are made possible without undue interference from the concerns raised in the previous stages. But learning is not confined to this particular time at school. Learning takes place before the latency period, and afterwards: in adolescence, in training, in adult education, including learning counselling and therapy through seminars, reading and supervision. What Hartung (1979) suggests, building upon the Erikson model in an article on learning psychotherapy, is that in order to be able to learn, adults need to be able to enter a 'latency mode', like children in the latency age.

Suppose then that we apply this also to children in what has been thought to be the latency stage. They too need to enter into a latency mode in order to be able to learn. When not over-stimulated by dependency needs (oral issues) those who learn can feed their growing appetite for understanding and information. Not too troubled by the need for perfection (anal issues) they can find fulfilment in the satisfactory completion of tasks, and in being able to make, do or understand things well. Relaxed about cooperation and not being unduly competitive (oedipal issues), learning presents opportunities to relate to and identify with others. In the latency mode, children and adults can learn to experiment with objects as well as with friendships and social groupings; to tolerate the frustration of results taking time; to ask questions, and look for proof of observations and explanations; and to alternate between passively receiving instruction, and actively investigating. But if children or adults are too stimulated at the same time as they are learning by other emotional issues (and Hartung illustrates how this can happen over issues of dependency, authority and rivalry, as in the first three stages of the Erikson model), then it becomes very much more difficult for them to learn, and to maximize the opportunities presented by the teacher.

The difficulties which interfere with the latency mode therefore apply to children and adults alike. To take a parallel example: the child who is able to control bowels and bladder is freed to engage in a whole range of activities at school; whereas the child who is still soiling him- or herself is likely to be so concerned with problems of staying clean and dry, that there will be less time at school available for concentration upon all the learning activities on offer. Most primary school children (unless disturbed by some family or classroom crisis) are relatively free of these physical anxieties. But some children (and many adolescents and some adults too) may have concerns which are less physical, and more to do with attitudes or anxieties, which can be detrimental to their learning. If there is continued over-stimulation of issues from previous stages, attitudes to learning as well as the learning itself may be influenced detrimentally. Although some children and adults sometimes use their work to defend against worries, most people, of any age, find it hard to concentrate when there are more pressing issues on their minds.

The concept of the 'latency mode' is an important one. It represents a quite distinct way of looking at what Freud calls a 'stage', which is different again from the 'inclusive' concept which for example, Hunter suggests, and which I have myself put forward above as a possible way of looking at each age of development. The idea of a 'mode', such as a 'latency mode', is a way of look-ing at and using the Erikson Ages, which I have come to think is the most valu-able one. Just as we have to enter into a latency mode to learn, so other aspects of relating to other people and other objects in the external world, as well as relating to ourselves, involve us in other 'modes': it might be possible there-fore to speak of a dependency mode, or an autonomous mode, a mode of inti-macy, or creativity – each one of which may involve different qualities and strengths, and different ways of relating, and which is informed by the more traditional stage models.

In the first edition of this book I was aware of some of the implications of such an approach: by setting the major part of the book out as 'Themes and Variations' I was conscious that I was outlining the major themes of young childhood and the way in which they were played out through later child-hood, adolescence and adult life. Those themes I related, as indeed I do also in this edition, to the first three Freud/Erikson stages, identifying the detailed aspects of oral themes of trust and dependency, anal themes of autonomy and authority, and genital themes of sexuality and rivalry. I was already in that edition including many examples from working with adult clients of the way in which these childhood themes were repeated. But I could not altogether let go of the chronological sequence of Erikson's Eight Ages, and I pursued it through the 'variations' in the latter part of the book. While I recognized the need to trace the three Erikson adult themes *throughout* adult life, and not con-fine them to early, mid- or late adulthood, I was still in a mid-way position, between 'stages' and 'themes', not altogether sure about making the move to themes complete. In this edition I take that decisive step, convinced now that there is more to be gained from it in the practice of psychodynamic therapy and counselling, than from adherence to a stage model.

Themes and positions

To use the idea of 'modes' or 'themes' as distinct from 'stages' to examine human development is to link in with other traditions of psychoanalytic theory, in which the apparently clear steps of a stage model have similarly been replaced by concepts, such as that of 'positions' in the formulations of Melanie Klein. While she claims to take up Freud's mantle, she alters his stage theory so that it bears her distinctive stamp. She demonstrates another way of looking at development that opens up further possibilities for the way in which psychodynamic concepts can be applied in practice. If in the past there have sometimes been battles about orthodoxy in the psychoanalytic tradition, particularly between the followers of Melanie Klein and the followers of Anna Freud, those of us who are outside the professional psychoanalytic societies that represent somewhat entrenched points of view can enjoy the opportunity to use the variety of insights that their arguments and discussions provide. Psychodynamic therapists and counsellors can be broad in their use of theory, without sacrificing the depth of knowledge which is represented by what is indeed a rich, if sometimes contentious, psychoanalytic tradition.

Julia Segal observes that Melanie Klein found too limiting Freud's concept of stages of development, through which a child passed 'in well-defined order' (1992: 33). Although she concurred with Freud that children's interest is focused upon oral, anal and genital concerns, 'there was constant movement from one to the other and back again' (Segal 1992: 33). The similarities to my adapted Erikson model are immediately obvious. Klein describes two particular sets of attitudes that react to and act upon these concerns, which she calls the 'paranoid–schizoid position' and the 'depressive position'. Unlike Freud's stage model, which supposes moving from one set of concerns (oral) to new tasks (anal, then genital or oedipal), Klein does not believe we are ever free of these issues: adults as well as young children oscillate between these two 'positions' time and again throughout their life – indeed in the course of any normal day.

I explain these positions more fully in Chapter 3, but at this point I refer to them to illustrate the way Klein suggests continuity of developmental concepts through all stages of life. She uses the term 'paranoid–schizoid position' as a way of describing the early state of mind in the newborn infant and in the first few months of life. Here good experiences and bad experiences are not yet understood as emanating from the same nurturing object (the mother's breast). Instead there is in phantasy (this particular spelling of a very important concept is Klein's) perception of an ideal breast, that provides food and comfort when it is needed; and a bad breast, that withdraws, or is unavailable to the baby when it is most wanted, and so is endowed by the child with an attacking quality. This attacking quality is reinforced, Klein believes, by the projection on to the breast of the child's rage at being frustrated. Thus the child feels persecuted by this bad breast, putting the young infant temporarily into a paranoid state, largely of its own making.

While we have to be careful, in any study of children, not to attribute to them adult states of mind without real evidence (and such phantasies as Klein supposes are virtually incapable of proof, and can only be surmised from other evidence), the term 'paranoid' as used by Klein can refer to the infant's state of mind; or to the paranoid schizophrenic who believes that everyone is against him and that the world is a hostile and dangerous place; or to the persecutory feelings that we can experience when we wake on a Monday morning (or any morning?) and think, 'Do I have to get up? I don't feel like facing "out there" – I'd sooner stay here where I am, cosy and warm.' These are of course different states in their intensity and their degree of permanence, but they are all related to that early experience of the infant. Similarly the term 'schizoid' applies to experiences throughout life. In infancy it refers to the way in which the breast that is perceived as persecutory is split off from the breast that is perceived to be beneficent. Schizoid feelings can range (and here I extend the term to include the way Fairbairn and Guntrip employ it) from the infant who needs to protect the vulnerable self from attack; to the adult person who is totally cut off from others, since others are perceived as dangerous because of their hate (Klein) or because of their love (Fairbairn/Guntrip); to the state of mind that says, 'Just leave me alone for a while. I need some space to myself.'

Klein's term 'depressive position' is first used of the child's growing perception that early good and bad experiences come from the same source. It has little to do with depression as it is normally understood. The child begins to integrate experience, able to contain loving and hating feelings, without such fear that the hating feelings will destroy the loving feelings. I explore this concept more fully in Chapter 3, and at this point wish to stress that the 'depressive position' similarly is one which we experience throughout life, as we work through phases of paranoid–schizoid experience, and phases of more constructive and integrated experience. Julia Segal sums it up as follows:

> Under the pressure of frustration of various kinds, the attacks of the paranoid–schizoid position continue throughout life, though mitigated more and more by a sense of love and reality which can no longer be denied . . . Klein saw the conflict between love and hatred as the motive force for much of what happens in life.
>
> (1992: 39–40)

The continuous conflict between love and hate, that Klein places at the centre of her theoretical system, is a reflection of the basic conflict that Freud also put forward between eros (love) and thanatos (death). Sexual desire (libidinal drives) is only one of the several forces or drives within each person. Aggressive drives are also part of our make-up. These can be linked in Freudian and post-Freudian theory, as in Anna Freud's 'developmental lines' (1973: 59–82), to the different stages: biting in the oral stage, sadism in the anal stage, domination in the phallic stage. Anna Freud's 'developmental lines' are more obviously linked to a stage model, although she makes important distinctions which merit further consideration than I can provide here. She makes it clear that the various developmental lines progress at different speeds. Add to this 'the interactions between progression and regression . . . [and] . . . the disharmonies, imbalances, intricacies of development, in short the *variations of normality*, become innumerable' (A. Freud 1973: 94, original italics). Her position, closer to her father's than Klein's, still lends some support to a fluid use of stage theory in working with individual children and adult clients.

Putting it together

We are now in a position to see how these different aspects of a psychodynamic model for therapy and counselling can be employed: that is, how the therapeutic relationship, models of human development, and the theories of personality structure might function in practice. Although in the example above the client Chris used the history of his birth and early childhood to reflect upon his present state of relating to others, the developmental model as I have developed it in this chapter is capable of yielding much more than actual history alone. Wide use can be made of ideas and images linked to psychodynamic theories of human development. With a sense of the content of these major themes (or modes, or positions, or lines or stages, since they can all be used in this creative way), the therapist and counsellor has a treasury of possibilities with which to understand, relate to, and communicate with the client. Linking past to present can be enlightening (psychodynamic therapists call this 'insight'), although showing the presence of past or present in the therapeutic relationship is frequently the most challenging and formative experience of all. The relationship of client to counsellor (and therapist to client) is, as Freud put it, 'a living laboratory'; or perhaps more aptly a 'stage' upon which in part is re-enacted (with the therapist) the story of a person's life:

Diane presented two issues at the start of her first session of therapy. The first was that she was binge-eating, and then making herself sick. The second was that her husband had left her, and she was unable to get him to say anything about his future intentions. He was unwilling to pronounce the relationship between them over and finished, but he would not return to her.

She did not say much about her childhood and adolescence, nor did the therapist ask any particular questions that might help him see whether the past might throw light upon the present. It was too early for that. Diane talked very fully about how she was reacting and feeling in her current situation; and the more she said, the more the therapist was able to connect up her words with one of the presenting symptoms – her problem over eating. Eating is clearly connected with 'feeding' and therefore perhaps with themes that are typical of the oral stage of development. He began to play with the language and images of the oral stage to see if this might throw light upon the way Diane felt and acted.

Diane told the therapist, for instance, that she desperately wanted her husband to come back so that she could have a baby to love: it would be sufficient for him to return long enough for her to become pregnant. She didn't appear to want a baby in order to tie her husband to their relationship. She also described their relationship when they were living together as one where she mothered him so much, and did everything for him, that he had said he had begun to feel hemmed in and dependent upon her.

As the session went on, the therapist began to experience Diane as very demanding. It wasn't that she was asking a lot of him in any obvious way: she talked very freely, and that should have made it easier for him. But she spoke at such speed and length that it was often impossible for the therapist to get a word in edgeways, and it was difficult to bring the session to a close. At the end, when she had left the room, the therapist felt quite drained; and this happened at the end of subsequent sessions, convincing him that this was something to do with Diane's impact upon him, and not his own tiredness. It was unwise in these early sessions to make explicit his counter-transference (feeling drained), but he used his awareness of it to consider the possibility that Diane needed to feed off his presence and his time, perhaps trying to build herself up in a way which no amount of physical eating could achieve.

What he did suggest more openly was whether Diane might need to *give* so much love because she *needed* love so much: 'You seem to put your unloved self into your husband, or into the baby you so much want, and try to love your self. I think you feel so empty inside, now your husband has gone away, and when you have no baby to feed and look after, and you are trying to fill that void by eating.'

Diane reacted to this interpretation with real understanding: it clearly made some sense to her. This was reflected in the sessions that followed, in that she talked about herself differently. She started to make what were now quite appropriate demands upon her husband: she asked him where she stood, and made him take a share in sorting out their money problems. They both began to accept responsibility for some of the domestic issues that had arisen since their separation. She began to make legitimate demands for herself, rather than to act them out through oblique, obscure, unsatisfying and potentially damaging means. Her eating steadily came under control, and she talked of beginning to feel a sense of her self once more. It was as yet a shadowy self, but she felt she had 'more substance'. In fact, Diane said, whereas before she had lived from point to point through each day – breakfast to lunch, lunch to tea, supper to bed – she was now able to look and plan further ahead. Whereas before 'my arms and legs seemed all over the place and not to belong to me now I am beginning to come together'.

What is of real interest here is not the history (we know very little of it) but the words Diane used, the feelings she evoked, and the images that come to the therapist's mind. This example shows how the 'oral stage' in a Freud/Erikson model can be used as a key to consider what we might call a psycho-dynamic picture of this client. The therapist did not know (and even if the therapy had been longer he may never have known) whether Diane was starved, or felt starved of love during her infancy. It did not matter, except as a question of intellectual interest, whether she had been or not. What helped the therapist, and consequently the client, were the associations he had to Diane, to her presenting issues, and to her language, which linked with his knowledge of the issues around feeding, emptiness, making demands, boundaries, etc. He was able to reflect back to her aspects of how she might feel, which she could accept, and which provided her with a different experience of herself. Perhaps she felt understood on a deeper level and not just at the level of presenting problems. If there had been some confirmatory knowledge from Diane's past, which supported the impressions he was receiving, the therapist might have wanted to add a tentative explanation to his interpretation of her emptiness. He had noted, for example, the short time span of her day (three to four hours, reminiscent of early feeding patterns) and the image of her body being 'all over the place', which was for him so like the baby's flailing limbs.

In this example, the oral and young infant imagery is the most obvious, although it is also possible to look at Diane and her issues from the imagery of another 'stage', or, as I prefer to call it, of another 'theme'. The oral theme can be matched by an anal theme – or at least images and associations which link to that stage of development, with its key features about order and control. It was obvious that Diane liked to organize her husband, and that he was a more disorganized person who needed to break free from her oppressive control. She described how she needed to keep people happy, by saying what she felt they wanted to hear; so she was unable to be assertive and autonomous, to be her own person. She dressed very smartly, even when she said she would have otherwise preferred to wear casual clothes. It was as if she had to look perfect for any casual visitor who might come unannounced. Her rapid speech in the session might have been interpreted as a way of keeping the therapist in his place, and controlling how much he was permitted to say. In this respect there was some confirmatory evidence of this anal stage material from Diane's descriptions of her parents: her mother was very controlled and could not show her feelings, particularly when she felt others might criticize her for them; and her father appeared to have been a strict disciplinarian – a severe authority figure. The therapist might therefore have chosen to make his opening interpretation around this 'control' theme, although he felt that the feeding imagery indicated that Diane had shifted from being controlled and controlling when she had been living with her husband, to a mode of being (an earlier stage?) in which she was not in control of her eating, and unable to make appropriate demands.

What about a third theme, the one that would be linked to the genital or oedipal stage of development? Were there rivalry or sexual issues here? Diane's husband left her in the first instance because he had a relationship with another woman. This was clearly a three-person situation, typical of problems related to that theme. But for the therapist that was almost the sole identifying issue around that theme. With some clients, the material brought to therapy or counselling can be understood in two or three different ways, different lenses with which to look at the presenting material. To avoid confusion in the therapist and for the client, it helps to listen carefully for the predominating theme in each session, and to address thinking and explicit interpretation to one set of issues at a time.

The triangle of insight

The presenting past is therefore seen not in the details of a client's personal history (although when these become known they often highlight the issues), but in the way that history is probably being relived in the present. The 'here-and-now' provides all the clues that are necessary to enable the present to be better understood, especially when those clues can be linked to developmental patterns. Psychodynamic theory includes a concept known as 'the triangle of insight', in which past and present, relationships outside therapy and within therapy, external world and internal world, are linked.

The triangle of insight describes a way of thinking and a type of interpretation which is open to the therapist, which links the client's past with significant people (including the way they have been internalized so that they 'live on' inside the person), and with the client's current relationships to others both in life 'outside' the consulting room, and in the relationship with the therapist or counsellor.

Making links between a client's current relationships and the relationship with the counsellor is not uncommon in much counselling practice, of whatever orientation. The psychodynamic school of counselling and therapy also links these two points of the triangle – out there and in here: for example, 'You've been saying today that you get very anxious when things in your room

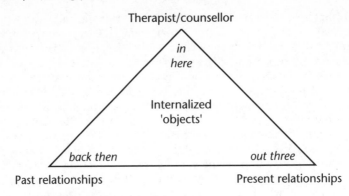

Figure 1.4 The triangle of insight

are out of place: I feel you are anxious here too, especially when I can't make things neat and tidy for you.'

Another link that can be made is between what a person describes in his or her current situation, and a past event or relationship: for example, 'You've been saying today that you get very anxious when things in your room are out of place: that reminds me of something you've said before, that your father was very fussy when anything got untidy at home when you were a child. It's as if he's still there, in your room, commenting on how untidy it looks.'

A third type of link can be made between the client's reported past and the present situation with the counsellor – known in psychodynamic theory as 'transference': for example, 'You say your mother always went around tidying everything up after you as a child. I wonder whether you're also saying that you wish I could put everything in order for you here and give you a neat answer.'

Finally there is the complete triangle, where what Freud calls a 'construction' (1937) attempts to make a link between all three points of the triangle of insight: 'You are clearly feeling that your life's a mess – it feels impossible to put any order on it. I think this is made worse because your father always insisted that you have everything ordered when you were a child, and your mother would make sure it was, to protect you from his rage. I'm wondering whether you're feeling really frustrated with me, because I don't seem to be helping you to get everything sorted out?'

When relevant links are made, whether it is between two or three points on the triangle of insight, this can bring relief, not least at being understood at a deeper level. Insight is not normally enough. It is the relationship between the therapist and the client that provides a safe place where old patterns of relating are re-experienced. The therapeutic relationship provides, of course, the possibility of a good experience, and a facilitating environment (Winnicott 1965b) in which a person may grow; but this is not just by providing *good* parenting. Counselling and therapy inevitably mirror parenting which is (and perhaps was) far from ideal: like the absent or preoccupied mother, a counsellor is not always on tap; like the parent who inadvertently fails to give enough reassurance, the therapist fails to provide enough ordered answers (as in the example above). Like the controlling parent, a counsellor sets limits on the time and availability of sessions; and like the parent in the oedipal triangle, he or she is not available to become the partner with whom the client might wish for an intimate relationship. Negative experiences from the past – frustrations, rejections and disappointments – will inevitably also be relived in the therapy relationship itself, providing the potentiality for the therapeutic experience to evoke, and in the end contain, good and bad feelings, dangerous fantasies, disturbing thoughts, as well as the fondness and freedom of a maturing sense of relatedness.

Looking ahead

The themes which form the central part of this book present material from childhood and adult life from which formulations might be made, illustrating the way the three main childhood developmental stages can be seen in adult clients. My objective is to relate patterns of human growth, emphasizing emotional and relational issues, to the content and process of the meetings between a therapist and a client, using the themes that arise from these three stages. They are linked, as I have argued is appropriate to a psychodynamic approach, to the presenting situations which young people and older adults bring to counselling and therapy, and which are playing a significant part in their life. Each age of life raises issues around trust and dependency, autonomy and authority, competition and cooperation, involving questions of intimacy, sexuality, learning, identity, intimacy, independence, creativity and integrity. Just as each age gives rise to occasions for reworking these basic themes and issues, so counselling and therapy provides opportunities for them to receive particular attention.

Chapters 3, 4 and 5 therefore draw out the three major themes as they appear developmentally, in childhood, in adolescence and adult life, as well as in the relationship with the therapist or counsellor. Chapter 6 traces how these themes are seen at various stages of the therapeutic relationship itself. The Appendix continues to perform the important function which readers of the first edition tell me it has had for them, as a constant source of reference. The Appendix summarizes the substance of the book, listing under each theme many of the difficulties that clients present or describe; it provides pointers to the type of relationship the client tries to create with, or seeks from, the therapist; and it suggests ways in which the therapist may need to be particularly attentive to the needs of the client. It hints at what might make for satisfactory and mature development, which may be said to be the aim of counselling and therapy. These sections, when related to the actual history of the client, help point to the different links that may be made through 'the triangle of insight'.

Terms like 'mature' and 'satisfactory' are of course relative. They are definitions which are bound by time and culture, and even by the value system of one particular subculture, or one person, the author, within it. I do not expect every reader to agree with all that is contained here. Each counsellor and therapist has their own value system, even if some like to think of themselves as neutral. The reader will wish to refine and amend these themes in the light of his or her own experience and philosophy. I argue in the next chapter that each client must be treated as a unique individual; and clearly each counsellor and therapist needs to develop an individual view of what constitutes maturity.

Psychodynamic theory helps the development and clarification of such a view, and can indeed be translated into the everyday practice of the counsellor and therapist. In the desire to make it clear, an author risks making it appear too simple, so before identifying the main elements of each of the themes of trust and dependency, autonomy and authority, and cooperation and competition, the next chapter reflects on ways in which theories of human development and their application to the therapeutic setting need to be qualified and used with care.

INTERPRETING THE
PRESENT AND
THE PAST

The relationship between the present and the past is a fascinating one, which needs to be more fully explored at this point if the main themes in the following chapters are to be used wisely and sensitively. The psychodynamic approach is of course not alone amongst the various therapies in relating past experience to present situations: the cognitive–behavioural approach, for example, in many ways seems diametrically opposed to the psychodynamic. Yet that approach also looks for reasons, often in past learning, that have led to a person's behavioural or thinking patterns. Where there are differences between the approaches they lie partly in explanations of the influence of the past experience, and in the methods they use to help a client alter these patterns in the present.

The concept of the past influencing the present owes something to the argument of cause and effect. Older philosophical thinking (metaphysics) used this as one of the arguments for the existence of God: that wherever there is an effect, there must be a cause; since behind every cause there must be another, this sequence extends into infinity until the prime cause is reached. Psychologists and psychotherapists similarly often look for cause and effect, although as in philosophical theology, any argument that pursues just one single line of cause and effect is too limited and unconvincing. Freud's original case histories show that he was rarely content with a single explanation for the conversion hysteria that many of his young women patients presented in their initial consultations with him. Elizabeth von R., for example, might attribute the pains in her leg to walking, and Freud likewise initially to the place where her sick father's leg rested when she was nursing him; but the most effective interpretation which he made brought together a number of different precipitating factors (Freud and Breuer 1895: 206–30).

A straightforward quest then for the single source of a presenting issue is like trying to find the source of the water at the mouth of the Amazon in a single Andean spring. Even when connecting past and present in an almost literal way, through the hypothesis that the past must influence the present, the counsellor and the therapist should never assume that he or she, or the client, can be content for long with a single explanation. That type of detection may appeal to the amateur sleuth, but is scarcely sufficient in seeking to understand human nature.

Questioning personal interpretation

The connection between past and present is made even more complex, because as well as our experience of the present being influenced by our past, we also have to recognize that our memory of the past is influenced by the present. Our perception and interpretation of people and events have a strong subjective element in them. The way we view the past can be distorted by current circumstances. For example, when we feel depressed, we tend to remember other occasions when we felt bad, and may perceive past events in that light: 'I remember that dreadful holiday after my mother died.' On another day, in another conversation, when we feel brighter, that same holiday may appear totally different in the way it is remembered: 'We stayed in some brilliant places during that holiday we went on after my mother died.'

As individuals we construct our personal history in much the same way as a nation or a people constructs its national or cultural history, in order to support our way of seeing things. However objective we try to be, and whatever facts we try to put forward to inform our judgements, all historical views are inevitably biased, since they consist not simply of facts, but of selected facts, one weighed against another, to support a particular position. No wonder then that a French view of British history, or a Scottish view of English history, or a Black view of British foreign or social history often challenges the commonly held view that the white British person has of his or her country's past. This bias in both the telling and the interpretation of history applies similarly to the way clients construct their personal stories, and to the way therapists hear and interpret them. As one study of contemporary thought suggests, history 'is always written from the perspective of the present; history fulfils a need of the present' (Lechte 1994: 111).

It does not follow that history is irrelevant. How people remember their history, how they relate their history and how they construct their history is a potentially valuable way of understanding them as they are now, or at the point of time in which they are telling their story. It is nevertheless impossible to 'take a history' (as psychiatrists and some therapists do) once-for-all. The history will change, sometimes subtly, sometimes with dramatic new revelations, as the person changes, and as the therapeutic relationship passes through its different phases. Sometimes there are new memories; but all the time there are possibilities of new interpretations. While not detracting from the need for therapists to affirm that certain events happened, and that memories are not playing tricks (especially in trauma work, such as with adult survivors of child abuse), there must always be open debate about the historical reality of all memories. This is true of academic cognitive psychology now, with its admission that we do not fully understand memory, as it was in

Freud's ambivalent position over the fact of actual abuse. Slogans against Freud's view of actual abuse (largely inaccurate, see Jacobs 1992: 101–3) obscure the fact that in the psychodynamic approach to history, there is an interweaving of fact and fantasy, actuality and interpretation: all are experienced as real, and all are essential aspects of the work. As Freud observed in one of his last papers, analysis is interminable (1937a), not just because some patients cannot leave analysis (although this is true) but also because interpretation and reinterpretation is the unfinished task of each person's lifetime.

Freud's work, despite its obvious weaknesses 100 years on, contains certain elements which make any therapist cautious about the status of knowledge: for example, unconscious processes include the repression of unacceptable thoughts and feelings, and make it impossible ever to know ourselves or others 'as we are' (if indeed that phrase actually means anything). We are constantly interpreting and reinterpreting ourselves and external perceptions, not infrequently opting to see the world as we want to see it rather than the way other people see it. It is questionable whether it is ever possible to say with conviction that we see it 'the way it is'. Human relationships are dogged by the problem of misperceptions and misrepresentations, leading inevitably to the conflicts that arise between individuals, groups and nations, each claiming that the way they see things is right and that the way the other sees them is wrong.

It is inevitable then that clients present themselves and their history from particular perspectives which sometimes may need to be questioned, and sometimes may need to be validated in the face of their own doubts about the accuracy of their memories. My concern at this point is to identify the different ways in which *therapists* too look through various distorting lenses at both the client and the content of the client's story and history. Without such qualifications, any approach which tries to use the so-called facts of personality development in work with clients is both dangerous and dishonest.

I take it for granted that one prerequisite for all psychodynamic work is that a counsellor or therapist engages in the continuous task of self-analysis, through personal therapy, through supervision, and through self-monitoring. We only ever perceive 'through a glass darkly', because personal factors affect the way we see everything. Even a period of personal therapy can never rid the individual of their subjective outlook; and indeed why should it? What it hopefully does is to highlight our individual propensity to distort, and our particular personal bias. Awareness of the ways in which the therapist's perception can be influenced by different factors minimizes the risk of believing that the therapist and her or his theoretical base must be right. The position of the therapist or counsellor is powerful enough in the eyes of the client without having to add grandiose self-deception. Many clients at first, and later in times of crisis, want the therapist to know all the answers, and they are ready to 'swallow' anything. (Notice the first theme of trust and dependency, with its metaphor of swallowing.) When a therapist or counsellor misinterprets a client, as inevitably he or she will, the situation is ripe for misuse of authority, especially since therapists tend to put their views across in ways which are warm, caring and beguiling. When Freud said that 'whatever in the doctor's conjectures is inaccurate . . . has to be withdrawn and replaced by something more correct' (1933: 505), the principle is sound; but his own practice does not always suggest such modesty. At times he appears to strive to convince his patients that his view is the correct one. I return to this aspect of his work later in the chapter.

Therapists learn through their own therapy how easy it is for them to be biased. They may learn the particular ways in which they subjectively react to and interpret particular material, and this can alert them to their capacity to mishear and misunderstand. Their formal training also involves academic as well as personal knowledge – about technique, about personality structure, and about human development. The vast literature about therapy and counselling serves this quest for knowledge, and it is of course my own intention in these chapters to make a further contribution to that search for greater understanding. I bear in mind that some of the leading writers in psychoanalytic literature have made it clear that there is also much that they do not know, and that therapy all too often involves tolerating 'not knowing'. One colleague commented on Winnicott, for example, that he had a 'monumental capacity . . . to contain unknowing' (Winnicott 1989). But the sheer volume of the literature on human development and personality structure carries a different message, that there is so much written that there must be so much known. It is difficult to 'not know' when so many books appear to claim expertise.

Winnicott wrote: 'It is more difficult for an analyst to be original than for anyone else, because everything we say truly has been taught us yesterday (i.e. by patients)' (1965b). This is an interesting statement, and one in the end which is essential to bear in mind, since it is learning from clients which constantly informs all the therapist's work, and carries the possibility of enhancing or correcting the misinformation of her or his training. Yet it is also a statement which needs unpacking, since the bias of the therapist, and the prevailing societal values and structures in the period of history in which he or she works, inevitably mean that learning tends to be selective, and that it is often made to fit preconceptions. Thus Freud's patriarchal view of women, or Winnicott's relative lack of reference to fathers in his work are each examples of the way in which ideas are influenced by the time in which they were written. Winnicott acknowledges that he is taught by his patients, but is less aware that the way he interprets what he believes he is being taught is also informed by the values of the society of which he is a part. This interplay of different pressures upon thinking make it essential to be cautious about 'learning from the patient' (this phrase is also the title of Casement's valuable book, 1985). Therapists and counsellors interpret their client's material not just in the light of personal bias, but also in the light of preconceived ideas which their training has taught them, and in the context of their social and political milieu. It is these influences which need to be identified, in order to demonstrate the questions which can validly be asked of developmental models generally, and in this instance of psychodynamic theory in particular.

Science or art?

Freud wished his new found discipline of psychoanalysis to be a science, although he suggested himself that some areas of scientific enquiry, such as biology, can never be as exact as others. The life sciences are generally less precise than the material sciences (Freud 1925a: 242). The scientist in Freud nevertheless seems at times to make universal statements on the basis of fairly limited evidence. While he is far less dogmatic in his writing than many people suppose (he frequently admits the limits of his knowledge, and anticipates the day when some of his theories will be overturned), some of his followers have not been so open-minded or so prepared to disagree with him. Others have questioned aspects of Freud's work theories, acknowledging his skill as an observer, but putting forward different ways of constructing theoretical models from the same observations.

Psychological and sociological research perhaps involves even more variables than life sciences such as biology and zoology. The information from research in these areas often acts as a guide to the way people think and behave, but it is less precise about the individual person than, for example, the chemical physicist can be about the structure of a particular atom. The social sciences themselves debate whether they are more an art than a science, although over this century they have emerged as a different type of discipline to traditional science on the one hand or the arts on the other. Psychotherapy and counselling may be located in that part of the map of knowledge, the social sciences, rather than in the physical sciences, even if it is in the latter sector that many university psychology departments like to see themselves.

Malan (1979) entitles one of his books *Individual Psychotherapy and the Science of Psychodynamics*. Storr (1979) on the other hand entitles one of his *The Art of Psychotherapy*. Art and science both start with observations, but then they diverge. Both interpret their observations, but science does this in order to *explain*, and to explain in such a way as may hold good for all occasions. Art also interprets, but does so to convey varieties of experience, each one unique. A work of art, unlike a scientific experiment, cannot be repeated, even if it can be copied. Science on the other hand relies upon replication in order to validate its hypotheses. Much of this has bearing upon how psychotherapists and counsellors understand the status of theory, and how they use it. Psychodynamic ideas, including the themes in this book, can be applied to many situations and many clients, but they must be interpreted in the light of the individual circumstances of each client. This leads to a uniqueness (as a fingerprint is also unique) in personality and in history, that may be similar to, but is never the same as, another's. It is this perhaps that makes therapy such a fascinating occupation, since every enquiry is different.

Inevitably, as Rayner observes in the second edition of his book *Human Development*, the helper who is 'case-loaded' pays a price, since

> his ideas are only tested informally through his experience, reading and conversation with others. [His ideas] do not meet the criterion of formal testability in an experimental design which is espoused by the research psychologist.
>
> (1978: 16)

In the third edition Rayner explains that his book is 'largely based upon the intimate, detailed work with individual people originated by Freud' (1986: 7), but that his book 'is not a gospel, it is limited in its data and vision. Think of it as asking pertinent questions, let yourself argue with it, think for yourself' (1986: 10–11). This writer would echo those words.

Winnicott or Casement write then of learning from their patients. We read that Freud's early discoveries were almost dictated to him by patients who demanded that he hear them rather than ask them questions about what interested him (Freud and Breuer 1895: 119–20). Counsellors and therapists encourage people to tell their stories, to describe their thoughts and feelings, and to share their experiences; even to put forward their own explanations. None of this is scientific theory, although it may be raw material for more general observations. In other contexts these stories could form the basis of a novel, a poem or drama. D. M. Thomas (1981) in a note prefacing his novel *The White Hotel* goes so far as to say of Freud's writings that they are 'masterly works of literature, apart from anything else', a quality which Freud recognized when he described some of his case histories as being like novellas. Thomas's fictitious case history is itself a masterly pastiche of Freud's style, which reflects with fascinating accuracy Freud's careful exploration of words, images and symptoms. He describes Freud as

> the discoverer of the great and beautiful modern myth of psychoanalysis. By myth I mean a poetic, dramatic expression of a hidden truth: and in placing this emphasis I do not intend to put into question the scientific validity of psychoanalysis.

He may not intend to, but he is permitted to question the scientific validity. Myths may sometimes start as early attempts at explanation (for example, of how the world came into being), but they are much more than this. Jungian therapists appear to give more attention to myths and symbols (both collective and personal) than do most other therapists; nevertheless psychodynamic therapists generally attach particular significance to the use of words and images – they are pointers to the way in which a person consciously constructs experience, and unconsciously processes hidden feelings and thoughts. We might say that we all live out various myths, whether they be stereotypes about others, or in the ways we construe ourselves. Many of our intellectual constructs are myths – expressions of a hidden truth, even if some of them can also be justified as having apparent objective validity.

Language and imagery lie at the centre of many counselling approaches, but nowhere perhaps as thoroughly examined as in the psychodynamic and psychoanalytic tradition. Words and sounds with more than one meaning (such as puns), metaphorical thinking, symbols in waking life and in dreams and narratives form the basis for constructing our understanding of individual people. Each person has a unique story to tell, using both idiosyncratic and shared images with which to illustrate it. Psychodynamic counsellors and therapists try to discern what the symbols, words and stories might mean, what 'truths' they may portray, or even mask. It is not unlike hearing a poem or reading a novel, and asking what the author is trying to convey of the way he or she sees the world, or this dilemma, or that relationship; or what the author is trying to express of his or her own personality, thoughts and emotions. No wonder psychoanalysis has become an important tool for literary criticism and film theory. Psychoanalytic thought is also given more credibility by many sociologists, in contrast to the scorn often heaped upon it by academic psychologists.

Like good art and literature, psychodynamic theory becomes relevant when it speaks (as often it appears to do) to our experience: 'I have felt that'; 'I know that fantasy myself'; 'That helps me understand myself'. Like great art and literature, good theory also leaves room for individual interpretation. The artist, the writer or the composer provides opportunity for each person to fill out the piece in her or his own way, so that it becomes special. Psychodynamic ideas similarly are approximations and pointers, which should leave space for the individual client and the individual therapist to make their own. Even the language used in the theory should not be taken literally. Just as metaphor and simile are common features of everyday speech, so they are constantly present in the therapeutic dialogue in phrases such as: 'It feels like . . .', 'It is as if . . .'. Images are there to be played with, not translated into psychological concepts:

> Eddie said of himself at one point, 'It feels as if I'm drifting through life.'
> I thought about the phrase 'drifting', and then reflected on how drifting takes place on currents, and not at random. I thought of the way his parents wanted him to move in a particular direction, so that his drifting might be passively going their way. When I replied I therefore said, 'Yes, drifting . . . but drifting perhaps on an undercurrent of what others have always told you you should be doing.'

Each person has his or her own imagery, as each has a unique experience of growing and living. At the same time there appear to be certain symbols that have universal appeal: light and dark, the circle, the pillar, the mountain, etc. Perhaps many of these universal images have been borrowed from the natural world and reflect the importance of the external environment, but analysts suggest that such powerful images also describe our internal world. Jungians in particular connect such symbols to the collective unconscious and to archetypes. A different view of imagery is put forward by Rayner who argues that many metaphors and symbols are linked to childhood fantasy. He gives examples of such fantasy in everyday speech, such as 'the evocative language of oral activity' in phrases like: 'I've bitten off more than I can chew', 'She's sweet', or (as I noted above) 'I can't swallow that' (1986: 43). There is of course a danger that this type of psychoanalytic thinking (whether Freudian or Jungian) can lead to standard interpretations of symbols, most commonly, for example, of the unconscious, of mother or father, or of penis, breast and womb. Sometimes such meanings appear to make sense, but it is every therapist's dilemma just how much weight to give to the individual, and how much to the general interpretation of the words and images which the client shares.

Structuring and deconstructing experience

Just as language or symbols can be understood as having certain meanings in common, but can also give rise to highly individual interpretations, similarly all discourse about personal development and character needs to honour the uniqueness of the individual on the one hand, and acknowledge the possibility of common elements on the other. At the simplest organic level, everyone is born; we need special nurturing for a considerable time (although by whom and for how long varies from culture to culture and from class to class); we develop physically at roughly the same pace (even though this depends to some extent on nutrition and therefore upon economic circumstances); we share certain basic needs (but there may be some dispute about which are basic and which are culturally conditioned); and there is no argument that we age and we die. That much (perhaps more) it can be said we hold in common. But already my qualifications show that there can be significant differences over something as apparently straightforward as physical development. Each person lives in a society, with cultural norms and societal expectations, and even a single culture can contain a number of subcultures, in which common cultural experiences are treated and understood differently.

While it is therefore possible, and largely helpful, for the therapist to learn from psychological and sociological studies (whether of large cohorts, or through casework and the individual 'living human document' favoured in psychoanalytic writing) there must be caution about the use of such learning. As Burman writes, 'ideas are tools for change, and they are certainly used to prevent change' (1994: 188). For example, Maguire draws attention to the way in which a strongly biological version of Freud's work was assimilated into the medical establishment in North America, 'where it was often used to bolster conservative ideals of "women's place"' (1995: 53). Burman's critical analysis of developmental psychology leads her to 'hope that at the very least some caution about the indiscriminate application of general models should follow' (1994: 188).

It is therefore vital, particularly with psychological and psychodynamic theories such as this book expounds, to recognize that all our knowledge is conditioned by the society in which we live. Burman illustrates how 'paradoxical, mixed conceptions of developmental psychology testify to the different aspects of its history' (1994: 9). She relates, for example, how in the late nineteenth century, when the observation of children was first taken seriously, only men were presumed objective enough to undertake this, since women would be too involved with children to make good scientific observers. The idea that a woman might understand children better because of her ability to relate closely to children was foreign to these male intellectuals (Burman 1994: 12). Amongst numerous examples which illustrate the need to be discriminating about what passes for evidence in developmental psychology, Burman also cites Bowlby's wartime studies of maternal deprivation (Bowlby 1947). Like other critics of Bowlby she shows how his studies not only imposed upon mothers the sole burden for the development of children, but also made apparently negligent mothers appear responsible for their children's psychopathology and criminal behaviour. Bowlby's findings meant that no account had to be taken of the prevailing economic and social forces, even though these might provide more cogent reasons for understanding crime and mental distress. Similarly in the 1990s, British government statements appeared to indicate that children of single parents did less well educationally, not (as could be put forward as an alternative explanation) because of lack of resources, but because of this single-parent status.

Those who manage society instinctively know how to use psychological pressure.

It is not simply the distortion of Bowlby's research (for example, extrapolating from institutional care to maternal care) that provides a warning. It is also the use to which it has been put: for example, apparently justifying the need for women to return to their home and children. They had proved their value as a workforce during the war, but conveniently for society (or at least the male half of society) this type of research justified women vacating their jobs, and making way for their men who were returning to civilian life (Walker 1990: 29). The lesson must be drawn from its brief history as an applied discipline, that the observations of psychologists are influenced by their historical context, and in turn may be reinforced by political and economic requirements.

Historical context and societal forces also influence the way in which normality and abnormality are understood. Homosexuality, for example, was an official diagnostic category in psychiatry until the third quarter of the twentieth century; and the understanding of schizophrenia, or even of people to whom the label of madness has been applied, differs not just from culture to culture, and from one generation to another, but also within one generation of psychiatrists (see, for example, Laing 1967). Mental illness can even be used to silence political argument, as in post-Stalin Soviet Russia, where the mental hospital replaced the labour camp as the means of dealing with dissent. To take another example: speaking with the spirits can be interpreted quite differently in different societies. In African Caribbean groups, for example, such phenomena are natural and healing; in some other religions speaking with the spirit(s) may be either a sign of particular sanctity or of satanic possession depending upon the extent of the person's orthodoxy; and in Western secular psychiatry, such phenomena are quite likely be seen as a sign of auditory hallucinations or (in a group) of mass delusion.

Further examples of the caution that needs to be applied to any study of human development and character arise in relation to gender, culture and race. Gender issues in counselling and therapy are examined further in Chapter 5, but at this point it is important to note how many studies of human development (especially of psycho-social stages) have been based on hypotheses by male scholars, using norms which may legitimately apply to men, but do not necessarily apply to women. An example of this is the sequence of Erikson's fifth and sixth ages, where he suggests that identity (becoming oneself) has to precede intimacy. He fails to draw a possible distinction between young men and young women. Feminist psychodynamic therapists distinguish between a general tendency in men to wish to separate and to be separate, and in women to wish to relate. 'The male's self . . . becomes based on a more fixed "me" – "not-me" distinction . . . By contrast, the female's self is less separate and involves a less fixed "me" – "not-me" distinction' (Chodorow 1989: 110).

Another important example of gender differences in psychological research arose from Kohlberg's study of moral development (1981), the way in which people make moral decisions. His own studies appear to rate men as more highly developed in their moral thinking than women, but this is on the basis of his assumption (as a man) that justice is the highest ethic. Gilligan, one of Kohlberg's colleagues, was puzzled at this finding, and found in her research that women think more in terms of care than justice, and that mature moral thinking combines fairness and care. Women, as the title of her book proclaims, speak *In a Different Voice* (1982). This distinction in moral thinking had already been observed by Freud as well ('for women what is ethically normal is different from what it is in men', 1925b: 342), which he put down to a less developed super-ego. Whether this explanation is sufficient is doubtful, but given that he equates super-ego development with the resolution of the Oedipus complex, and that feminist psychoanalytic thinking has followed him in recognizing significant differences in mother–son and mother–daughter relationships (see Chapter 5), Freud's early views seem to have received some confirmation two generations later.

Despite the criticism of his developmental sequence Erikson has recognized, as have other analysts who emigrated from Europe to North America, the significance of cultural differences on personal development. In *Childhood and Society*, for instance, he contrasts two North American Indian tribes, the Sioux and the Yurok (1965: 127–41, 169–80). There he links the economic and environmental conditions of each tribe with their ways of rearing children: in one case he shows the similarity between living in conditions of abundance of the prairies and the generosity of Sioux mothers in breastfeeding, together with their lack of concern for rigid anal training; and in the other Erikson observes how the salmon fishermen of the Yurok have to protect the cleanliness of the river and conserve the stocks of fish, which appears to be reflected in their child-rearing in greater oral prohibition, as well as what might be called 'anal' features such as cleanliness in toilet training, and conservation. In recognizing the inseparable link between economic, environmental and family conditions Erikson reminds us that we must look for the same relationship in working as therapists and counsellors with clients in and from different subcultures. This includes awareness of the dissonance caused when those who have been brought up in one culture are compelled (by social pressure as well as economic circumstances) to adapt to a different set of norms and values.

These cultural differences in child-rearing patterns are important. I suspect that the experience of child–parent relationships is necessarily influential in adult character and relationships (and indeed will often be reflected in caring for one's own children, especially when these patterns are reinforced culturally). But whether one method of child-rearing is superior to another in its care and in its promotion of personal development can only be answered from within a culturally determined position – in other words, most of us are biased towards thinking our own culture's values are normal. But other ways of child-rearing may lead to much the same adult characteristics. The book *Children in Collectives* records the visit of a largely American group of child psychiatrists, psychologists and analysts to Israel to study and discuss the effects of the kibbutzim on growing children. It is clear from the record of the observations and the discussion that 'psychologically and psychopathologically, there appeared to be very little difference between the kibbutz and the non-kibbutz child, even though they had been brought up in radically different ways and in radically different surroundings' (Neubauer 1965: 128). While there clearly *are* 'radically different' practices, such as the separation of babies from mothers,

group care, different sleeping arrangements etc., many of the issues underlying the concerns of the observers and the kibbutzim themselves are similar:
for example, the need for a constant and reliable figure for the baby, questions
of transference, sexuality, oedipal issues, etc. 'None of us was really talking of
all-or-none phenomena – that is "no one but the mother" or "the mother not
at all". We were concerned with *degrees* of contact, with a *spectrum* of
mother–child transactions' (Neubauer, 1965: 130, original italics). This study
is a good example of how psychodynamic concepts promote understanding,
in different cultural settings, of the way in which parent–child relationships
affect childhood, adolescence and adult life, but without being used as a set of
moralistic or normative standards.

Yet what are we to make of another way of child-rearing, as in the Alorese
tribe in the former Dutch East Indies? Here the newborn baby is left during the
day in the care of a sibling or adult relative some two weeks after birth, when
the mother returns to work in the fields. During that time the infant is not fed
at the breast, despite attempts to suckle. When the mother returns in the
evening, the baby is nursed and fondled all evening, but this does not make
up for the lack of nursing while she was away working. By one year of age the
infant has to beg for food during the day until he or she is old enough to
forage. The effect of this irregular care pattern is seen in the rage shown by
children between two and five years old, at which point 'the ineffectual rages
cease' (Munroe and Munroe 1975: 42).

The effect of this on the adult Alorese is not surprising. Interpersonal
relations are shallow, grief is brief, marriages are brittle, suspicion and distrust
are endemic, and the Alorese are noticeable for their passivity in the face of
problems (Munroe and Munroe 1975: 42–5). Interpretation of Western
Rorschach tests used with the Alorese show these same characteristics. The
data is clear: the effect of childhood on the adult is obvious; even Western
psychological tests prove valid in use with this tribe. But are we able to assert
that the Alorese are not good at child-rearing as we shift from observation and
explanation to making value judgements? The Alorese way of life is very different, partly determined as it is by the particular agronomy; but it is also their
norm. An adult who dwelt upon feelings or who developed close relationships
might be viewed by them as deviant. Other practices of child-rearing might be
viewed by the Alorese as over-indulgent. But then is female circumcision, cli-
toridectomy, or the masturbation of infants to help them to sleep acceptable
because it accords with a different set of cultural norms, or not? Or in our own
society is it acceptable to send little children away from home to school? These
are not just political questions. They are areas of concern where feelings run
high, but where knowledge and interpretation is relative. Just as Erikson does
not appear to single out either the Sioux or the Yurok Indians for preference
in their child-rearing patterns, so the therapist and counsellor cannot assume
there is only one type of development or one definition of maturity. But there
are also some practices and behaviours which appear to go against more universal norms.

Clearly these questions are particularly important when working with
clients from different races and cultures, but they are also important in
reading psychodynamic, psychoanalytic and psychological texts. Children

brought up to different cultural patterns, or by single parents, or by gay or lesbian couples, or in a kibbutz *may* develop different strengths, or show different weaknesses from children brought up in the mythical normal nuclear
family. It is not the task of the therapist or counsellor to pontificate on
whether these strengths and weaknesses are better or worse for the child and
subsequent adult. These fascinating areas of divergence must be borne in mind
throughout this book, even when they are not specifically explored. Inevitably
any one writer works from her or his own experience, knowledge, and cultural
background. In time it is to be hoped that studies will trace psychodynamic
development from other perspectives, but it must be carried through by those
who indwell that perspective.

For the time being, until alternative studies of human development are written, there will always be a series of question marks over the working concepts
in psychodynamic thought (e.g. the incest taboo and the problem of oedipal
relationships), and whether they are universally applicable. Melanie Klein
writes of a discussion with an anthropologist who objected to her assumption
of a general foundation for character development (1975: 262–3). She appears
to find common ground in the relationship to the primal good object, the
mother, whatever other 'distortions of character are accepted or admired'. Her
use of the word 'distortions' is an interesting one, as if, despite her belief that
there is a common foundation, anything which differs from her own view of
character is in some way deviant. On the other hand, in her example she uses
the idea of the tent and the sanctuary in another community as a symbol of
the good and protective mother in her own. What we may find is that some
of these psychodynamic concepts are metaphors or symbols of aspects of relating, which have value as long as they always open translation into other cultural patterns. In later chapters it will become clear that other psychoanalytic
concepts (such as penis envy and castration, or Lacan's use of the word 'phallus' as something distinct from the penis) also need to be understood symbolically, if they are to have any general value.

Other books specialize in discussing the issues raised about cross-cultural
and gender awareness, bias and prejudice (e.g. Pedersen 1994; Burck and Speed
1995; Maguire 1995; Lago 1996). I assume all this to be vital in terms of therapeutic approach and technique. In this book I wish to underline that therapists and counsellors must also be aware that every aspect of the study of
personal development is open to similar bias.

The danger of labelling

It is an indication of the cultural bias of Western psychotherapy and counselling that I turn at this point to the application of psychodynamic knowledge to the individual client. Individualism is typical of the Western view of
the person, as well as being indicative of the political climate at the end of the
twentieth century. (Lago (1996: 78) neatly summarizes this culturally determined outlook.) Nevertheless, while in no way wishing to neglect the individual's relationship to others and to society as a whole, as a therapist I need
to validate the uniqueness of each client's personal history and present

circumstances. Even when we have taken into account the relativity of much psychological knowledge, gender and cultural variations, conscious and unconscious bias, and the political and social context in which therapists function, it is important to look at how we apply theories of personal development to individual clients. There is a danger, in a text which sets out ways of identifying major psychodynamic themes, of promoting a type of 'pathology-spotting', or labelling of clients, which fails to do justice to the individual situation.

This is especially so in an occupation where it can feel essential to cling to a sense of order in the midst of the prevailing chaos or disturbance of a client's presentation. There is safety in labelling people; and there is a false security in technical language and jargon, of which there is plenty in psychodynamic literature. Such technical and impersonal language is of course present in the medical and psychological disciplines from which psychotherapy and counselling have sprung. Counsellors can sometimes feel that their own explanations, attitudes and feelings are amateurish and simplistic; and in their communication with colleagues in the medical or psychotherapy setting, they may feel obliged to use a technical vocabulary and diagnostic categories. When others are using words such as psychotic, neurotic, character disorder, depressive, manic, obsessional or hysteric like the rest of us use prepositions and conjunctions, counsellors and therapists who are trying to prove their value and demonstrate their expertise do not simply have to learn to understand these terms, but also feel under pressure to adopt them as labels for their clients.

Categorization, which labelling to some extent represents, is of course an inevitable part of every intellectual discipline. This chapter has already cast doubt on how objective research can be in this area of human enquiry, although in practice therapists and counsellors are bound to go on using theories and technical terms to communicate more clearly and precisely with each other. Yet it is important to challenge some of the assumptions that go with the use of categories, labels and technical language; and there is a more relevant and effective way of using this process of identifying where the client is.

I have already shown in the example of Diane (pp. 21–2) how one client's material can be approached from a number of different angles, and interpreted in the light of a number of themes. What the therapist perceives, and sometimes what the client chooses to present, can vary due to the individuality of the therapist (what one sees one way another will see differently), and sometimes from interview to interview. Counsellors and therapists whose work permits access to medical case-notes, particularly the fat files of patients who have seen several consultants, doctors or psychologists, may be aware of how many of them have been placed in a variety of diagnostic categories. I recall one client, whose notes I saw, who had been diagnosed in four different ways by the same psychiatrist on four different occasions. Given the qualifications made above about the status of knowledge, that should not be surprising.

There may be value in finding the right label, or diagnosis. It is particularly important, for example, that counsellors and therapists involved in assessing whether or not clients are suitable for therapy are able to identify factors which help clarify a person's psychological state; when, for example, there is some suspicion of conditions which are beyond the scope of the counsellor, the agency or the individual psychotherapist. In this context a certain amount of labelling is inevitable. Nevertheless the need to label can also lead to stretching labels beyond recognition. One such instance presented in supervision involved a client whose psychiatrist had labelled her an 'atypical bulimic'. In fact she only occasionally ate too much, and then might take laxatives. But it was not a major part of her presenting problem, and, as the supervisor said to the therapist discussing this client, since he had dreams which contained 'mad' elements, he might as well be labelled an 'atypical schizophrenic'!

Effective labelling may help a client. In another context, for example, it is reassuring to the patient with a pain in his chest to be told by his doctor that it is not cancer or heart trouble as he feared, but that he has strained a muscle decorating while painting a high ceiling. Or if the cause of the pain is indeed more serious, it is probably not only the doctor, but also the patient, who will want a definite label to be attached as soon as possible. Even when the prognosis looks unfavourable, identifying the illness may carry some reassurance for the patient. Counsellors and therapists have less opportunity to provide such definite information, although it can be extremely relieving to a client to be assured that he or she is not 'mad'. Knowledge, however, in this area of work, is always much less precise than it is in medicine or the law. Psychodynamic theories may help therapists identify what is going on in the client or in the therapeutic relationship; but they are not so easy to share with clients: while saying, 'You are clearly depressed' may be an effective empathic response, even if it does not constitute a very clear diagnosis, saying, 'I can see you've got a narcissistic personality' is not going to get the therapeutic relationship very far!

The themes which I explore in the following chapters are not intended as means of labelling or even diagnosing clients. The aim is rather to provide a way of looking at, and understanding, the therapeutic relationship as it concentrates upon a person's inner world, with all its emotions and internal objects. Since this is an area which abounds with confusion and contradiction, and which is full of intense and often disturbing feelings, for clients as well as for therapists, the various themes and sub-themes may sometimes provide an important sense of security, a reference point in the midst of bewilderment, to which a therapist might look, and from which there may come some sense of direction. As long as the themes and the terms used within them do not become simple catchphrases, but represent a way into the complex network of presenting problems and past issues, they can also provide a range of possible clues to look out for in the material with which the therapist is presented. The label 'depression', for instance, is little use in itself, but might lead the therapist to look further, for a sense of loss, or guilt-feeling, or self-loathing, or repressed anger, or over-zealous conscience, or a morally or physically punitive upbringing, or any combination of such factors.

The label in these circumstances is not used to foreclose the issue, or fob off the client, but to widen the horizon, and to trigger off a series of associations and questions which can extend the therapeutic plan. But there is another approach which might be used, which obviates the disadvantages and dangers of labelling, and which provides more opportunities for translating the general theories of psychodynamic psychotherapy and counselling into the particular work with each client.

Naming

There is clearly some value in labelling, and therefore in learning both the language and the method which psychodynamic practitioners use, and used well, both can benefit the therapist as well as the client. But the idea of identifying what is happening in the client and the therapeutic relationship is capable of a much richer way of working and of understanding than general application of theory permits. I therefore introduce an alternative term, which also promotes a distinctly different concept, and which appropriately (given the need to think across cultures) is seen in many non-Western societies. It is the concept of 'naming'.

> The different use of the concepts of labelling and naming is illustrated by a client who had seen me for quite a long time. Freda opened one session by asking, 'What's wrong with me? Am I a manic depressive? Am I neurotic? Do I have an anxiety-state?' I was rather concerned how best to answer this, wondering which she wished me to pronounce. But I decided to reply honestly (and partly because I was not sure I really knew!) that I was not normally interested in attaching such labels to people. To my relief Freda replied that if I did, she would want a category all to herself! The reason was obvious: she came from a large family, in which she was the very middle child; time and again she had talked of situations both in her family and in present relationships where she felt that she did not matter. She saw herself as always left out of invitations to parties, she felt people ignored her, she recalled how her parents had teased her when she showed early signs of intellectual promise, which marked her out from their other children. She desperately wanted recognition, and yet she also felt guilty when she got it. She wanted to be treated as a unique individual. And she was prepared, had I labelled her, to insist on that too in any 'diagnosis'.

It is the uniqueness of the individual which lies behind the ancient concept of 'naming'. Ursula Le Guin, in her fantasy novel *A Wizard of Earthsea* (1971) employs this concept in a remarkably powerful way. Although each person, each animate object and each inanimate object has a common name – one which is used in normal speech – each also has a special and secret name. In the case of animals and objects this name has been passed down from ancient times in ancient speech. People are given their true name either in infancy or at puberty.

Salman Rushdie uses a similar concept, in his case clearly part of Muslim thought, in his novel *Haroun and the Sea of Stories* (1990). In one scene the Water Genie asks Haroun to pick a bird to travel upon. Haroun looks around the room but only sees a peacock carved in wood. The Water Genie tells Haroun that he can choose what he cannot see.

A person may mention a bird's name even if the creature is not present and correct... A person may even select a flying creature of his own invention... To give a thing a name, a label, a handle; to rescue it from anonymity, to pluck it out of the Place of Namelessness, in short to identify it – well, that's a way of bringing the said thing into being.

(Rushdie 1990: 63)

There is a positive and a negative side to this concept of naming and bringing into being. Haroun clearly benefits when he can name his means of flying; but by the same token naming may bring the more feared imaginations into being. I return to this danger below. Naming is an awesome act, and this is seen in the way in which Ursula Le Guin develops her story. She observes that those who are wise are able to control objects and people only when they are able to give them their true name. Because of the power of the name people only give their true name to those whom they can trust. 'A man never speaks his own name aloud, until more than his life's safety is at stake' (1971: 46). The giving of your name to the other gives the other a certain power over you.

Such a fictional concept is shown to have a real basis in many cultures, in Africa, in the East and the Middle East and in Polynesia. In his book on psychology and religion, Leslie Weatherhead similarly writes about the significance of a person's name. He describes how in the East giving one's name is felt to be the surrender of power to another (1963: 64). He cites as evidence a number of Indians in a regiment in which he served in the Great War, who would not give their true name lest their officers should acquire an uncanny power over them. In case of their death they kept their true name in a little cylinder on their person. Similarly, he says an Indian bride would not give her true name to her bridegroom until after the marriage ceremony. Weatherhead is particularly interested in the way these examples reflect the significance of naming in the Judaeo-Christian tradition. He cites the episode in the Old Testament where the angel wrestles with Jacob and asks Jacob his name. Jacob gives it, but when he asks the angel his name, none is given. Similarly the power of the name is seen in the New Testament, for example in the healing of the man possessed by many devils. It does not matter whether this story is true or not. As I have indicated earlier, myths contain hidden truth. What is crucial in that story is the question, 'What is your name?'; and the devils' reply, 'Our name is Legion', because it is this name which gives Jesus power over them.

The power involved in the act of naming is the central feature of Le Guin's story *A Wizard of Earthsea*. The story is of a young hero, Sparrowhawk, who, in a fit of youthful pride, conjures up a shadow from the dead, which nearly destroys him. The shadow follows him and he tries to flee from it, without success. An old wizard, the one who had given Sparrowhawk his true name, tells him that he must stop running, and turn and face the shadow, and name it. Sparrowhawk protests, 'The evil thing, the shadow that hunts me, has no name.' '*All* things have a name' is the reply. Sparrowhawk turns and now becomes the pursuer, while the shadow becomes the pursued, until at the ends of the earth he names it. Without revealing the climax of the story, there is enough here to show the relevance of this concept of naming for therapy and counselling.

Naming forms an important part of the therapeutic process – far more relevant to the individual client than labelling. First, it is an essential part of the initial session when clients are able to name what is troubling them. This process not only brings inner distress into the open, but it also begins the process of removing the fear and anxiety aroused by and associated with their present experience. Naming starts the process of owning and controlling the person's fear of what is happening to them, in their external or internal world.

Second, naming is seen in the way the therapist responds, in recognizing individuality, treating the client not as 'another depressive' but as a unique individual, with her or his own particular problems, and her or his own life experience contributing to those problems.

Third, naming provides the opportunity of naming those parts of the self which frighten the client. In the ongoing process of naming, as in the initial naming of what troubles them, clients can experience considerable relief from the power that these parts of themselves have over them. Such naming takes place in a variety of ways. Parts of the body, for instance, may be given their proper name by the therapist or the client, and rescued from their association with guilt and shame – particularly the sexual. Words like 'homosexual', 'gay/lesbian', 'masturbation', which even in a more liberal society still trouble many, cease when named to hold the same power in an individual's conscience. Similarly other parts of the self, 'forbidden' feelings like hate, jealousy, revenge, envy, even perhaps for some people love, when named come within the compass of an individual's ego-control, rather than being repressed or suppressed. Anxiety and guilt about feelings, actions, thoughts, parts of the mind and parts of the body are lessened as each one can be named and brought into the open.

However, this is a subtle process. It is not enough, any more than it is enough with simple labelling, for the therapist to hammer the client into submissive acceptance by technical language or by clever interpretation. Naming takes place when something which is already known by the client is given that final push into consciousness or into words. In her novel *Possession*, A. S. Byatt writes of the recognition that takes place when we see something which at the point of seeing we realize was always there:

> Now and then there are readings which make the hairs on the neck, the non-existent pelt, stand upon end and tremble, when every word burns and shines hard and clear and infinite and exact, like stones of fire, like points of stars in the dark – readings when the knowledge that we *shall know* the writing differently or better or satisfactorily, runs ahead of any capacity to say what we know, or how. In these readings, a sense that the text has appeared to be wholly new, never before seen, is followed almost immediately, by the sense that it was *always* there, that we the readers, knew that it was always there, and have *always known* it was as it was, though we have now for the first time recognised, become fully cognisant of, our knowledge.
>
> (1990: 471–2, original italics)

There is no magic, no secret formula, no clever interpretation which can reach that depth of a person unless that person is already near to self-recognition. 'A mage can control only what is near him, what he can name exactly and wholly' (Le Guin 1971: 60). Therapists and counsellors can only speak of what is known (how can they presume to do otherwise?), not from a theoretical background but from the client, however much theory may inform their practice. Theory sometimes proves to be true, and sometimes proves not to be true. Unless it is translated into an individual's current presentation, it is likely to give rise to interpretations that make the therapist feel more secure than the client. Naming on the basis of theory alone may give the therapist the feeling of being helpful, but it probably also colludes with the client's fantasy that as an expert the counsellor has only magically to 'speak the word' and the client will be healed. Interpretation, especially if it is based on guesswork and not what the therapist 'can name exactly and wholly', may even give the counsellor the sort of power over the client that the person most fears. It is vital, when naming takes place, whether by therapist or client, that power should remain with the client, and that power should be based on self-recognition. As psychotherapists and counsellors we must not replace repression with oppression. Winnicott writes that premature interpretation 'annihilates the creativity of the patient and is traumatic in the sense of being against the maturational process' (1971: 117).

One of the misconceptions about psychoanalysis and psychodynamic psychotherapy is that analysts and therapists make standard interpretations. It is true that at times it seems that Freud equates all dream symbols with representations of sex; and Melanie Klein in some of her case histories appears to make what can only be called leading interpretations. Psychoanalysts in particular tend to write for other analysts, and often frame what they have to say in technical language, failing to give us a true picture of the give-and-take of the consulting room. In what is otherwise a technical book on groups, the French psychoanalyst Anzieu underlines in his opening pages that 'in everyday practice . . . [the analyst] expresses himself as much as possible in everyday language' (1984: 4). Freud writes about the need to get close to what the client is trying to express, rather than interpreting indiscriminately. In one of his papers on technique he warns against the analyst imposing ideas upon the patient. 'It is not difficult for a skilled analyst to read the patient's secret wishes plainly between the lines of his complaints and the story of his illness' (Freud 1913: 140). But he stresses the danger of plunging in with interpretations when the patient is a 'stranger', adding that 'even in the later stages of analysis one must be careful not to give a patient the solution of a symptom or a translation of a wish until he is already so close to it that he has only one short step more to make in order to get hold of the explanation for himself' (1913: 140). He even appears to acknowledge mistakes in his own practice when he writes, 'In former years I often had occasion to find that the premature communication of a solution brought the treatment to an untimely end, on account not only of the resistances which it thus suddenly awakened but also of the relief which the solution brought with it' (1913: 140–1).

Freud appears to have forgotten this in one of his very last papers, where he asserts that the patient or client is always able to reject the wrong construction, and that no harm will be done if the analyst makes a mistake. He adds that if the analyst realizes that a mistake had been made 'we shall admit as much to the patient at some suitable opportunity without sacrificing any of our authority' (1937b: 261–2). There is false reassurance when Freud says in the same paper that 'an analyst would have had to behave very incorrectly' (1937b: 262) before the danger arose of leading the patient astray by suggestion. He also appears blind to his former admission of error when he adds, 'I can assert without boasting that such an abuse of "suggestion" has never occurred in my practice' (1937b: 262).

What Freud fails to do in this paper, written only a few years before his death, is to recognize just how powerful the authority of the analyst, the therapist or counsellor can be, particularly where the process of naming is involved. The description of naming which Rushdie's Water Genie gives Haroun contains an implicit notion that *anything* can be created by naming it: 'A person may even select a flying creature of his own invention . . . in short to identify it – well, that's a way of bringing the said thing into being' (Rushdie 1990: 63). Therapists and counsellors will know clients who have been damaged by carrying around with them a psychiatric label which some tactless doctor or psychologist has given them in the past – the correctness or not of the initial label is immaterial. If naming is therapeutically so much more powerful than labelling, then wrongly used it is by the same token more dangerous. It is not difficult to see how a counsellor or therapist can create in the client what may indeed have been dimly part of the client's unconscious, but which should have been allowed to remain there, by being strictly contained within the boundaries of the therapist's imagination. In his old age Freud fails to recognize the ability to misuse the power of the interpretation.

Another old man, a very knowledgeable but largely self-taught naturalist, once spoke (in a personal communication) about what he called 'sweet power'. This is not power over others or, in the context in which he was speaking, power over the environment. 'Sweet power' comes from being able to stand at a particular point in the country, and looking around, naming the geographical and natural features, being able to recognize the plant and animal life, and the relationship of the parts – including the observer – to the whole, in that microcosm of the natural world. It is perhaps something like the naming of the beasts in the Genesis story of creation. It is not merely a scientific exercise, nor (he made it quite clear) is it a way of showing off knowledge – as some labelling is. It is a process whereby a person feels in touch with, and in tune with, the environment of which he or she is but one part. Ursula Le Guin puts similar words into the mouth of the old wizard in Earthsea:

'When you know the fourfoil in all its seasons, root and leaf and flower, by sight and scent and seed, then you may learn its true name, knowing its being; which is more than its use. What, after all, is the use of you? or myself?' Ogon went on a half-mile or so, and said at last, 'To hear, one must be silent.' The boy frowned . . . kept back his resentment and impatience . . . For he hungered to learn, to gain power.

(Le Guin 1971: 269)

There is one last aspect of 'naming' which links with the frequent reference made in this chapter to metaphor. I refer above to the Genesis story of creation, and to the power given to Adam to name the creatures. One interpretation of this is to see in the act of naming that Adam was not himself the creator, but was given a share of power over creation. In one of the poems in *Possession* A. S. Byatt alludes to this Genesis story, echoing in her own way the power of naming which Rushdie and Le Guin also describe:

> The first men named this place and named the world.
> They made the words for it: garden and tree
> Dragon or snake and woman, grass and gold
> And apples. They made names and poetry.
> The things *were* what they named and made them . . .

The significant words follow:

> . . . Next

> They mixed the names and made a metaphor
> Or truth, or visible truth, apples of gold.
> The golden apples brought a rush of words
> The silvery water and the horrent scales
> Upon the serpentining beast, the leaves
> All green and shining on the curving boughs
> (The serpentining boughs) that called to mind
> The lovely gestures of the woman's arms
> Her curving arms, her serpentining arms . . .

> (Byatt 1990: 464)

In this beautiful playing with words, A. S. Byatt reminds us that 'naming' (and indeed 'labelling') is itself a metaphor, and that all language is a means of trying to bridge the gap between inner experience and outer reality. It is also important to recognize that therapists, counsellors and clients use words, as indeed a writer uses words, because it is probably the most convenient means of expression. This means that what therapists, clients and writers identify and name is still only an approximation to inner experience. Since psychodynamic theory therapy is full of metaphor, there is a point with clients when it becomes essential to make it clear that what they and we speak and name may be better than a label, and may carry more force and feeling than a label, but that it is still only a fallible and one-dimensional expression of the inner world.

Conclusion

Given this important proviso about psychodynamic language and the power of the interpretation, we may summarize the argument of this chapter: psychodynamic theory meets our desire for greater knowledge as therapists, to explore further the inner and outer worlds of human relationships. Much as this knowledge may prove valuable, it has limitations, not only because of what is not known, but because even what appears to be known is embedded in societal, cultural, and gender assumptions, which must always cast some doubt upon the permanence or objectivity of these and other theoretical concepts.

Seen as metaphors, sometimes even as symbols, which can enhance the art and skill of the therapist and counsellor, psychodynamic ideas and language have much to offer therapists and clients. The terminology itself may promote clearer communication between practitioners, although using the theory and language to label clients runs the risk of merely giving therapists power over their clients, whether to pronounce upon what is wrong, or to analyse what they are like. There is always the risk inherent in any categorization of losing sight of the individual, but there is also the danger of burdening the individual for life with a misleading or even damaging self-image.

Naming, on the other hand, ultimately provides deeper security to clients, for in the end they are helped to do the naming themselves. Naming gives them a sense of control, that is based less on head knowledge, and more on insight and on acceptance of more hidden parts of themselves. Naming recognizes and explores the 'being' and the uniqueness of each individual, for ultimately it is by name we are known, not by label. By recognizing how even naming itself is a metaphor and that what we name are also metaphors, then as counsellors and therapists we are less tempted to use our knowledge to become as gods.

Developmental models and themes provide many clues to possibilities which ultimately only the client can confirm or deny. If the themes inherent in human development are to have any value, it will not simply be because they promote knowledge, but because they can be integrated with those inner senses of which counsellors and therapists are already aware from their training. Combining the knowledge of the theorist, the insight of the artist and the humanity of the therapist is a delicate skill. Theory only serves therapists and counsellors well if it serves the client well. It is primarily clients who make theory, and not theory that makes therapy.

TRUST AND DEPENDENCY

Introduction

Since it is one of the axioms of psychodynamic counselling and therapy that past experience (both of external events and as subjective perception of those events) strongly influences reactions to the present, it is not surprising that in psychodynamic thinking the earliest experiences of human life are reckoned to form the foundations for all subsequent development. Indeed psycho-analytic theory, even if it may take different forms in different writers, is in agreement that the first relationships between a baby and her environment (particularly the person(s) who provide infant care) can be either very beneficial (when the care is good) or very damaging (when it is bad or neglectful). There is within psychoanalysis, as elsewhere, debate about the relative strength of the influences upon personal development of nature and nurture: how important is genetic inheritance, natural temperament, and the environment in which the child grows, especially that provided by parents or parental figures? Melanie Klein, for example, appears to stress innate factors, and others such as Bowlby, Fairbairn, Winnicott and Guntrip prefer to emphasize environmental factors. Winnicott wrote: 'Environmental influences can start at a very early age to determine whether a person will go out for experience or withdraw from the world when seeking a reassurance that life is worth living' (1988b: 128).

The relevance of this for the practice of counselling and psychotherapy is twofold. First, and most obviously, there is a parallel between the start of a therapeutic relationship, and the starting point of human relating in infancy. These parallels will become clear in this chapter. The way in which people make or break other relationships, particularly close or intimate relationships, similarly depends upon the way in which other earlier relationships have been experienced. Both trust and the capacity to be dependent (or interdependent) are obviously key factors in the way people relate. Second, the attempt to enter into the experience of the infant may be relevant to understanding not just how positive experiences strengthen the formation of the growing personality, but also towards understanding some of the long-standing and severe disturbances from which some people can suffer. Some of these people may not be suited to psychodynamic counselling, or may require the skill of an experienced and extraordinarily careful psychodynamic therapist. But all those who work in this field need to have some comprehension of the effects of early deprivation, abuse, and neglect.

Trust and dependency can be difficult issues in therapy. They are also very difficult to imagine when contemplating how an infant experiences her early situation. How difficult, perhaps even impossible, it is to enter the experience of the baby, even for those whose detailed observations have described the relationship between a baby and her tiny world. It is tempting (unless you are the parent of a young child) to imagine that life is straightforward for the infant, consisting as it does of the round of sleeping, feeding, bathing, playing and sleeping. While we know that life gets more complicated with age, infancy itself is imbued with the adult fantasy of innocence. A more dynamic picture of a baby is far from sweet and charming. Indeed, those who study the writings of Melanie Klein may at times find it difficult to believe the horrifying picture she appears to paint of the child, until, perhaps, parents remember the times when only partly in jest they have called their child a 'little monster'. Most parents have seen their baby's rage, and they are only too aware of how powerfully a baby can make her demands felt.

It is well recognized that the long period of dependency of the human child upon its parents makes for particular features in the process of development. For a considerable time (although it often feels longer than in fact it is) babies need others to feed them, to give them security and warmth, and to make them comfortable. What goes on inside their minds in those early months? Just as it is very difficult to imagine a state of being unborn, or of being dead, so it is hard to imagine the thoughts and feelings of a baby. Very few people have memories of being a baby, and some psychologists might be very sceptical about how much supposed early memories can be called genuine memories. But if the leap of imagination is hard, it is useful to attempt it.

Much psychoanalytic writing helps us, almost poetically, to imagine what it may be like to be content and full, and what it may be like to feel the pangs of hunger; what it may be like to be held by someone who loves, and what it is like to be held by someone who is anxious or angry; or what it may be like not to be held at all. The language that describes these experiences is of course drawn from later life, from those times that counsellors and therapists and their clients can more readily imagine or remember, and when they have words to describe that experience. While we cannot be sure whether it is right to describe infancy by using the language about thoughts and feelings that arise in later childhood and adult life, it is worth making the attempt, especially if later adult experience uses these metaphors to describe innermost thoughts and feelings. The amalgam of information and speculation in psychoanalysis about the earliest months of life has sometimes been criticized as reading back into childhood the experience of adult clients. Certainly we have to be very careful of interpreting childhood from the perspective of the adult; but one aspect of the richness of psychoanalytic writing on infancy is that it provides a language with which to conceptualize the inner experience of seriously disturbed adults (generally known as psychotic or borderline personalities, or as those with personality disorders). It may also help us to achieve a better understanding of clients (and ourselves) whose life may generally be less severely disturbed, but who experience intense episodes of need, fear and despair. It may be of course that in the continuous process of living, our early days are little different from our later ones in terms of inner experience. It is the same pleasure or despair, differing not in degree, but in the circumstances that cause it, because later knowledge acquired as an adult can sometimes set a single experience in a wider context. Adults may know why they feel the way they do; babies do not.

Starting from nothing

One of the differences between analysts in their understanding of the earliest weeks of infancy is over the question of the precise nature of early relationship between baby and mother ('mother' being the most common and straightforward term to use here, although of course 'mother' may include father, or may not be the natural mother). Before birth, of course, mother and baby are intimately linked, and at birth that physical link is, in one sense, severed. But are they still intimately linked psychologically, as one person? Is there perhaps a type of symbiotic relationship, as for example Winnicott claims, or does the baby have to bond with the mother, as Stern or others have observed? Winnicott, for example, writes that 'there is no such thing as a baby' (1964: 88), but rather a nursing couple, as if the baby does not (and cannot) exist on her own. Daniel Stern finds this idea of undifferentiation between mother and baby 'very problematic . . . at the same time . . . it has great appeal' (1985: 240). The idea appeals perhaps because it touches an early memory – but we cannot know whether this memory is of the womb or after birth.

The problem here is that it is not easy for us to unlearn years of experience and perspective, in order to try and imagine what it may feel like to be a newborn child: a state where there is virtually no knowledge, and not yet enough experience to constitute memory and learning. As adults we have many frames of reference. We know, for example, that night follows day, and we can visualize summer when it is winter. We have memories which support our knowledge so that we can recall times and seasons, and we know that they will return. At the same time some painful feelings can be so strong that it is impossible to imagine that good feelings will return – and if that is true for adults, it is probably no less true for infants and children. It is of course impossible to imagine a time when we knew nothing, and did not know how to make sense of each new experience. For a newborn baby this lack of knowledge gives rise to 'fantasy' – primitive attempts to make sense of experience without any knowledge as yet of 'reality'.

Perhaps the closest we get to this in imagination is when we are due to visit a new place, or to meet a person with whom we have only spoken on the 'phone. We form an idea of what the place or the person will be like, and very often we are surprised that the reality is not at all like we imagined it in our fantasy. The disjunction between fantasy and reality may even (temporarily) be quite disturbing, although we quickly adjust to the new situation. As adults we take for granted this ability to imagine, or, to use psychodynamic language, 'to fantasize'. We have sufficient knowledge and experience for our fantasized expectations not to become too wild. Similarly most day-to-day experiences in adult life can be assimilated readily into some frame of reference.

A newborn baby, however, has no frames of reference, and has to learn to set her experiences in perspective. What interests the psychodynamic observer is what the baby experiences as that learning takes place. The baby learns that the pain of hunger is relieved by sucking, when sucking produces something warm, sweet and wet; and that the discomfort of cold disappears when wrapped in something warm and secure. But if the reader's picture here is immediately of a mother's breast, or a soft blanket, a new baby has no such knowledge. Milk, a blanket, mother's skin – none of these have as yet any objectivity. A baby does not know whether they belong to her or whether are outside her. It is in this sense that it can therefore be said that all experience is unitary: there is no division between 'me' and 'not-me'. A baby's thumb (in her perception) may be no more or less attached to her than the mother's nipple. The boundary between what is me and not-me, between self and not-self, the space between the body of the baby and the body of the mother – all these are only gradually distinguished.

Self and not-self

The relationship between mother and baby is sometimes called 'symbiotic' not because of this deep sense of primitive unity, but because each is depen-dent upon the other. As such it is a misnomer: although a baby will not sur-vive without mothering, a mother can survive without her baby, although not without real pain. Viewed psychologically, however, it may be the right word to use of some mother–baby relationships. Many mothers, in the period of pregnancy, birth and early weeks, are primarily preoccupied with their baby, not just because of their baby's demands, but because they need the baby as much as the baby needs them. Some mothers describe this as 'being in love' with their baby. Danah Zohar writes of her pregnancy:

> I experienced what for me was a strange new way of being. In many ways, I lost the sense of myself as an individual, while at the same time gaining a sense of myself as part of some larger and ongoing process.
>
> At first the boundaries of my body extended inwards to embrace and become one with the new life growing inside me. I felt complete and self-contained, a microcosm within which *all* life was enfolded.
>
> I experienced myself as extending in all directions, backwards into 'before time' and forwards into 'all time', inwards towards all possibility and outwards towards all existence.
>
> (1991: 193)

We catch glimpses of such a state in adult life in those moments where we experience 'oceanic feelings', when for a fraction of a minute time itself seems suspended and we feel a sense of harmony which cannot adequately be conveyed in words: the harmonies of music sometimes express it better. It is also seen in the confusion of space and time boundaries which can result from the use of hallucinogenic drugs, both in good and bad 'trips'. It is generally the bad experience that might bring people to the counsellor or therapist:

> Gemma had been slipped LSD in a drink. She described the terror of time sliding backwards and forwards, together with a frighteningly vivid conflation and confusion of herself with two people whose deaths she had witnessed years before. At one moment she felt she was them, at another that they were her, and she was convinced that she was going to die too. Fortunately this was an isolated incident, and after she had been able to describe the terror, she was able in a more grounded way to look at her memories of these two deaths, and some of the (unjustified) guilt she was still experiencing over them.

The effects, or even the after-effects, of drugs may be responsible for these types of frightening experience. But confusion about the boundaries between self and other, or over time or space, may be a sign of a deeper level of disturbance than is appropriate for a counsellor and some therapists to consider working with. When a client refers to such a confusion, particularly to feeling apart from the world about them, or even from their own body (such as physically experiencing looking down upon their body), a therapist needs to consider various possibilities:

- it may be an example of dissociation (often linked with a history of severe trauma or abuse);
- or of a borderline personality, where generally the person can relate to the therapist, but describes experiences which can feel to the client and to the therapist as 'over an edge', too far out of touch with reality;
- or of psychotic disturbance, particularly when the person apparently has no awareness that what they are describing is strange; or when, even if they are disturbed by the content of their thoughts, they are not actually disturbed that they are functioning in such a way.

It is vital to be aware of these levels of disturbance, particularly at a time when counsellors and therapists are at times asked to take on clients who in an earlier generation would have been cared for elsewhere. In the first two instances (dissociation and borderline personality), developed skills, considerable experience and good supervision are essential in the therapist. An over-interpretative technique might trigger off psychosis. In the third instance of psychotic states, psychiatric assessment and cover is essential. There are only a few psychodynamic therapists experienced enough in working with people who are psychotic. Where there is evidence of drug or other substance abuse, again specialized help might be necessary.

Symbiosis is of course not all bliss. Mothers can experience pain along with their troubled babies. And other mothers, it is important to add, do not necessarily view their pregnancy and/or their newborn baby with joy. Indeed, pregnancy and/or birth may lead to a particular type of depression. Some psychoanalytic or psychological observations about mothering, particularly by male writers who can easily idealize motherhood, have contributed to women feeling inadequate and depressed if they do not experience the pleasure of being a mother. On the other hand some analytic writers have made it quite clear that the emotions of motherhood include hate as well as love: e.g. Winnicott's list of reasons why a mother can be said to hate her baby (1975: 201), which he links to the hate which therapists can also feel for their patients. Dana Breen describes in detail the different experiences in pregnancy and the early weeks from actual conversations in *Talking with Mothers* (1989).

The confusion of self and not-self is not confined to the mother–baby relationship, nor in adult life to the seriously disturbed. It is part of all relationships. It will not always be troublesome, although it may lead to strained relations – when, for instance, we attribute to another person a thought or feeling which we cannot see is in fact a part of ourselves; this is known as 'projection'. A similar psychological phenomenon is 'projective identification'. This can be seen at work when we find ourselves experiencing feelings, which somehow seem to be ours, but at the same time make us wonder where they have come from: 'Why am I reacting to this person this way?' There are, of course, many explanations for this, but projective identification suggests that such feelings have been 'put into' us by the other. I may therefore disown my angry feelings for my partner, by 'making' her the one who becomes angry with me (and most subtly of all, without her realizing, or even me realizing, that I have made this happen). Projective identification is not unusual in close relationships, such as between sexual partners, or in the therapeutic partnership.

Projection and projective identification are reckoned in psychodynamic theory to be early (or 'primitive') defences, although in the early weeks of life they are thought to be natural defences against overwhelming pain or terror, occurring as feelings and experiences pass almost without barriers between mother and baby. One of the tasks of psychodynamic therapy and counselling with adults is to receive such projections and identifications, to hold them, and at the right moment to help clients receive them back. In some instances they will be able to take back what belongs to them. Those who project can be helped to own their feelings and responsibility. In other instances clients have swallowed what others say negatively about them, taken on board the projections of others, and in such cases may be helped to recognize that other people have contributed to their difficulties. So these clients may be helped to temper their sense of over-responsibility for things that have gone wrong. As one counsellor described her client in supervision: 'It's almost as if she became part of her father's mental illness.'

Here again we see the significance of the phrase 'me/not-me': what belongs to me, and what belongs to not-me? The term 'self' has similar connotations, as can be seen from the way it is used in everyday language: 'I seem to have lost myself'; 'I don't understand myself'; 'I am not myself anymore.' The concept of the 'self' certainly has complex psychological and philosophical problems attached to it, but ordinary life too is full of different types of problems around the self. The self can get lost, for example, in love. When people fall in love their personal boundaries seem to merge. Absence of the other 'half' (the term is an interesting one) is like losing part of oneself. The language of love (as much as the act of love) frequently expresses the interpenetrating of each one by the other. If this phase of love is perpetuated, not permitting separateness to be re-established, a person may fear losing him- or herself in the other:

> Harry became desperate when he realized how his love for Isabel made him so dependent upon her that she was able to play him along, always calling the tune. He needed Isabel so much that he was afraid to say anything which might destroy the relationship. At the same time he felt resentful at being treated like an object that could be picked up and dropped at her whim. Things got to such a pitch that he resolved to break off seeing her, and was able to do so. Immediately he felt so different that he told the counsellor, 'I have got my self back again.' He had feared being desolate and alone, but found himself able to relate to others much more easily. Harry was then, and only then, able to see parallels between the confusion of his self with Isabel's, and the relationship between his parents. He remembered a time when his father was cutting a piece of wood, but cut it to the wrong length. Father had immediately blamed Harry's mother, with the result that Harry was bewildered. He could not understand what his mother had done. His mother also confused him, because she would say, 'If you do this, or don't do that, you'll kill me.' He remembered feeling puzzled as a child about how such things could happen, and what it meant about the way people interacted. He had had to distance himself from his home before he found any sense of identity for himself; and he had lost it again in his relationship with Isabel. One of the aims of counselling was to help Harry to establish the boundaries of his own identity. Only when he had done this would he be able to get close to another without fearing the loss of himself.

Omnipotence

In his construction of the early relationship between mother and baby Winnicott suggests that a baby is born with a mental conception of the breast. There is little doubt suckling is an instinctive act. The baby searches for something that should be there, and knows what to do as soon as she has found the nipple, or has been presented with it. But Winnicott's observation is about more than an instinctual process. It is the mental process which is also important. When a mother presents her breast to her baby, her baby is looking for the breast she needs, and the baby 'thinks' that she has 'created' the breast. All these of course are metaphors: we can scarcely call this 'thinking', as (for example) the reader is presently thinking. But Winnicott is making an observation which is particularly relevant for understanding the nature of omnipotence.

'I thought it, and it was there.' Finding the breast of which she had conceived perhaps leads a baby to believe in the power of her thought, or her wish to make things happen. She is, in a sense, omnipotent. 'I have only to think it, and it is there.' This type of thinking lays a basis for later belief in oneself, or for trust and faith – these terms might at this point be interchangeable. While we may think of these early months of life as engendering trust in the mother (and indeed this must be part of the experience), the baby's sense of being able to create something lays down an even earlier sense of trust – belief in oneself. Since mother is not yet perceived as a separate person, this trust is in 'everything' – the baby, the mother and indeed the whole (little) world the baby experiences. 'When I want it, it is there.' In fact, this early sense of omnipotence will not last. Winnicott calls it an illusion, and it is indeed the first of a whole series of illusions which we experience throughout life, some of which we come to question. It is one function of a mother to provide the basis for such illusions to take place, and it is soon her task to help her baby towards disillusionment, as the baby learns that the breast is not always there, and that life is not always there for the wishing. But at the beginning it is the mother's provision of herself, at the point at which a baby seeks the breast or needs to feed, which creates this sense of confidence in the nascent self, and which forms a foundation for the maturing sense of self. By contrast, a baby who does not find her needs met not only feels frustrated, but is also denied an early lesson about her ability to create.

There are two sides to this in our work as therapists with adult clients. People can have sufficient sense of confidence in themselves, laid down in infancy and no doubt reinforced in their childhood. They believe in themselves and trust others, and in some sense have confidence in life itself, even if life can be unpredictable. Others incline to pessimism or cynicism, even when life is going well. It is not that those who are confident think they can make every-thing happen; but they know that (often as a result of working at it) some of what they wish for can happen. There is in them a basic optimism that life is on their side, and that it is worth living. They may be knocked by events, but the counsellor senses enough basic strength or confidence to merit some opti-mism in the process. This can be contrasted with the much more difficult task of working with those whose mental conceptions of themselves are either bleakly pessimistic ('I never get anything I want'; 'I am powerless, and can do nothing'); or are frighteningly omnipotent: that is, frightening to others ('I am going to have whatever I want'); or frightening to themselves ('I thought that, and so it must have been me that caused it to happen').

An example of such an omnipotent fantasy could be seen at work in John. He had met the girl of his dreams, but his difficulty – as the counsellor saw it – was that it *was* all a dream or a daydream. John *believed* that she would marry him, but she (who had also seen the same counsellor because she was unable to handle John's attentions) was clearly angry at the way he was pestering her – not quite as threatening as stalking, but almost as troublesome. She had tolerated his calls at her flat, but she made it quite clear that she already had a relationship. She had said, 'Let's just be friends', even though she did not like John at all and only felt sorry for him. Such a slender straw was enough for John to cling to; he read this as her wish being the same as his; and he redoubled his efforts. She moved, and she refused to answer his telephone calls. He wrote, but she did not answer, until one day she grew tired of his persistence and replied, to tell him about her new job. Once more John grabbed the straw, and sent by return an erotic love letter. Nothing could shake John's conviction that he was going to marry her. 'But he's not in love with me', she said despairingly, 'he's in love with himself.'

John was certainly in love, but in love with an illusion, an object of wish-fulfilment, an idealization of the girl and of their relationship. When John himself saw his counsellor he provided an opening in what could so easily have been an intractable situation when he said, 'It's God's will that I marry her.' John had a religious faith, which enabled the counsellor to address him in a slightly different way: 'You seem to be very sure that you know God's will . . . Perhaps you are trying to tell God what you want.' This oblique reference to John's wish for things to go his way (even taking on God's omnipotence) implied that he did not stop to think what the other person might wish. The shock tactic of this intervention seemed to make a slight impact upon his thoughts about the girl. Perhaps suitably reminded of his own fallibility John replied at that point, 'Perhaps I should wait and see what happens between us, and try not to push it too much.' The counsellor was not very confident that things were resolved, but thought it was a step in the right direction.

The facilitating and containing mother

This way of thinking about a baby, her mother and the environment suggests that the small world of the baby is as Balint describes it, a 'primitive, harmonious, interpenetrating mix-up' (1968: 72) – although of course sometimes the mix-up is not all that harmonious. It is quite hard to imagine what it might be like for her, when this is the only 'world' a baby knows. 'The horizon of the baby extends at first a few inches, and later only a few feet from his body. Its adequacy is determined by the very restricted exchange between mother and child' (Scharff 1988: 15). When the baby feels good, even though the source of that feeling is not yet clear, the world as a whole is good; when she feels bad, everything is bad. It is like being caught in a hall of mirrors, which almost infinitely reflects either good or bad feelings. It is this that is a baby's first experience of her environment. That little world enlarges of course as the child grows, but first impressions count for much, especially at such an impressionable stage. It is probably an all-or-nothing existence, which is not unfamiliar in adult life:

> Kate was talking about the last few months, which she had spent in Africa: 'When I first arrived I was almost worshipped by the people in the village – I was put on a pedestal, and I felt really great. But after a couple of months they got used to me, and me to them, and I started to feel ordinary – well, not ordinary, but really criticized by some of the people there. I'm like that. Things can be pretty wonderful, and then all of a sudden they go off, and I have to find something new. I'm an all or nothing person.' Perhaps this linked with the issues which she first brought to therapy – alternately over-eating and then starving herself: all or nothing.

There will be times, then, when everything feels very good for a baby, but also times when everything feels bad. It is impossible for a mother to be ever-present or ever-attentive, even though most mothers are very alert to their baby's needs. The points of frustration are important for the baby's development, the beginning of learning that in the end there is nothing simply on tap. There are some pains which mother can do little to relieve, when nature must simply take its course, and her baby will not be comforted, however hard she tries. What matters is that the mothering is reliable and dependable, so that where there is pain there can also be comfort, and that where there is waiting there is also satisfaction.

It must sometimes feel impossible to get it right, because too anxious a mother may also give rise to an anxious baby. It is not only the neglectful mother who nurtures the seeds of doubt. A mother may be too preoccupied with her baby, for too long 'lending her own self to her infant' rather than encouraging the development of the infant's self and 'recover[ing] her self-interest' (Winnicott 1965a: 15). Winnicott uses the phrase 'the good-enough mother', or 'the ordinary devoted mother' (1988a: 3–14), meaning by this one who is attentive and adaptive to her baby's needs, but who also knows when she is not wanted; one who contains the painful feelings in her baby, but who gradually introduces the wider world, so that it gradually impinges upon her infant. She provides the foundation for the emerging view of the world that in later life is recognized as sometimes heavenly, and sometimes hellish, and on balance a good enough place to be. Trust in oneself comes from a dependable mother-figure, whose reliability gives rise to a broad sense of trust in the ever-widening world beyond her.

Issues about trust and dependability are present to some extent in every client. The parallel between the reliable and sensitive mother and the reliable and sensitive counsellor is obvious here, although only in the work which some experienced therapists undertake with deeply regressed clients is there any real replication of the daily attention which a mother gives her child. The reliability of the counsellor or the therapist is maintained by keeping to appointments, by being able to listen without making the client anxious, and by being able to contain 'bad' experiences and feelings. The therapeutic relationship provides the milieu in which, in Alice Miller's words, there is 'freedom to experience feelings which are spontaneous. It is part of the kaleidoscope of life that these feelings are not only cheerful, beautiful and good, but that they can display the whole scale of human experience including envy, jealousy, rage, disgust, greed, despair and mourning' (1979).

The need for reliability perhaps goes without saying. Yet no therapist can be so reliable as to be constantly present for the client. Apart from illness and those occasional but unavoidable times when they cannot keep an appointment, counsellors and therapists build time breaks into the contract, both through regulating the frequency of appointments, and through holidays. Neither can therapists hope to avoid lapses of concentration, or the failure to understand, any of which shows therapists to be fallible. Counsellors and therapists cannot fulfil the wish some clients have for a substitute mother. Such moments of 'failure' provide important points to take up clients' feelings of disappointment, anger or sense of loss in relation to the therapist. When such feelings can be vented, they can sometimes be linked to past experience (without in any sense letting the therapist 'off the hook'); or they may be opportunities for enquiring into past disappointments.

In some writers on counselling and therapy (more often from a humanistic perspective) there is a tendency towards idealization of the role of the thera-pist, whose main task is providing all the right conditions that will enable the client to grow naturally. Clients can also idealize their therapist, and counsel-lors need to be wary of colluding with such a picture in order to boost their self-esteem. While it is the endeavour of all therapists to provide what Winni-cott called (in respect of mothering) 'a facilitating environment' or the 'environment-mother' (Winnicott 1965b: 75), therapists inevitably fail to do this. To describe the therapist–client relationship with any accuracy, especially in terms of trust and dependency, we need to set alongside each other two con-tradictory statements of Winnicott's:

> It is the mother–infant couple that can teach us the basic principles on which we base our therapeutic work.
>
> (Quoted by Guntrip 1968: 361)

> He can never make up to clients for what they have suffered in the past, but what he can do is to repeat the failure to love them enough . . . and then share with them and help them work through their feelings about his failure.
>
> (Quoted by Malan 1979: 141)

Dependency and attachment

Psychoanalytic literature refers not just to dependency (and the more arguable term 'symbiosis') but also to 'attachment'. Dependency is a relationship which gradually alters so that a person becomes more independent. Winnicott describes three states, the absolute dependence of early infancy, relative dependence, and 'towards independence' (1965b: 84). Relative dependence involves the child learning to tolerate anxiety when mother is temporarily absent; and learning about loss, all within the bounds of what a child can take. Winnicott's phrase 'towards independence' indicates that this is never an absolute state: it is not isolation (which I describe below) but interdependence between the individual and the environment.

Unlike dependency, the concept of attachment is one which applies throughout life (Parkes *et al.* 1991), although types of attachment vary, in reac-tion to early experience of the mother–child relationship. Attachment theory owes much to the work of Bowlby (1969, 1973, 1980). Secure attachment is seen when an infant is able to use mother as a base from which to explore the world, being willing to separate from her for brief periods. As an adult a securely attached person is confident of those with whom he or she closely relates. By contrast, anxious attachment can be seen in the person who clings and is over-dependent upon others, because of their anxiety about the reliability of attachment figures. Detachment is a third way of dealing with relationships, particularly likely to result from long and repeated separations from key figures in childhood. Detachment is a defence against the anxiety and pain of anticipated loss in relationships.

In reaction or response to mothering which is either neglectful or over-indulgent, a child may become clinging, or withdrawn. Both defences can be seen in adolescent and adult life in those who cling to drugs, alcohol or food, or who live in a fantasy world, in extreme cases becoming psychotic (see below). They may at the same time withdraw from intimate contact with people. It is probably the case, especially where there is evidence of a disturbance to the continuity and effectiveness of early mothering, that clients who present in this way require long-term counselling or psychotherapy, or other specialized help. There will of course be less extreme examples of withdrawal or dependency in every short-term counselling practice:

Lara had fallen in love: everything was heavenly, her boyfriend was 'super', her work going 'very well'. Even her terminally ill father had begun to rally. But none of this eased her problem of overeating. When she was on her own she ate and ate. She could not see anything that caused it, except to acknowledge that the only cloud on the horizon was her fear of being let down when she was so happy. A previous boyfriend had left her when she had least expected it. Her counsellor wondered whether eating was a way of trying to store up happiness. He made several interpretations along these lines, although they had no effect on her voracious appetite, until one session in which he suggested that it was almost as if she were saying of her boyfriend and her father (both of whom she feared losing), 'I'll eat you up – I love you so much.' This remark appeared to have a dramatic effect; from that session on Lara's eating became more normal. She was also able to move towards getting in touch with her discontent at her boyfriend's lack of consideration for her.

In this instance the counsellor knew little of Lara's early life, upon which to base any idea about her early experiences of attachment. He concentrated on the present situation, but he used imagery which appeared to suit one of the presenting issues.

In the following example, the family history had some relevance in what was also short-term work:

Mike had fallen in love. This had created some turmoil for him, because he was a 'fiercely independent' late adolescent, following his father who had laid great stress upon that particular virtue. Mike's father was the child of a broken home, and had been shunted from one part of the wider family to another, and from one institution to another. Subsequently he had been successful in his career, and he brought his sons up to think of career first, and relationships a long way second. Mike too had been successful to date, ahead of his peers in many of his achievements, but afraid of being caught up in a close relationship. He was not only worried what his father would think; he was scared in case he ceased to love his girlfriend, or she stopped loving him. Mike described their relationship in this way: 'She has got into the pool, whereas up to now I have only allowed my close friends to dip their feet in.' The way she had 'got inside him' was a disconcertingly new feeling, though it only appeared temporarily to throw him.

Some clients fear dependency on their therapist or on the process of counselling. This can be expressed openly at assessment, but may be expressed obliquely, as in the reference made by one client to the anxiety he felt about becoming dependent on the tablets the doctor prescribed. There may also be clues to anxieties about dependency in the client's pattern of relating to others:

> Nan said in her first session that she tended to see people two or three times, and then break off relationships. The therapist was therefore alerted to the possibility that this might also happen with her. Indeed after four meetings Nan aired the idea of stopping. The therapist reminded Nan of what she had said in the first session, and looked with her at her present anxiety about closeness.
>
> Nan illustrates the withdrawn person well. She feared close relationships, but deep down longed for comfort. She sought therapy because she was so isolated, spending much of her time on her own, eating and sleeping. Her early history demonstrated that her infancy had been traumatic. She had been born prematurely, and her mother died soon afterwards. Her first weeks of life were spent in an incubator, and it was several weeks after that before she left hospital. Father had been looking for somewhere to place her. She went into a foster home, where food or a dummy was used whenever one of the children was upset. When Nan's father married again, and she was taken back by the new family he now had, she rejected her stepmother. Nan later experienced further losses of other members of the family whom she had allowed to become important for her. Little wonder that she could not allow herself to depend upon another person, for fear of losing them. She found herself hating people once she had got to know them a little, and this seemed to be a way of forestalling any rejection they might first make of her.

This presentation was typical of the personality type that is known in psychoanalytic terminology as 'schizoid'. A schizoid person maintains an emotional distance, even in what might otherwise be a close and intimate relationship. Although long-term therapy may be necessary for shifting a schizoid pattern of relationships, such clients can of course seek counselling for other reasons than their relationships, in which case short-term work may be possible. A counsellor may be able to build a relationship with such a client of sufficient trust to make long-term therapy for the deeper issues a possibility.

Sometimes a client uses an intellectual defence in order to avoid closeness, which may prove difficult for the therapist, since the 'feeling mode' is kept at a safe distance:

> Oliver found solace in his books, and passed his exams at school well ahead of his own age group. He had been brought up in a home where there was not simply material poverty, but also extreme poverty in the quality of relationships. His parents' constant rows drove him to his room and to study. At school he made friends, but never close friends. It was not until his mother died that the dearth of love in his life hit him, although his presenting problem was complete inability to progress with his doctoral thesis. He tended to talk intellectually in his counselling sessions, looking all the time for explanation – and always in a most affable way – but unable to get near to any feelings of sadness or of closeness. The most obvious feeling he experienced was anxiety about closeness, but he

avoided that socially by keeping people at a comfortable distance. It took many months before he could begin to show any glimmer of sadness; the counsellor did not push for feelings to emerge, but rather used the 'intellectual' style of the sessions to point out constantly the fears which Oliver might have. Helping those who have deeper levels of pain can take a very long time, and requires respect for the defences that protect them.

If one of the difficulties in working with a detached person is creating a relationship in the first place, the opposite is true of the clinging, dependent client, who might be said to latch on to the relationship offered by the therapist, and hungrily demands more and more time, help and attention.

Peter had been four years in therapy in an outpatient department of the local psychiatric unit when he came to the counselling centre. The therapy had terminated six months before, and he was still feeling depressed. What was noticeable was how quickly he raised questions about what he and the counsellor would do when it came to the summer break; how difficult it was to get a word in edgewise with him (although he also did not give away much about his deeper feelings); and although he was on the surface very warm and friendly, the counsellor soon recognized how difficult it was to end sessions. Peter always wanted to take them over time. Thinking about what he said, one of the clearest themes that emerged was his experience of being let down when he thought he was in a committed relationship, and the counsellor tried to identify this as the anxiety Peter felt about any thought or talk of endings.

The therapist can easily feel 'drained' and empty, frustrated and angry, perhaps mirroring in her or his counter-transference the dependent client's own feelings of emptiness and anger, neither of which can be assuaged. But dependency takes many forms, and the inner compulsion to make demands can make some people feel so guilty or ashamed that they become afraid of expressing their needs, or are constantly apologetic about 'taking up your time'. They are afraid of their hunger for love in case it drives people away – which, of course, is what a demanding person often does.

Counsellors, and indeed many therapists, are not in the course of their training given sufficient experience in handling a full regression, as in the really damaged and demanding clients, who may call upon the therapist at all hours. Where such demands are experienced, therapists need to be able to preserve their own and their client's boundaries, remaining steady but reliable over time limits and frequency of meetings. It is important to remember that in such cases more frequent meetings do not usually stem the demand, and even suggest that boundaries can be pushed even further. Supervision is clearly vital for working with such phases in counselling or therapy.

Less regressed but similarly demanding clients may indicate their need and their discontent through quiet grumbling or open hostility. If this can be brought out into the open and accepted by a counsellor or therapist, without retaliation on their part, a client can often appreciate the security of firm boundaries, whereas wavering and flexible times often make the client feel even more anxious. A reliable and stable therapist who cannot be shaken by the client's demands or by their attacks enables a client to feel more secure and less fearful that the needed relationship will be snatched away. A therapist who constantly tries to reassure by acceding to requests can make a client feel anxious and guilty. Winnicott writes of this: 'In the analytic situation the analyst is much more reliable than people are in ordinary life; on the whole punctual, free from temper tantrums, free from compulsive falling in love, etc.' (1975: 285).

It needs to be said, however, that it is easier to write about the balance between setting limits and showing care than it is to effect it. It can be difficult to weather the storms which blow up, hard on both the therapist and the client. Until a client feels secure in the relationship with the therapist, and understands that the frustrations involved in the relationship are not the therapist's retaliation towards the client as 'bad' or 'needing to be punished', it is difficult to move from the intensity of the therapy relationship itself to look at other relationships outside the session, and to wider areas of concern.

The link between being 'bad' and being demanding is seen in the following example:

> As a child, Quia clung to her mother for many years at those times when mother was home from the mental hospital. She was a frequent non-attender at school, until the age of ten, when she overheard her mother saying to a neighbour that her most recent spell in hospital was because she was worried about Quia's clinging behaviour. Although it was initially mother's absences which had made Quia so dependent, the situation was now turned on its head; it appeared to her that it was her demands that were driving mother away. She also recalled an early occasion of mother's absence when an aunt with whom she was staying refused to let her see 'Watch with Mother' on the television, because she had not 'performed' on the potty after lunch. We might restate that situation as: 'If I cling on to what is in me (i.e. my faeces), that prevents me seeing mother too.' After Quia had heard mother speaking to the neighbour she determined to become self-reliant, and went to school without making any fuss. But the problem had been pushed underground, because in her first session with her counsellor she several times used the phrase, 'You can't rely on anyone.' The counsellor observed that Quia was probably wondering if she could even rely upon her: but in this instance even this was not enough to help her return for a second session.

Reliability and dependability are important with all clients. With demanding clients it will help them to learn that however badly they think of themselves this does not alter the constancy of the therapist. With those who are fearful of making demands and allowing themselves to become dependent, the steady attention of the therapist may help them to make the first moves towards the trust that they need to engage in the therapeutic relationship.

Narcissism and self-respect

Demanding people often treat people as if the sole purpose of the other is to serve them. Difficult though it is to be treated in this way, it is easier to understand such expectations if they can be linked to a natural and normal stage in early infancy, before a baby has learned to recognize limits and boundaries, or the necessity of living with the realities of other people's independent concerns. The following words, which Winnicott first broadcast in a series of talks to new mothers, are just as applicable to new babies:

> Enjoy yourself. Enjoy being thought important. Enjoy letting other people look after the world . . . Enjoy being turned in and almost in love with yourself . . . Enjoy having more right than you have ever had before or will have again to do just what you feel is good.
>
> (1964: 26)

When older children, adolescents or adults behave in such a way we call them selfish, or more technically, narcissistic. It is perhaps unfortunate that psychoanalysis uses the term of infants too, where it is usually called 'primary narcissism', since it has such a pejorative ring to it. But whatever the merits or drawbacks of the term, it can be used in this descriptive way of babies and young children, since they need to have sufficient narcissistic 'supplies' for themselves (to use a somewhat unsatisfactory psychoanalytic image) before they can show concern for those who care for them. It is from the security of being loved that we acquire both the confidence and the wish to love others. In adults it is this same unfulfilled narcissistic need that lies behind egocentricity. The narcissistic person, so often criticized as self-centred, has not in fact acquired sufficiently strong a sense of self-love to be able to express concern for others and for their well-being. What appears as self-opinionated talk frequently masks lack of confidence, vulnerability and lack of self-esteem. Although a narcissistic adolescent or adult can easily become at the very least a bore and at worst an object of hostility, we might be more tolerant if we could understand that what we call selfishness is in fact a sign of the opposite, a depleted sense of self.

Raoul was described by a psychiatrist who had once seen him, as one of the most narcissistic people he had met. Popular opinion might venture that it was being an only child which had 'spoiled' him (the word carries an interesting *double-entendre*); but in fact Raoul's mother had had little time for him, and had sent him out of her room whenever he went to talk to her when he was small. He keenly felt the status of an outsider, which in his case was reinforced by his nationality and his religion. One of the issues he presented was his anger with others whenever his 'private space' was threatened: for example, when he lost sole use of his office at work and had to share it with another; or at the presence of his (third) wife in the living room, bedroom or kitchen which he felt interfered with his wish to watch television, sleep or cook a meal; and when doctors refused to take his hypochondriacal symptoms as evidence of physical illness. All this made Raoul go wild. He saw himself as looking after his wife in a generous and selfless way, although it appeared that she represented a part of himself that wished to be looked after. In his fantasies he had devised schemes for robbing banks of money – they had plenty and they would not miss it. He was always looking for an ideal job with high status, yet he gave up opportunities where he could have done very well for himself after only a short time, when negative aspects of the job appeared. Although Raoul liked to think of himself as important, he was taken aback when the counsellor offered to see him for a year: he clearly believed that no one would ever offer so generous a time. Indeed it took that year before he began to recognize how badly he had treated people. It was only in the penultimate session that he acknowledged how he had made each of his three wives feel insecure. The counsellor pointed out that Raoul too, as a child, had been made to feel insecure, and that much of his behaviour sprang from his insecurity. It was important to support his self-respect at those times when he was able to be honest with himself, because the inflated sense of self hid a fragile and frightened person.

Kohut is one of several psychoanalysts who have made a particular contribution to working with what we should more accurately call narcissistically damaged clients. Josephine Klein explains his thinking in an admirably clear chapter called 'Feeling Grand' (1987: 203–27). In summary, a baby needs to 'feel grand' when her needs are met by the parent. But where there is narcissistic injury, the child may grow into a 'grandiose' person, as if they are always struggling to feel grand, but never succeed in this, whatever their external achievements. Kohut's clinical practice suggests generous empathic responses to the narcissistic client as the main form of intervention, without attempting to make the usual type of interpretations in which a client is encouraged to link present feelings to past experience. The exception to the empathic response will be when the therapist in some way fails in being empathic and has therefore been unresponsive to the client's needs. The client is at such times particularly encouraged to look at the limitations in the imagined grandness of the therapist. Thus the therapist concentrates upon accurate empathy; and only as a second stage, when the client feels really understood, on explanation.

Since a narcissistic person has a fragile sense of self, which constantly needs boosting, there may be real difficulties for the self-absorbed person in mid-life, when physical well-being begins to wane, illness becomes more common and the signs of ageing are more apparent.

In an article on mid-life, Chessick describes one such person: a 48-year-old married woman, unusually talented, presented with tension and arthritic pain in various joints, and a morbid fear of growing old and dying. In her relationships with her husband, her teenage children and with friends there were no major disturbances. Her history revealed a mother who had resented having her as a baby, because of the mess that was inevitable with an infant. But both mother and father had encouraged the growing child in her considerable musical and other talents, although this left her little space for ordinary play. Her parents fostered her 'infantile grandiosity' and her being 'outstanding and unique', which must have been a welcome change from feeling mother's rejection of her (at least in some respects) as a baby. Instead she found her sense of self through having to be brilliant at everything, and through being praised for it.

In her adult life she gave many successful musical performances. But with the growing evidence of ageing, in terms of her physical appearance and creative power, her arthritic joints making her playing music less fluid, and the death of some friends and relatives, this woman had to face weakness and limitations in the immediate future, and mortality in the long term. Chessick writes that she was 'what we might call a "successful narcissist" until the second half of her life', but her sense of self was bound up in body-image, and in achievements that were now less easily achievable. The sense of self she had developed as a child and as a younger adult could no longer be sustained. Her therapy, over four years, proved successful, partly through her coming to understand the deprivation in her childhood and her need for 'empathic soothing and relaxation in the parent–child interaction'; partly because she was able to internalize the actual experience of this which she received from her therapist.

(All quotations in this example are from Chessick 1983: 5–12.)

Winnicott describes this type of personality as a 'false self', and suggests it is not uncommon: 'The defence is massive and may carry with it considerable social success. The indication for analysis is that the patient asks for help because of feeling unreal or futile in spite of the apparent success of the defence' (1965b: 134). In Winnicott's terms we might understand this as being a major crisis of disillusionment, because the prospect of death, certainly no respecter of persons, and the thought of dissolution of the self, puts an intolerable strain on the illusion of omnipotence. 'Death exposes the superficiality and triviality of many of the ambitions and aspirations on which men spend their energies' (Macquarrie 1966). Letting go (in many of life's events) is more gracefully accomplished when we feel secure enough in ourselves. In dying, and in loss and disappointment of all kinds, acceptance is more possible (although never easy) when we have a strong enough sense of our own value and the value of others to tolerate the wounding of our narcissistic pride. Some will react angrily, even showing paranoid concerns about ageing and death, as if both are 'out to get me' and have to be defeated: a quite different reaction to that will to survive which can bring some people through life-threatening situations. Other narcissistic personalities, on the other hand, might be able to bask in being looked after and cared for, as if they were once again children – as long as this caring is sustained, because even the contented older person, enjoying such nurturing, can of course turn bitter and demanding if the care is not as continuous or as great as is needed.

Pride (at least of an inflated kind, because in other ways children and adults need to feel proud of themselves and their achievements) is often a defence against feelings of worthlessness. The narcissistic client may find it difficult to accept what the counsellor says, not simply because it appears critical, but because it strikes at the root of his or her being. What I am describing here is different from guilt, although it is near to shame. People who show narcissistic damage may feel bad about their whole self, whereas when they feel guilty or in some instances ashamed, they are more likely to dislike or feel bad about one particular aspect or action. Broucek concludes an article linking shame to early narcissistic developments with these words:

Shame experiences disrupt the silent automatic functioning of the sense of self, and shame is therefore considered to be the basic form of unpleasure in disturbances of narcissism. The grandiose self is viewed as an evolving compensatory formation instigated in large part by primitive shame experiences.

(Broucek 1982)

It is perhaps cynical to suggest it, but there are certainly some clients who so enjoy talking about themselves that therapy seems to feed their narcissistic needs in an unhealthy way. Their talking about themselves may of course be confined to more acceptable concerns, as they defend against deeper feelings of worthlessness. But there are other clients who, far from seeking praise and attention, demonstrate a real devaluing of their self-worth. This is typically heard in the protest, 'You must have people who are much more in need of your time than me.' This may indeed partly be a defence against self-explor- ation, but it is often also a demonstration of inability to claim time and atten- tion for themselves. They may be afraid of their wish for love and affection, in case it is never achieved, or in case it is lost as soon as it is found; their low self- esteem is a form self-denial, to prevent intense feelings later of disappoint- ment.

Simon expressed doubts early in the first session about therapy being self- indulgent. He went on to talk at length of various family situations in which, as a child, he had to defend his mother against his father, his sister against his mother, and look after a sick brother. Such concerns meant that in late adolescence he had to abandon his own plans and wishes. He could see how he had had to assume an adult's responsibility for others, which did not permit him to enjoy his own childhood. The therapist related all this material to Simon's difficulty of having anyone for himself: 'You seem to be saying that no one cared for you, you had to care for them, and you aren't at all sure you can allow someone to show care for you.' Simon's eyes filled with tears, confirming the accuracy of this inter- vention.

A middle-aged woman introduced herself to the counsellor as 'second- hand Topsy'. In the session which followed there were many examples of allowing others to be indulgent at her expense. When the counsellor had to alter the times of their meetings two sessions running, she acquiesced and denied any feeling of being put out. She was grateful that she was able to see her at all. 'You have to put yourself second here too, even though it would be natural to feel something about my changes of time', the coun- sellor observed, 'just as you put yourself second with others.' Topsy often said that she felt selfish coming to counselling, although later she was able to accept that she could sometimes put herself first. She found it difficult to relate freely to others: she was continually concerned not to offend them, needing to make sure of their favour, but at the same time suffering because they (often themselves more obviously narcissistic) took advan- tage of her.

The complaint that counselling or therapy is too self-centred, individualis- tic and introverted is by no means rare, and it contains some truth. Therapists need to tread a narrow path which involves giving generously of their attention to clients, and encouraging in them an awareness of their own needs; yet also challenging them to look at areas of emptiness and of distress, as well as at their impact (or lack of it) upon other people. Given that the term 'narcissistic' is used in two quite distinct ways in psychoanalytic discourse, the one positively to describe an essential aspect of development, and the other somewhat pejoratively to describe a form of inflated esteem, this ambivalent view of narcissism must surely have to be wrestled with throughout the process of therapy and counselling. Certainly the point at which egocentric clients show concern for the therapist or for others in their life is a rewarding one.

Idealization and splitting

In the early stages of life, then, with good enough nurturing, a baby acquires an early sense of well-being in the face of the natural vicissitudes of experience, so as not to be afraid of the world that is around her, or that is part of her (depending upon which perspective we take). It is a very small world, but it is her whole world. Her experience is still very limited, it is all she knows, but it is upon this that much else has yet to be built.

In the face of distress and discomfort, especially when it is more than the disposition of the baby can tolerate (because individual babies tolerate different degrees of stress), different ways of trying to preserve or find a basic sense of a good self and a good world may be adopted. These ways of defending the self can be seen more clearly in adult frames of reference than they can actually be observed in infants. So, for example, a dependent person continually needs to 'top up' a rapidly draining sense of worth; a withdrawn or schizoid person tries to keep well away from the risk of rejection and the wish to be dependent; a narcissistic person surrounds the undervalued self with self-praise and flattery – or even puts others first and meets his or her needs by meeting them in others.

I have already indicated above that a particularly significant aspect in developing a harmonious sense of self is learning to integrate good and bad experiences, so that a growing child learns that while life is good, it is not invariably good, and that it is not all bad either. On balance, for most people, the good outweighs the bad (although what is felt to be good and what is felt to be bad is partly culturally determined varying from society to society, and from age to age). If we are to make realistic assessments of the relative merits and faults of ourselves, of others and of the situations in which we find ourselves, we have to learn a sense of perspective and balance. This is probably a lifetime's task, but writing of her own adolescence, in *Lark Rise to Candleford*, Flora Thompson records that 'older people saw things more in proportion, for they had lived long enough to learn that human nature is a curious mixture of good and evil – the good fortunately predominating' (1973: 479). It is not surprising therefore if it is difficult to learn this in the early months of life.

In normal discourse the term 'ambivalence' is often used to mean having mixed feelings, but psychoanalytic discourse uses it slightly differently. It means the capacity to contain more extreme swings of feeling and reaction, and then to hold together these opposite emotions or 'affects', such as love and hate. For some people, relationships are 'all or nothing', by which we mean that they must be all good, or they then become all bad – just like the infant's experience of pleasure and frustration that we tried to imagine earlier. Many people find it difficult to reconcile quite contradictory reactions to the same situation: for example, anger and sadness at times of grief; or pleasure and envy at another's success; relief and anger when someone has caused us worry and all turns out well. Flora Thompson, following on from her words in the previous paragraph, continues that 'tart and tears should be separated by at least a decent interval' (1973: 479). We might think of adolescents, as I observe later, as swinging *par excellence* both in mood and in their views, but consider then how much more might young children, and babies, find different life experiences confusing and puzzling, with mixed emotions that might be difficult to reconcile.

Although it might be difficult it is possible to imagine what it is like to feel full and comfortable and therefore complete at one point of time; and hungry, cold, frightened and angry at another. It has been suggested by child analysts such as Melanie Klein (Segal: 1973) that a baby copes with this, as yet incomprehensible, phenomenon by splitting: believing that good experiences have come from a good mother, and that bad experiences must come from a bad mother – so separating into distinct compartments their own positive and negative feelings. This way they isolate the bad feelings so that they cannot damage the good feelings. We must not of course confuse 'feeling' with 'thinking', although perhaps in the infant these two processes are much closer than in an older person. Although it may be difficult as an adult to imagine such a way of dealing with confusing experiences, it may be helpful to see splitting as a primitive form of logic, which is somewhat like a computer programme, in which everything has to be split up into clear-cut compartments. Computers cannot cope with contradictions without crashing.

But this type of 'primitive' thinking or feeling is not confined to babies and children. It is also seen in adults. Some religious belief systems resort to splitting in an attempt to resolve the problem of how a good God can allow evil: so that it is a 'demi-god', Satan, or a devil, who is held responsible for everything that is bad, preserving God as the source of all that is good. Despite their claims to be monotheistic, some such religions encourage a type of dualism: the belief in two gods, each with a different attitude to creation. Splitting is also seen in much 'cold-war' political rhetoric, where it is combined with paranoia and projection. The external enemy is pilloried as all bad, threatening the all-good homeland; or one section of society promises to save 'us' from the machinations of 'them', 'us' being all good, and 'them' being all bad. Realistic attitudes towards others are not as common as we would like to think, even amongst apparently thoughtful men and women.

At its most extreme, such splitting therefore leads to idealization of the one party, and denigration of the other. A therapist may be idealized, while the client speaks of theirself or perhaps their partner as lacking in understanding, uncaring, and unhelpful. When faced with such idealization, a counsellor may respond in a number of ways:

- s/he may observe that s/he is being elevated into a perfect person/object;
- s/he may suggest that the client is endowing him/her with all that is good but is denying his/her own value and strengths;

- s/he can identify the negative feelings that are voiced towards those outside the therapeutic relationship as belonging also within the relationship between them – although the greater the idealization of the counsellor, the more rigorous is likely to be the defence against admitting discontent and anger with her or him;
- s/he may try to balance the picture by pointing to positive features in those people whom the client runs down, so that ambivalent feelings can be more fully recognized in those relationships.

There may be occasions, albeit fairly rare in counsellor–client relationships, but less so in longer term and more intensive therapy, when this idealization can become so highly charged that the therapist finds herself worshipped like a god, with strong needy and dependent feelings focused upon her. One indication of such strong feelings is a sense of how impossible it is to meet the expectations of the client. This has been called the 'eroticized transference', although the term is a weak one, since the origin of such feelings in the client appears to be less connected with genital sexuality than with early oral dependency needs. Sexual feelings may be felt and indeed expressed, although it would be a mistake to see such a highly charged relationship as purely about the physical expression of love. Such situations are delicate, partly because there is also explosive anger not far beneath the surface, which needs to be handled with sensitivity. It is impossible to give general advice on handling these intense relationships, except to observe that in such cases the counsellor or therapist has to maintain firm but caring boundaries, and has to be prepared for the fiercest of attacks from the client for doing so. Such work also requires regular supervision, preferably with a therapist who is experienced in more intensive psychotherapy.

These extreme emotional attachments are of course at one end of a spectrum. I have no wish to underestimate the strength of feelings and the employment of primitive defences which counsellors and therapists are likely to encounter in some of their clients – especially when caring professionals are frequently asked to take on work which a generation ago would have been considered only suitable for the most lengthily trained (and highly paid). Counsellors, especially in counselling centres, are often engaged of necessity in containing and supporting those for whom no other professional service now exists. Neither do I wish this more extreme end of the spectrum to be dismissed as applying only to certain very disturbing clients. A spectrum means that what we see in some extreme cases is also present, to a lesser extent, in so-called normality. Idealization occurs even when it is not always 'eroticized', where the good and the knowledgeable is ascribed by the client to the counsellor, leaving the client feeling depleted and inadequate.

Hate and paranoia

The child – or the child in the adult – struggles to preserve the good against the ravages of bad experiences, and idealization is one defence. It is difficult to know whether the opposite of idealization is narcissism or paranoia, although of course the latter two may be linked. Like the person who idealizes, the person who expresses paranoid ideas also uses the defence of splitting, although in this instance he or she projects all the bad feelings away from the self, seeing either the world, some individuals, or people generally as hostile and persecutory, set on attacking the innocent and good self. Such a person is struggling to keep negative feelings at bay, by denying ownership of them and putting them into others. In extreme cases paranoia takes the form of para- noid delusion, where the person perceives plots and machinations, human or otherwise, which are 'real' to the client even if the counsellor can only under- stand them as fantasy. Such fantasies suggest the need for a full psychiatric assessment.

Although paranoid delusions indicate an extremely disturbing state of mind, paranoid feelings are part and parcel of everyday experience, even if they do not usually render us suspicious and impotent for long. When life takes a turn for the worse, it is not unusual to project our frustration and anger outwards, and to wonder why others, or indeed why life itself, should have it in for us. This is a common way of dealing with negative feelings, paranoia being a defence against dealing with one's hate. (In some psychoanalytic thinking paranoia is also interpreted as a way of defending against forbidden love: 'I love him. No, that is forbidden. Therefore I must hate him. No, that also is forbidden. Therefore he hates me.')

It is possible to jib at the way in which the word 'hate' is used so frequently in psychoanalytic writing. Winnicott's list of reasons why a mother might hate her baby, for example, accurate though it is in its examples, strains the use of the word 'hate' (1975: 201). But then parents *can* momentarily hate their babies (and each other), and we might presume (as both Melanie Klein and Winnicott would have us do) that babies can hate their carers. Because hate seems such a destructive emotion – as indeed it is when it is acted upon – we tend to suppress our expression of hate almost as soon as we have thought or said it. Nevertheless, 'I hate you' is not just an expression of speech (such as 'I hate spinach' might be) but at the very least a momentary flash of murderous rage.

The paranoia of some severely damaged clients is not momentary, and because it is so pervasive it often has the effect of making others wary and rejecting, which of course compounds in reality what are otherwise paranoid fantasies. Those who experience paranoid delusions are not suitable clients for the generic therapist or counsellor. Yet making a referral, even for an assess- ment by a specialist, can be very difficult. While the idealizing client might see a referral as rejection, the truly paranoid person may see it as confirmation of the plot against him, and as a way of delivering him into the hands of the enemy – especially if he or she has received psychiatric treatment in the past. The skill of referral lies in trying to become and then remaining a good enough person, supporting every hint of the central rational part in the client, so as to quell, at least temporarily, any irrational fears. Careful choice of words, a gentle manner, avoidance of irritation, and refusal to show panic oneself are all helpful. This is easier to set down than to effect when under pressure, although it is important to recognize that a seriously disturbing person is also feeling under great pressure him- or herself. Empathic responses, without col- luding with irrational ideas, may help create sufficient trust for a referral to be made: this is a significant role for any counsellor or therapist, even if it is a fairly brief one. Where it can be carried through well, a referral provides an example of an alternative experience and world-view, more positive than the one which the client has come to fear. Badly done, it simply confirms a negative world-view and makes the task of the next helper even more difficult.

A therapist or counsellor also needs to discriminate between paranoid feelings which have little basis in present reality, and more justifiable ones. Attitudes in society towards racial minorities and around gender issues often are prejudiced, and may give some substance to a client's paranoid anxiety. There are equally other forms of prejudice and discrimination which every therapist should be aware of: against disability, sexual orientation, religion and age. At the same time, we cannot rule out the possibility that some people invite or incite hostile reaction, or interpret current situations adversely on the basis of earlier experiences which were all too real, but are not now so. Such situations are often complicated when clients showing some degree of paranoia select as their persecutory figures people who genuinely demonstrate hostility to them. A counsellor therefore needs to disentangle genuine from fantasized examples of prejudice, and to help clients to own and express their own feelings of anger, even when their paranoid feelings have some basis in reality. The history of psychoanalysis and psychotherapy contains too many examples of experiences being misinterpreted by therapists as fantasy, when they were only too real, for today's counsellor to be anything other than cautious in attributing cause and motive to the victim rather than to the persecutor.

Paranoid feelings are a particular way of handling negative emotions. The nature of anger and the origins of the capacity for aggression are still much debated, particularly how much aggression is innate and necessary for development and survival, and how much it is a response to frustration or fear (Heimann and Valenstein 1972; Malan 1979: 185–92). Anger can of course take many forms, although in this chapter it is extreme expressions of anger that are the major concern, such as the angry client whose forceful expression or threats actually scares the therapist.

Malan observes that there are certain patients who show the following linked phenomena:

1 A history of emotional deprivation, sometimes severe, often occurring relatively late in childhood.
2 Impulses of almost unbelievable primitive savagery and destructiveness, side by side with love of equal intensity.
3 Incontrovertible cumulative evidence that the deprivation is felt to be mainly directed towards the mother.
4 Prominent themes to do with breast-feeding.

(Malan 1979: 189)

We are once more up against the difficulty of envisaging what a baby's experience of frustration might be like. We can observe that at such a time a baby's whole body can become contorted with what we could call rage. If the force behind her physical expression, kicking and flailing limbs, were translated uncontrolled into an adult body, the damage that could be done would certainly be immense. Malan asks, given that aggression is millions of years older than personal love, if it is possible that a baby's first relation to her mother is aggressive rather than loving, and (we might add) getting rather than giving? If the mother then in some way fails to meet the demands of the baby, could it be that her baby then thinks that her aggressiveness (or her greed) has in some way damaged or even destroyed the good mother?

Any such statements can appear extreme, although the nature of this description is symbolic. It is only when we pursue such ideas in the experience of the child or adult who can verbalize internal experience, that we conceive how they may have parallels in infancy. As an adult, I may be kept waiting by someone who does not arrive as arranged. If this person is special to me, I begin to wonder if they are all right. I may then wonder if they are hurt. It may not be long before concern gives way to frustration: how dare they keep me waiting! Then, perhaps, there follows a different concern: did I say or do anything last time that might have put them off?

Readers will be able to add other constructions and fantasies of their own, which, when the person arrives, are fairly soon forgotten in the relief at seeing them again. The resentment may continue rather longer, but beneath the surface. Children are not always so good at dissembling or disguising their feeling, and Bettelheim observes how much the thoughts of revenge in the mind of the fairy tale 'genie in the bottle' may reflect a child's feelings:

> This is exactly how a young child feels when he has been 'deserted'. First he thinks to himself how happy he will be when his mother comes back; or when sent to his room, how glad he will be when permitted to leave it again, and how he will reward Mother. But as time passes, the child becomes angrier and angrier, and he fantasizes the terrible revenge he will take on those who have deprived him. The fact that, in reality, he may be very happy when reprieved does not change how his thoughts move from rewarding to punishing those who have inflicted discomfort on him.
>
> (Bettelheim 1978)

Feeling hungry or uncomfortable, the baby cries, but mother does not immediately respond. Her frustration rises, and her cries become more angry and frightened. Still mother does not come. What does the baby make of mother's absence? If adults can put wild constructions upon a person's lateness, it is quite possible infants and children will too. Various fantasies are suggested by child analysts, in that a baby may wonder: is it my need for her, my greed for her, my frustration with her, is it my anger with her that has driven her away? Of course mother eventually comes (only minutes late in her eyes, but an eternity in the baby's); and such fantastic thoughts are largely set to rest. The repetition of this experience enables most babies to learn that mother comes, even if they have to wait, as surely as an adult knows the sun will rise each morning. Yet in babies with low levels of toleration, or where the intensity of the frustration continually goes beyond what they can take, a residue of fear may be left that it is they themselves who have driven mother away.

Perhaps this seems far-fetched. Perhaps not, when we remember mythical tales in animistic societies that purport to explain what has happened to the sun as it rises and falls in the sky, or the fact that an uninformed people may hold themselves responsible for the sun's disappearance and reappearance in an eclipse. Neither is it far-fetched when we recognize that in bereavement the words 'if only I hadn't thought, said or done that' can be the precursor of thoughts that in some way the bereaved was responsible for the death. Nor, yet again, when we remember those occasions when we have become so angry that we have wished someone dead. Of course we did not mean it, but that is easily said as long as the person survives and reconciliation lays the thought to rest. It does not prevent memories of such thoughts surfacing when a death occurs; and some adults feel, even if rationally they know otherwise, that their death wishes might have been responsible. It is not far-fetched to surmise that the mind of the infant and child can also make false assumptions, including those suggested above. Theorists differ in the relative weight they ascribe to anger, greed, or even love, as the imagined cause of loss, but they all accept the enduring power of fantasy.

As the degree of idealization seems to be equal and opposite to the force of negative feelings, unconsciously repressed, and sometimes split off on to another person, so rage seems proportionate to the degree of need and its consequent frustration:

Urwin collected clocks and watches – his room was full of them. But whenever he detected a blemish in one he had bought, or when one of his time-pieces went wrong, he got into a frenzied rage, in which he smashed the offending object to pieces. His early history threw light on his behaviour. His parents had divorced soon after he was born, and he was sent to live with a spinster aunt who spoiled him and, in his own words, 'let me get away with murder'. He was visited occasionally by his mother, and once by his father. It was his earliest memory that father had tried to comfort him when he was distraught by holding a watch to his ear, soothing him to sleep with its rhythmic ticking. From the age of three Urwin remembered wanting clocks and watches, and when she visited him, his mother would bring him old clocks that no longer worked.

We have to guess that the old aunt, while giving him much, was unable to give him the body-contact and the nurturing which he needed. Being 'Victorian' in her own upbringing, she may even have been of the school that felt babies should not be given too much attention. Father's watch became a symbol of closeness, comfort and intimacy; perhaps of the beat of the heart beneath the breast? It resembles Winnicott's 'transitional object' (1975: 229–42), a representation, like a thumb or a teddy bear, of mothering. But whereas most children grow away from their transitional object, Urwin was always looking for the perfect one. He could not get enough watches in his search, and when the objects he thought were perfect showed their obvious imperfections, they had to be destroyed. Urwin was not so disturbed as to think that the clocks and watches which were imperfect actually became persecutory objects (as does the Duke in James Thurber's tale *The Thirteen Clocks* (1962), where time itself is the persecutor). But the borderline between his thinking and paranoia was thin. It was only Urwin's fear of his new father and his mother, when she remarried and he returned home, which prevented him from smashing them up when they frustrated his wishes. It was ominous that his old aunt had been the person he continued to attack physically right into adolescence. As he became more frightened of his aggression, he sought help.

When a counsellor or therapist works with a client who demonstrates or fears this destructive anger there are a number of key aspects to be borne in mind:

- Help the client to keep hold of characteristics and achievements that are positive and good, presenting that side of the picture alongside any reference to aspects which might otherwise overwhelm the client with fear or guilt.
- Encourage the client to verbalize the anger in the session, rather than act it out in self-destructiveness or damage to objects or people outside, perhaps observing how expressing it verbally in the safety of the session harms no one.
- Demonstrate, through the relationship with the client, that verbally expressing anger (especially towards the therapist) or describing destructive fantasies does not destroy either the therapist or the client, or their relationship – the client can even 'bite the hand that feeds', and learn that it will not be taken away.
- Where necessary (and the threat of this happens only very occasionally) maintain a firm stance against any physical expression of destructiveness in the session.
- Make connections between the past and the present that may explain the intensity of the anger or the guilt about experiencing it; at the same time draw a distinction between what was an age-appropriate response in infancy or childhood and what is inappropriate now (in Urwin's case, the imperfect watch is *not* his mother as he experienced her as a child).
- Support the client in expressing appropriate anger to the right degree about current situations: Urwin was in therapy for some time before he was able to go back to the shop to complain about a clock which turned out to have a fault.
- Clarify the distinction between realistic guilt, resulting from expression of anger which has hurt others (such as Urwin's aunt) and inappropriate guilt, where the damage is much more to the client's sense of well-being.
- Where there appears to be reason for realistic guilt, encourage and support the client's wish to make direct or indirect reparation: being able to mend situations and repair relationships is a sign that destructiveness need not be final.
- Remember that beneath the anger there is probably deep sadness, emptiness or a profound sense of helplessness and weakness, all of which are defended against by rage. The person who is wounded may prefer to respond angrily rather than show how hurt or weak they really are. Acknowledging their own pain may help them more.
- Certainly not last, acknowledge that therapists and counsellors also hate their clients, especially those who make them feel incompetent or afraid (Winnicott 1975: 194–203; Prodgers 1991). Appropriate channelling of aggression in the therapist towards therapeutic ends will minimize the split between the 'bad' client and the 'good 'therapist.
- Finally, Malan adds a fifth observation to those listed above in relation to

severely damaged clients and aggression: 'that integrating the love and hate leads to moments of extraordinary transformation, in which the world, both past and present, changes from "bad" to "good" ' (Malan 1979: 189).

Those who act out their aggression are in the minority amongst the normal client group that counsellors work with, unless they practise in a forensic or mental health unit setting: many clients in a counselling practice find it more difficult generally to show feelings than they do to control them. Indeed a good number of clients who find it difficult to express their hostility openly fear that if they do so, they will be too destructive. Their aggression is often turned instead upon themselves, in depression or in self-damaging behaviours; breaking off relationships, for instance, before they get angry with others.

Vickie was more typical than Urwin. She had great difficulty acknowledging her own anger, more usually feeling that it was others who were angry with her. She was constantly trying to please others in order to stay in their good books. After a year's therapy she was able to acknowledge her destructive fantasies, and even said to her therapist on one occasion: 'If you say that again, I'll go for your jugular.' Having said what she felt, she went on to say, 'It's been good to find the anger in me, and to begin showing it here without feeling so guilty.'

Envy and destructiveness

There can be an angry, sometimes destructive, component in envy, an emotion which is thought to be experienced in infancy. Envy is similar to, but not the same as, jealousy, since the latter normally involves three or more persons: for example, where a husband is jealous of his wife's attention to their baby. Envy more usually describes a two-person situation, where one person envies what another person has and which they do not believe they themselves possess: usually an object, or a quality, rather than 'possession' of a third person. Melanie Klein uses envy in this sense, such as a baby's wish to possess all the good milk in the breast, while Freud uses it in a similar sense when he writes of penis-envy in women (and as will be seen in Chapter 5, others have suggested envy in men of the breast or the womb).

Klein sees envy as innate, and closely linked to aggression: 'I consider that envy is an oral–sadistic and anal–sadistic expression of destructive impulses, operative from the beginning of life, and that it has a constitutional basis' (1957; see also Segal 1973). Yet there is no single psychoanalytic view on the origin and characteristics of envy, and it is also possible to see it as a product of a sense of being small, and helpless, yet aspiring to want to develop and grow – to have what the other or others have. Unresolved it can lead to feelings of inferiority, sometimes accompanied by the wish to destroy what others have on the principle: 'If I can't have it, then I'll make damned sure he doesn't have it either.' Joffe believes that envy can be accompanied by admiration, and that envy, unlike depression, carries a sense of hope. Its presence signals aspiration (1969: 533).

Wanda told the counsellor how angry she had been the previous week. She had returned from a break to find him suntanned and relaxed and, so she felt, not even listening to her. She envied him such a good life, when hers seemed to be full of disasters. She denied that she wanted him to suffer as she did, but the counsellor nevertheless took up Wanda's anger with him for being away and withholding his attention from her. He later linked her feelings about his inaccessibility while on holiday with the anger she felt at her mother's withholding herself from Wanda when she was little and mother was so often ill. His own looking so well, of course, compounded the situation. But her envy also gave an indication of what she would like to achieve for herself.

There can however be a destructive component in envy as can be seen in the following example, together with clear indications of jealousy, because whenever Xavier got close to a woman, he found himself so possessive of her, and so jealous of other men, that it always led to the break-up of the relationship. One of his therapy sessions illustrates the type of envy which Melanie Klein describes. It has to be said that Kleinian ideas are not always appropriate, and can be puzzling to the client; but in this (and other instances, of course) they really can provide the most helpful images of what the client has felt or is experiencing:

Xavier was remembering incidents in early childhood. When he was five he was taken by some slightly older boys to a wood which was out of bounds. They were going to collect birds' eggs. The other boys said there were dinosaurs in the wood, and hid behind bushes making roaring noises. Xavier became so frightened that he ran home, and arrived there crying. He could not tell his mother why he was upset because he should not have gone to the woods in the first place. In her frustration with him, she shook him to try and find out what had happened. When he wanted comfort from her, she only succeeded in making him more frightened.

The therapist responded, 'Perhaps it also felt bad to have stolen birds' eggs.' Xavier paused, agreed, and then went on: 'I've just remembered something else, but I'm too embarrassed to tell you.' The therapist tried to understand this resistance, saying: 'Perhaps you are afraid if you tell me that I'll then shake you like your mother did.' This appeared to free Xavier to speak of this further memory. When he was very young he was sent off to bed early, and lay in bed thinking that he wanted to cut off mother's nipples. He went on himself to wonder if what he felt then as a little boy, and re-experienced now in his possessiveness of girlfriends and his jealousy of other men, was associated with the birth of his younger brother, who always (so Xavier felt) received more understanding from mother than he felt he did. He also wondered whether brother's arrival had meant that he felt pushed away from his mother's breast. Xavier's thoughts certainly made sense to the therapist in terms of Kleinian theory. We can speculate further, although in the session it was not immediately relevant to Xavier to express it openly, whether stealing birds' eggs, and then experiencing guilt (as a result of the persecutory dinosaurs?), was linked to an envious wish to destroy too the eggs in mother's body, and so prevent a rival appearing on the scene. Such associations in the therapist's mind needed further evidence from the client before they could be shared, especially since the therapist was keen that Xavier should make the links, not herself.

Psychoanalytic thinking sometimes associates the expression of aggression with the three psycho-sexual stages (oral, anal and genital): witness Klein's words quoted above about 'oral–sadistic and anal–sadistic expression of destructive impulses'. Klein might be said to have done for infantile aggression what Freud did for infantile sexuality, resulting in the same horrified responses from many who cannot conceive of babies and children as being either destructive or sexual.

It is perhaps unfortunate that these terms get muddled with adult behaviour and responses, and with the intentions and active expression of aggression in adolescents and adults. Klein's language often sums up well the sadistic aggression of those who have reached an age when they can wreak havoc with others' lives and property. Applied to infants her terms need to be understood as her understanding of the fantasized meanings attached to normal relationships: so that when cutting teeth makes feeding more painful for the mother and in our European culture weaning often takes place, the removal of the breast may be associated for a baby with her biting at the nipple – in turn perhaps leading to concern for having damaged the mother. Such biting, or 'tearing' the mother's body with teeth and nails, is what Klein means by oral–sadism. Anal–sadism is associated with defecation and the way in which this too can be used as a 'weapon' (see the next chapter). Genital sadism is seen in rape, abuse, and other aggressive sexual relations, particularly where the penis (or its substitute) is used to hurt and damage (see Chapter 5).

These violent images (and Klein's interpretations are full of them) make real sense when linked to aggressive and destructive impulses, fantasies and actions as they are described by adult clients. The link to the stages of infancy does not have to be made explicit, although it often helps the therapist to be able to understand violent reactions in such ways. Trauma in early life can regularly be traced in those who act out their destructive impulses, although sometimes even if the link is not clear, the metaphors are still useful:

> Yvette was a desperately unhappy young woman. She found making relationships very difficult, and her shyness and awkwardness in company tended to put people off. She admired people from afar but could never approach them. Once she entered therapy she became deeply attached to her therapist, and as a result huge storms arose whenever the therapist had a break or rearranged a session. Yvette's attacks on the therapist were bitter and cruel – she accused him of deliberately taking her on in therapy in order to torture her with the pain of his absence; she at times rubbished everything he said, that it was all therapy-speak, and worthless; she made one or two attempts at suicide just when the therapist was going away; she threatened suicide at other times and left him in suspense until the next session; she would slap at her face and head in the session (although the therapist firmly asked her to stop acting out in this way); she sometimes sat silently and shot vicious looks at him from her chair.

All in all Yvette succeeded in making her therapist feel dreadful, drained, and worthless.

All attempts at understanding this from her past met with a blank refusal to believe the past was of any importance. Although there were some occasions when Yvette might have felt furious with her mother or father, most of these fell within the usual range of family events; and since she was the youngest there was not even the birth of a sibling to explain just how thrown she was by breaks or changed arrangements. When invited to reflect on why she might react this way Yvette's fury could see no point in exploring her history.

Alternating with these episodes (and there were many of them) were other sessions when she was charming, or when she was good to be with. She never seemed to show concern for her previous behaviour at these times, but she would make things right by her manner. The therapist nonetheless felt that this was not true 'depressive position' concern (see below) but an attempt to make things better so that Yvette should not lose him altogether.

This style of therapy went on for many months – and eventually an ending had to be faced, because the therapist was leaving the area. The attacks intensified, and it was all he could do to sit out the sessions, interpreting when he could, but feeling that at such times his words were unheard, or if heard were spat out again and turned against him. Perhaps what made it worth it was that in her outside life things were steadily if slowly changing: she began to make friends; she received praise in her work; she became more bold in arranging to go out socially, etc.; although none of this would she acknowledge as progress. And some time after they had finished (and the last session went reasonably well) Yvette got in touch with the therapist and genuinely shared some really good news about her first intimate relationship.

The example bears out Segal's comment on a Kleinian approach of allowing fantasies to be expressed in a relatively uncontrolled way. Following comments on therapy with children, Segal goes on:

> With adults, too, expression of fantasies can be facilitated in therapy. Lack of restriction on what is said and felt is combined with firm holding of safe boundaries. These reduce the fear of powerfully loving or aggressive feelings spilling over into action. If the therapist is firmly in control the patient can 'let go' more. If the therapist can recognise unwanted feelings and ideas, the patient may be able to too.
>
> (Segal 1992: 61)

Klein's powerful imagery is immediately recognizable in the behaviour of some clients (especially in forensic work). It is also possible to detect it, if they are honest with themselves, in most people's fantasies. These destructive feelings can also be seen in infancy, where they are expressed in nightmares, in some play, and most clearly in the delight of children in stories which often have a somewhat sadistic quality to them. The traditional fairy tales (of the Brothers Grimm for instance) and their modern equivalents often contain in symbolic language issues around the developmental conflicts first encountered in our early years. Perhaps this is why such gruesome stories are so popular, even as bed-time stories when they might be thought to fuel dreams. Perhaps the expression at one remove of these feelings in fact clears the way for sweeter sleep.

One modern example of this type of story is *Where the Wild Things Are* by Maurice Sendak (1970), which is well worth looking at, for its illustrations as well as its highly significant text. When it was first published, it evoked a minor storm of protest from some protective parents as being too frightening for their children. In this story the young boy Max behaves like a 'little monster' and his mother sends him to bed without any supper. Alone in his room Max 'dreams' (we are not sure whether it is a dream or a waking fantasy) that he travels to the land of the Wild Things, where he tames them despite their terrifying attempts to frighten him. He then gets them to join in a wild rumpus to which he calls a halt, sending them off to bed (as he was himself) without their supper. Then he feels lonely, and wants to be somewhere he is loved 'best of all'. He leaves the Wild Things, despite their protest that they will eat him up (words he himself had used to his mother when she got angry with him), and he returns to his room where his hot supper is waiting for him.

Max's own wildness at home is thus relived and relieved in the dream, projected on to the terrifying Wild Things of his own imaginative world. Through taming them and controlling the start and finish of their rumpus, he tames the wildness that has got him into trouble. Having punished them (as he was punished and as he might have wished to punish his mother in revenge) he feels unloved and empty, and needs to return to reality, where he finds his supper, a sign that the loving relationship between the destructive Max and his angry mother has been repaired and restored.

Such a story encapsulates some of the principles of therapy and counselling, through which clients are helped to face both the strength and cause of their own feared or actual wildness, by coming face to face with it, as Max himself does when he first encounters the Wild Things; by expressing it (as in the rumpus) and by finding they can exercise control, as Max does when he commands the rumpus to stop. The constancy of the therapist, who stays with the client, even when the client has been angry with them, helps to show in action that relationships need not be broken irreparably if aggression is expressed, and that care and love, as they become internalized through time, need never be permanently cut off.

Guilt, concern and reparation

Following their expression of feelings, whether in action, or through words or in fantasy, people can feel guilty. Although psychoanalytic writing varies in where and when it places the origin of guilt, it is possible to cluster a number of terms which are similar, and may have a common root in early infancy. Klein therefore writes of guilt, and Winnicott of concern, while generally there is also agreement that anxiety soon follows the expression of aggression or other powerful feelings.

Since the themes of trust and dependency are not limited to a particular stage of life, debates about the origin of guilt are not particularly relevant. What is more appropriate is to consider the possibility that in therapy and counselling, relating powerful fantasies and feelings may be followed by anxiety, for example, lest the trusting relationship between therapist and client has been broken. Guilt may take the form of anxious concern for oneself, such as Yvette in the example above showed following most of her outbursts. She feared losing her therapist. Similarly some 'neurotic' guilt, that appears out of proportion to its precipitating circumstances, seems to show more anxiety for the welfare of the self than genuine concern for the person who has been hurt. Making reparation is sometimes an attempt to restore the needed relationship, although it can, especially where guilt is justified, include genuine concern for the person who has been damaged.

It may therefore be useful to distinguish between guilt and concern, with the latter more clearly showing the capacity to imagine how the other may be left as a result of one's actions. Concern for the other, and anxiety about the damage done to the other, are indications in Kleinian terms of the 'depressive position'. The phrase is confusing, given that it bears little relation to the clinical term 'depression'. Nevertheless what the term stands for is important to grasp in psychodynamic work. In contrast to the split between 'good' and 'bad' object, to schizoid or paranoid states, and the defence of projection, Klein posits a state of mind where others are perceived as whole persons (or whole objects as the terminology often puts it), and where the self is perceived as containing both loving and hating feelings. It is an expression of the ambivalence referred to above. There is also a greater sense of reality: 'damage is no longer feared as total destruction. A good experience does not mean heaven forever; its loss is not the end of the world, but is a real manageable grief mitigated by hope for good experiences in the future' (Segal 1992: 38). To those who rightly object that a major loss often seems like the end of the world, it is important to recognize that even when the depressive position is reached (as Klein suggests it is for most of us in the first year of life), it is never permanent: daily life and developmental crises continuously unsettle us, whether through large or small difficulties, with the result that we move between feeling anxious, paranoid, helpless, cut off, hateful, desperate and needy (for example) and recovering a sense of proportion, security, attachment, hope, satisfaction and love. However, the achievement of a more integrated state, with a sense of hope, having once been achieved, sets a marker for the reachievement of it, even if from time to time we descend into what seems like the deepest pit of despair. This movement is familiar in therapy and counselling, in which the peaks and troughs of experience can neither be engineered nor prevented; but where the achievement of a more whole sense of self provides both the goal for climbing back when things slip back, and also the strength with which to do it.

Empathy is closely linked to concern, and it is probable that the capacity for empathy is engendered in the developing concern of the baby for the one who cares for her, as the closeness of the relationship shifts into the identification of the other as a separate person, with separate needs. Empathy also proceeds from the relatively selfless concern of the mother for her baby, with which the infant identifies, in her concern first for the mother and then by extension for others. As the sense of self becomes more secure this is a stronger position from which to feel concern for others. This can also be described as a form of identification, in which I am able to identify with how another person may be feeling, and relatively altruistically show my concern for them. This usage is somewhat different from that form of identification in which I project my own needs on to the other, identify with the other, and then care for my self through caring for the other. In analytic terms, the infant moves from primary identification, where the distinction between 'me' and 'you' does not exist, to secondary identification, where separate identity leads to the ability to identify with the other person.

There is apparent confusion in analytic writing between terms such as 'identification', 'internalization', and 'introjection', reflecting perhaps the difficulty we have in identifying and expressing what is special to us, and what belongs to another; whether we act from our own unique identity or are influenced by another who has become so much part of us that the difference is undetectable; and whether in understanding others we are ever able to understand them as they are, unless in some respects we can identify their experience with part of ours. Perhaps these semantic distinctions need not interfere with therapeutic practice, where the capacity to know what another might be feeling needs self-understanding, and a healthy questioning attitude towards our own perceptions, if we are to avoid projecting on to another person parts of ourselves which bear little or no relation to what is being offered us by them. The confusion also reflects the difficulty of putting into words that intuitive capacity and emotional rapport which Winnicott calls 'primary maternal preoccupation': 'she knows what the baby could be feeling' (1965a: 15).

These concepts are therefore particularly relevant to counsellors and therapists, who, when they feel relatively secure within themselves and relatively free from anxiety about themselves, are more free to attend to the client, and to the client's needs, without projecting their own concerns on to the client. Whatever else is written in these pages about theoretical knowledge, there is no substitute for that intuitive way of knowing: the counsellor and therapist in the maternal role. When a therapist lacks a strong inner core it is much harder, not only to identify and empathize with the client, but also, for instance, to allow the expression of the frustration, the anger and the love which the client can feel towards the counsellor, or to be open to criticism and attack.

Loneliness and being alone

The processes which have been described to this point – such as the internalizing of good experiences, and the ability to integrate experiences into a whole which is fundamentally positive – are seen also in the ability which people have to be content within themselves when on their own. I refer here not necessarily to the physical proximity of others – it is easy to feel lonely in a crowd, or contentedly self-contained in the company of others. Loneliness in a crowd describes the inward feeling of being at odds with oneself, no matter how much external affirmation is forthcoming from other people. A person in such a state could be said to have become their own worst enemy (a not uncommon description of people who are depressed). The movement through dependency towards independence or interdependence, the affirmation of oneself through the meeting of needs for primary narcissism, and the internalizing of the love of the care-taker all enable a person to say, 'I feel comfortable with myself.' Notice here how the two personal pronouns, 'I' and 'myself', indicate an internal relationship between two parts of the one person. The capacity to be alone without discomfort depends upon this inner relationship, which is not to be confused either with narcissism on the one hand (a desperate attempt to like oneself), or with schizoid withdrawal upon the other (the need to be alone because relationships with others present too great a threat).

Winnicott throws light on the capacity to be alone when he describes the need for a mother and her baby to be on their own, and yet in the same room, without the mother needing to fuss the baby, and without the baby needing mother's active attention (1971: 50). Dunne describes well the ability to be solitary and yet content:

> What makes a man happy when he's alone and happy? What makes a child happy when he is playing alone? There may be a clue in the word 'alone'. The word is a combination of the two words 'all' and 'one'.
>
> (1979: 104–5)

In a moving passage where he draws upon the image of Greek theatre, and two actors alongside each other, Dunne goes on to suggest that loneliness can never be cured by another person: 'We are alone, you and I, and we cannot make one another unalone' (1979: 106). Winnicott's words fit this image, when he writes of the paradox of 'the experience of being alone, as an infant and small child, in the presence of the mother' (1965b: 30). He, like Dunne, sees this as a very positive experience, although some writers on psychotherapy and counselling (including psychoanalytic writers) seem to see it as axiomatic for maturity that a person has to be in a good relationship with another. Being in relationship to others is a value which our society, and psychotherapy, supports, but it is of course possible that, in Winnicott's words, in the end what we have to encounter is 'the essential aloneness of the human being' (1988b: 114).

The capacity to be alone therefore depends upon being content with oneself, yet not being self-content; and upon loving oneself, yet not upon self-love. It is another of those delicate balances that are seen at many points when we try to define health. It is important both for intimate relationships and in the state of being single. As Rayner writes, in a section on 'Being Alone' (1986: 229–36), 'Looking back over the course of life from birth, we can detect a continuous ebb and flow between intimate intermingling with other people on the one hand, and self-contained, even solitary, thought and action on the other . . . Without such solitary exploration a person can be little more than a cypher, an echo of others with no ideas of his own to contribute' (1986: 229). Winnicott, Klein (1963), Segal (1992: 40) and, from a Jungian perspective, Anthony Storr (1989), similarly link the capacity to be alone with creativity. (For a study of the ending of therapy, separation anxiety and solitude, see Quinodoz 1993.)

However, there are others for whom education provides opportunities of living in 'a world of their own'; it is not unusual to find that some of those whose minds are top-class also find difficulty in relating closely to others – their books, their research, or their laboratories exercise a greater pull on them than their family at home. Whether or not this is defensively schizoid or positively creative is perhaps not for the therapist to judge, although at the right time, therapy and counselling may prove to be a means of enlarging horizons:

Zara had been pushed back to school at the age of nine after a serious road accident which led to some facial disfigurement. Following the accident and a spell in hospital where she was seriously ill, her wish to stay at home close to her mother was very understandable. Yet her mother (as she later told her) was in a dilemma: she wanted to comfort her daughter, and at the same time felt she should respect the child psychiatrist's advice that Zara should go back to school as soon as possible. It felt hard for her to have to push her daughter out in this way.

But Zara did not know her mother's concern at that time. Having to go to school, she reacted by immersing herself in her books, and staying on the edge of the groupings of her school friends. In her books she found some consolation. Her reading meant that her schoolwork progressed well, and eventually she went to university. Perhaps it was going away from home that triggered off the separation anxiety, or perhaps her intellectual defences had worn thin; but once she arrived at university she stopped going out, she stayed in her room, even in her bed, and she read novels. When she first saw the counsellor she jokingly asked for 'magic pills' to make her less depressed. Following her mother's earlier pressure, she wanted to 'go out' because that was the healthy thing to do; but also she honestly wanted to stay away from people.

It was only later that Zara told her counsellor that when she first went to see him she was concerned about him as another professional person who might meddle with her mind. The child psychiatrist she had seen before had prescribed 'magic pills' to tranquillize her, after he had misunderstood her childlike way of expressing her school refusal ('It's like a voice telling me not to go', she had said) for incipient psychosis. So the counsellor, who at first had thought in terms of encouraging her to go out and begin mixing with people, soon realized that Zara needed to be able to retreat and find some safety; and that she needed to come out in her own good time, not under pressure. He was therefore content to link the dilemma which she felt, whether to 'stay in' or 'go out', with her mother's dilemma, and indeed his own.

Fantasy and reality

The inner world of each one of us – the conscious, pre-conscious and unconscious – is immeasurable and unknowable in its depth and breadth. To be able to be alone comfortably within one's inner world is therefore essential for health, since fantasy sometimes imposes as much threat as the external realities of living. Dreams and nightmares touch the surface of this hidden world, while tales such as *Where the Wild Things Are*, fairy stories and science fiction draw upon fantasy and the fantastic more than many other works of literature. In all of these expressions of imagination there may be little obvious semblance to the reality of the world as we think we know it, although they speak also about human situations which are indeed found in fact and fiction. The fantastic sometimes symbolize aspects of the 'inner world' – like the dinosaurs in Xavier's memory (pp. 76–7) or the Wild Things in Max's dream (p. 79).

Dreams are personal stories, which serve the purpose of preserving sleep, while at the same time working over unfinished anxieties, most commonly from the previous day. Clients' dreams are not usually an easy medium to work with, and in any case dreams are not usually in once-weekly psychotherapy or counselling the 'royal road to the unconscious', which Freud called them. In her introduction to a collection of papers on the significance of dreams, Flanders observes first that 'the dream no longer occupies the centre of psychoanalytical debate' (1993: 1), and later that 'the focus of contemporary analysis is emphatically the dreamer, not the dream' (1993: 20). Some clients spontaneously relate their dreams, although for others it is their experience of the day-to-day, and sometimes the links they make with their past, which are more likely to occupy the weekly session. Those who report dreams can be encouraged to associate freely to their own dream images as a way towards finding their own clues to the dream's meaning. The temptation with dreams is to try and understand them straight away: yet often it is later material in the session which throws light upon a particular dream image. There is never one single meaning to a dream, and what in the end matters most is less the dream itself, than having dreamt it. Dreaming is healthy, whether or not the dream is remembered or analysed.

If relating the images and symbols in dreams, and the feelings associated with them, adds further relief, this surely is a bonus, but it is not the only path to personal exploration and insight. Those clients who do not present dreams in fact present in many other ways the symbols, metaphors and images that are also the stuff of dreams: in their daydreams and fantasies, in the plays, novels, films and art that have moved them and which they speak about in therapy, as well as in their use of language. All these, especially language, can be as replete with double meanings, condensations of meaning, and all the other means of disguised communication which Freud initially recognized in dreams (1900), and of course later saw were also part of what he called the psychopathology of everyday life (1901).

Fantasies of other kinds can also provide glimpses into our internal world, although they do not always have to be deeply analysed and understood. Daydreaming of a good meal helps a hungry person go without food during the day so as to enjoy going out to dinner that evening. Picturing a loved person from whom someone is temporarily separated usually helps make the interval and absence tolerable. Imagining anticipated situations can act as a useful way of rehearsing words and actions, so as to be better prepared for different eventualities.

At other times fantasy is less helpful. The nightmare is the dream which has gone too far, when the fantasy becomes too much and uncontrollable, even in sleep. Some of the examples from therapy in this chapter demonstrate fantasy constructions upon experience which often lead to false conclusions, and may lead to perceptions of the world, and of people, as hostile or fearful, or both. Some fantasies provide security and satisfaction, but, because they keep a person introverted and collude with anxieties about real relationships, impoverish the opportunities for fuller and more mature relationships.

Psychotic and borderline states

What is important in all therapeutic work is to distinguish between fantasies which are recognized as such (and which may provide the opportunity for different insights into the major concerns and patterns in a client's inner world) and fantasies that have become so real that the world of make-believe has become confused with the realities of the external world. There are some people who seek help in whom fantasy has become so close to being their reality that they are unlikely to benefit from the counsellor's skills, and will need a very special kind of therapist. The distinguishing marks have been variously described, although it is often the therapist's own profound feelings of concern for the sanity of the client which are the most revealing. In working with the majority of adult clients, a therapist or counsellor knows that they can use metaphors and that the client will understand them as symbolic language. A common phrase to introduce a therapeutic intervention is 'It's like . . .', or 'It's as if . . .'. Clients similarly use such phrases in describing their ideas and feelings: 'You are just like my father when you say that . . .', 'She treats me as if I were a little girl . . .'. Some of the fantasies which people have they introduce with a qualification such as 'I know it's silly to think so, but . . .'. In other words, they are aware that there is a difference in kind between some of their thoughts and reactions and what they would regard as more normal or realistic constructions.

Furthermore, as I have described above, some fairly common traits are likely to be seen at work in most people: paranoid feelings, which are known to be unreasonable, but are nevertheless uncomfortable and need to be expressed and understood; schizoid traits in which people cut themselves off from some aspects of intimate relationships, but know they would like it to be different. These are minor, more common versions of more full-blown disturbing states, such as paranoia, schizophrenia, and other forms of psychosis. In such cases there is usually a clear sign that something much more inaccessible is present, and the feelings engendered by the client in the therapist or counsellor are often such as to raise serious questions about the suitability of the client for the help which can be offered by the therapist. The phrase 'as if' is missing; things are what they are, not what they seem; fantasy has become reality. There are indications of disturbed, chaotic thinking; words and ideas do not appear to connect; any sense of a personal relationship is remote.

The old somewhat 'black' joke runs: the neurotic builds castles in the air, the psychotic lives in them, while the psychiatrist collects the rent. It illustrates the difference between the neurotic person's acknowledgement of the difference between fantasy and reality (which in itself can lead to discomfort), and the psychotic person's confusion of the two. In fact a psychotic person's world and their strange ideas have their own logic, and meaning, while at the same time protecting them from the feared devastating effects of the real world. One of the compelling attractions of staying in their uniquely constructed world is that it is more capable of being controlled than the intolerable external world.

These severe disturbances appear to go back to equally intolerable childcare, abuse and neglect, where not only has there been little or no chance of building up trust in a dependable world and dependable relationships, but where the nurturing has failed to protect the vulnerable infant from the genuine harshness of the external world. Winnicott observes that the failure of the environment to facilitate the maturational processes in the infant is linked to psychosis, a failure which he calls 'privation' (1965b: 226). He distinguishes privation from deprivation, where there is an initial good-enough environment, which then for some reason ceases. These differences are noticeable in therapy and counselling: clients who have started off well, and then suffer traumatic circumstances, have a core which helps them climb back up. Those who have never had this, or have had to develop a false self with which to cope, will need, if they can get to the point of asking for it, a much more intense kind of help, beyond the range of what I can describe in this book.

As with other defences, such as those of the more normal neurotic predisposition, attempting to argue a psychotic person out of his or her bizarre thinking will be felt to be too threatening, and therefore is likely to be strongly resisted. Sometimes there is a thread of common sense, or the psychotic symptoms are part of a picture which has some signs of more ordinary neuroticism, and this might suggest what is often called a borderline personality. Definitions of the borderline personality differ, with psychiatrists listing a number of indications (as they do for all personality disorders) which place borderline personality more on the side of psychosis than neurosis. Psychoanalytic thinking represents a position which is closer to what we might think should be the use of the term 'borderline'; for example: 'persons who have achieved a kind of stability of personality organization in which they live a most limited and abnormal emotional life which is neither neurotic nor psychotic but a sort of frontier state' (Rey 1988: 203). The experience of being with a borderline personality might be described as sensing a person who is on the edge, who could, given undue pressure from the therapist as well as from outside sources or adverse circumstances, tip over into an even more disturbing state. Yet communicating with the borderline personality might be somewhat less fraught than with the person in a full-blown psychotic state. Where there are some signs of more realistic thinking, for instance, they may be used to guide the client towards more specialized help:

> Andrew presented his preoccupation with washing his hands to a counsellor in a Family Practice setting. This might be seen as an compulsive–obsessional symptom, related to other themes about guilt and control; but in Andrew's case there were some worrying psychotic features. He believed, for example, that when he was walking down the street he might

tread on glass; and when he came to take off his shoes, splinters of glass might get transferred to his hands; and that if he then rubbed his eyes, he might damage them. That was why he washed his hands so often. He asked the counsellor whether getting glass in his eyes was a possibility, an interesting invitation for a second opinion which suggested a degree of willingness to listen to what the counsellor thought. The counsellor replied that it was a possibility and that it certainly made sense to wash his hands from time to time, but that the chances of damage to his eyes were very slight indeed. Perhaps, the counsellor asked, there were other worries? Might it be wise for Andrew to go back to see the doctor? This degree of support appeared to encourage the client to return to the doctor, who was forewarned by the counsellor, and was able to prescribe medication to calm Andrew's obvious anxiety and 'erratic' thinking. Notice that Andrew's thinking was not illogical – it had a type of logical sequence to it. But it was too literal. Fortunately words like 'might' and 'possibility' indicated less rigid a fantasy in Andrew's mind than words like 'must' or 'probability', which he might have used had he been in a true psychotic state.

Turmoil or serious disturbance?

Diagnostic indications used in psychiatry sometimes make it clear the usual symptoms of different types of personality disorder cannot be applied to someone under the age of eighteen. This somewhat arbitrary line is a reminder that adolescence can be an extremely turbulent time, where what might be indications of more serious disturbance in adult clients are within the normal parameters for adolescent behaviour. The nature of the adolescent process therefore makes it difficult to distinguish between what lies within the norm, and what might indicate a more serious disturbance. Psychiatric illness is notoriously difficult to diagnose in persons of this age. What in the adult could be indications of the manic–depressive personality, in the young person might be normal mood swings. What is felt to be deviant or outrageous behaviour in adults might be seen as more usual (if not always acceptable) in an adolescent, and may even be called 'high spirits'. Dieting is the concern of many a young woman, without it having to tip over into anorexia or other eating disorders. Depression is common, without it being more than moodiness. Heavy drinking may even only be a feature of student life, part of a youth culture that can be left behind when the young person graduates.

The process of adolescence, which some authors see as finding an identity (Erikson 1965, 1968; Marcia 1975), may mean a period of confused identity, with a negative view of self: 'I am nobody. I'm stupid. I'm confused' are amongst the answers such a young person can give to the question 'Who are you?' The confused adolescent readily changes values, is vulnerable to feedback because of low self-esteem, and has difficulties in personal relationships. Although some young people may get stuck in such a position, for most of them this is a phase through which they develop. One of the virtues of adolescence is its fluidity: many young people are always on the move, changing, adapting, reworking situations, making and breaking relationships, experimenting, striving towards an identity. This is why counselling young people can bring rapid results, since they are less tied by conventions, permanent relationships and fixed attitudes.

At the same time there *are* pointers to deeper disturbance, which might indicate the desirability of referral to more specialist resources. When anarchic words and fantasies are acted out, a young person can be frightened of their destructiveness or self-destructiveness. Where work and relationships cease to matter or function, introversion is more extreme. Where a strong mood or behaviour pattern extends over a long period without showing signs of changing, this may indicate more serious problems. Where imagination runs riot and fantasies begin to feel too real, then psychotic features may be apparent. When unconventional dress and normal untidiness give way to a failure to care for themselves, and young people withdraw from contact with others, it is probably wise to seek psychiatric opinion (see Ryle 1973: ch. 6). The following client illustrates such severe disturbance:

> Basil initially presented with feelings of isolation from people, but at the time he seemed to be functioning well at work, and in any case was reluctant to see the counsellor, so the counsellor did not pursue the missed second appointment. When he returned a year later, with the same problem, he was more ready for counselling, although more out of a sense of desperation than of hope. Basil described himself: 'I'm cut off from people . . . it's like going down a spiral staircase and passing people on their way up . . . I have no sense of time . . . I couldn't work out what was real at the theatre last evening, whether it was happening on stage or whether it was what was going on in me . . . I saw a dead cat yesterday lying in the road, and went up to it and felt nothing . . . going from one place to another is dangerous . . . I'm losing my marbles . . .'
>
> Condensing his speech in this way masks the erratic pattern of the sessions; some were clear, and others confused; in some the counsellor felt they were communicating (especially when he could empathize with Basil by drawing upon images related to trust and dependency themes), but in others the counsellor, like Basil, felt hopeless and helpless.
>
> In the event, he only saw him until he could find Basil a place in a therapeutic community. The psychiatrist who interviewed Basil confirmed the counsellor's opinion that Basil showed some signs of being a schizoid personality, but said that the disturbance was difficult to describe or to understand. He added, 'The problem about once-a-week therapy is not so much that it is not enough, as that Basil has to be "open" at those times. A therapeutic community offers the advantage of any opening that occurs, no matter at what time.'

There are certain areas of work, in addition to working with the fluctuations of adolescent mood and behaviour, which present difficulties to the generic counsellor or therapist: disturbing behaviours or features, such as self-harm and mutilation, eating disorders, multiple personality, hard drugs and severe substance abuse, in adults as well as young people. Many of them have connections with the themes of trust and dependency, although control issues (part of the next theme) are also present. It is relatively easy to throw around labels (see my warnings in Chapter 2) that are likely to be carried for life, whether or not they are accurate. Insensitive referrals for medical or psychiatric help can break trust in the caring professions, since doctors (like parents) may not be trusted to understand, or a psychiatric assessment suggests the terror of mental illness. It is hard for a counsellor to know whether these indications of disturbance are extreme yet short-lived episodes, or more ongoing borderline features. It is also apparent that sometimes a sensitive counsellor or self-help group is able to do more good than hard-stretched and therefore inadequate professional resources. These are extremely difficult areas for the counsellors and therapists, as much as they are for their clients, where it can be hard to know what is best. Again supervision provides a way of checking out possibilities, and support with what can be confusing and disturbing material.

Trust and faith

Erikson sees faith – in its broadest sense, not simply religious faith – as one of the needs of any society, and as rooted in the mother–baby relationship. Winnicott likewise linked adult belief to an infant's trust in the mother, saying, 'The point is, can they believe? I don't care what it's about. The capacity to believe is more important than what you believe' (quoted in Rudnytsky 1991: 181). Arriving at their own value-system or set of beliefs is one feature of adolescents' questioning, an extension of their optimistic belief in themselves. Launching into the world of work, of relationships, and wider society requires this confident sometimes idealistic thinking, a confidence which needs to be affirmed through the response of others. Not surprisingly lack of opportunities to work and earn a living, rejection in relationships and other adverse circumstances can lead to the undermining of self-confidence, lack of faith in the social order, and in turn to destructive attacks on self, or other people and society. Early trauma and neglect in infancy can also lead to deep cynicism and a totally pessimistic attitude towards life. There is no sense of hope, only of worse to come. In such a frame of mind it is scarcely surprising that some people have only their frustration to express.

Apart from *what* people believe, it is also possible to distinguish *how* they believe. There are significant shifts in the way children, young people and adults express and conceptualize their beliefs. Concrete images in children develop into conceptual and abstract thinking, applied not only in their studies at school and perhaps thereafter in the major academic subjects, but also in making value judgements and in their moral thinking (Piaget 1950; Kohlberg 1981). Styles of belief, as well as the beliefs themselves, can be approached through developing Winnicott's ideas about 'illusion'. His use of the term is quite distinct from Freud's assumption of religious belief, for example, as an illusion, a wish-fulfilment, a sign that a person seeks to return to the primary dependent relationship of parent and child (1927). Winnicott sees illusion as much more positive, and as a lifelong transitional phenomenon (1975: 240). Although a baby has to given up early illusions of symbiosis and omnipotence, the growing child develops new illusions, some of which in time also have to undergo disillusion, making way for fresh illusions. We are engaged in a life-long process of illusion, disillusion and new illusion.

The implications of this idea for a psychology of belief, and for understanding the different ways in which people construct their sense of meaning, are examined more fully in my book *Living Illusions* (Jacobs 1993a; see also Fowler 1981, who draws upon Erikson, Kohlberg and Piaget, but appears not to be aware of the importance of Winnicott's ideas). Briefly summarized, it is possible to see parallels between the major themes in this book, and styles of believing. Therefore unquestioning, simple faith can be associated with early trust and dependency issues; beliefs which are accepted because of the authority of others (religious or political leaders, or academic experts) tend to mirror issues around authority, while a further style of belief challenges authority and seeks more autonomous ideas, sometimes at the risk of self-aggrandizement. Other styles of belief include more universalistic ways of thinking, real interest in alternative belief systems, and the willingness to accept the immensity of what is unknown – much of which finds parallels in the third set of themes about co-operation, wider social concern, and deeper self-exploration.

Becker similarly outlines different levels of meaning by which an individual can choose to live (1972: 185):

1 The basic level of the Personal – who one is, the 'true' self, what makes a person special, whom he feels the self to be deep down, 'the person he talks to when he is alone'. (This ties in with much that has been described in this chapter about confidence and trust in oneself.)
2 The higher level of the Social – the extension of the self to include those with whom a person is close or intimate: partner, friends, children.
3 The next higher level of the Secular – symbols and allegiance at greater personal distance which are often of a compelling quality – the corporation, the party, the nation, knowledge (science and the humanities), or humanity itself. Levels 2 and 3 take us into the next two sets of themes.
4 The highest level of the Sacred – 'the invisible and unknown level of power, the insides of nature, the source of creation, God'. (My own argument is that this level in some way represents a return to issues of trust and dependency, but on a far wider and deeper scale than the personal or the inter-personal.)

Becker concludes: 'The ideal critique of any faith must always be whether it embodies within itself the fundamental contradictions of the human paradox and yet is able to support them without fanaticism, sadism and narcissism, but with openness and trust. Religion itself is an ideal of strength and of potential for growth, of what man might become by assuming the burden of his life, as well as by being partly relieved of it' (1972: 196). His words apply of course as much to faith in political ideologies and humanism as they do to religious faith.

Trust and dependency through the life cycle

It has been a principle of this chapter that what might be seen as issues mainly related to the earliest weeks and months of life must not be confined to chronological age, but be seen as relevant to all other ages or stages. I have made it clear how a psychodynamic view of personal development sees the first few weeks and months of life as involving finding trust and faith, both in a dependable other, and, through that person, also in oneself and in the ever-enlarging world around the rudimentary self. These early experiences make all the difference between viewing life itself as basically beneficent, or as basically persecutory. At the same time, the achievement of healthy ambivalence comes not from an infancy or childhood free from frustration, but from learning how to integrate painful and difficult experiences with satisfying and pleasurable ones. In later life such a foundation permits the development of a multi-faceted view of life and the world.

The theme of trust and dependency that can be traced from this beginning is repeated and tested time and again in life as the growing child moves into a widening world, other relationships and new experiences. It is an aspect of all new developmental tasks. Basic trust, for example, leads to more refined forms of trust. Blind trust may be appropriate for babies, but it is not for toddlers and older children. It is important for awareness to develop that the world can also be a dangerous place, and that some people are not to be trusted. Being dependent intertwined with learning independence, and attachment as well as separation, are also part of a continuous process, from birth, through weaning, through taking first steps, in going to play group and school, into adolescence and on to the many other occasions for change in adult life, including leaving the parental home, changes in job and location, and the different stages of intimate partnerships.

There is a romantic view of love that dominates our culture, which is to some extent culturally determined, even if it has a longer tradition in litera-ture than in real life. The desire for this particular form of love tends to rein-force the idealization both of relationships themselves, and the expectation of how individuals in relationships should be. It is of course often the quite legiti-mate first stage of many partnerships today, sometimes popularly called the honeymoon stage. It was not so in the days of arranged marriages, which in some cultures are still the norm: there love comes through a longer process of getting to know one another, and is only occasionally 'at first sight'. Counsel-lors and therapists will work with clients who are still searching for their ideal partner; who seem neither to have learned that in most partnerships the sym-biotic mother–baby phase is only one aspect of a total relationship, nor that in their search they may in fact be looking for something missing in them-selves which an external other can never replace. Couples grow together as they learn to embrace and value the ordinariness of life, as well as the high points, to work through differences as well as enjoy agreement. Living with ambivalence, finding a type of 'depressive position' in a relationship, is as important to a couple as it is to individual maturity.

Some partners so much seek a symbiotic relationship that they cannot be separated or cannot permit each other individuality. There can be other diffi-culties where one or both partners are so narcissistic that they are concerned only for themselves, and have not developed sufficient awareness of the other's needs to accept their differences, or sufficient toleration of frustration of their own needs. It is as if the other exists like the early mother figure, simply to serve them. One partner becomes demanding, while the other struggles to meet those demands. In other partnerships one or both may be withdrawn emotionally, and find difficulty in abandoning themselves to sexual and loving feelings, and therefore to each other. In any intimate relationship there has to be shared caring (with each able to care for the other at different times), and therefore a balance between concern for the other and claiming some care for oneself. The most stressful times are often when each needs care from the other, and neither has the emotional resources to provide it.

This chapter has described much from the perspective of mother and baby, although it has not specifically looked at the different experiences around childbearing. In Western society pregnancy is more often than not from choice, therefore it is usually welcomed, even if it inevitably also gives rise to fears – for example, for the safety and health of baby and mother, as well as even more primitive anxieties. All kinds of dependency issues, even if worked through in the process of growing up, raise themselves again. For some women their pregnancy provides them with their first real opportunity to project their own needs for mothering on to their baby. If this serves the baby well at the start, keeping the baby dependent may not be so healthy later on. The need to love in order to find love may be one motive for an early pregnancy, although there are others: as a way of avoiding being alone, or even of avoiding adult relationships, as a means of gaining some independence from the family, and of making one's own home, etc. Nor should we forget that would-be and actual fathers also have their agenda, as in the following example, where the wish to find something for himself seemed important to Ced:

Ced's casual relationship with a young woman had led to her becoming pregnant. Ced was certainly not callous, and he helped to arrange the abortion with her. This was strange since at first he seemed delighted to have fathered a child, even if it was her wish not to continue with the pregnancy. He was in fact less concerned about her feelings than his own, perhaps because his own issues in this situation were considerable: Ced's father had simply walked out on the family when he was still small, and had not been heard of since; so perhaps Ced was trying to find the 'father' in himself, and that mattered more to him than any sense of how much difficulty and distress he had caused the young woman.

Even if an abortion is necessary, it obviously involves a very special kind of loss, and usually more so, one has to say, for a woman than for a man. It is hard to discuss abortion without religious and moral issues arising, even if there is not strong religious feeling in a particular client's background. Often guilt is intermingled with grief and relief. This is one obvious instance of a life crisis where it is difficult for a person to own and hold in tension very differ-ent, sometimes conflicting, feelings. Even without the type of moral teaching which might lead to particular expressions of guilt, abortion can trigger off anxiety about murderous fantasies (which this chapter has argued are very common in all of us, including that of wishing to get rid of potential siblings from mother's body). The pain and the guilt (where it is voiced) can be allevi-ated somewhat by being permitted to give expression in therapy to the con-cern about and existence of such fantasies, recognizing both that concern about procreation *is* appropriate, and that past murderous wishes *can* become inappropriately linked to real current events.

Dora was one of those gentle people who could never harm a fly. Another side of her came out when she got drunk at a party and afterwards slept with a man whom she did not even know by name. But when she found she was pregnant she was very upset at the thought of an abortion, although she recognized that it was necessary. She saw a counsellor to clarify her decision, and they arranged to meet again after she had been to the clinic. Dora went alone to the clinic in another city, and returned alone. On the train back, a goods train passed the other way, laden with military tanks, an image that stayed in her mind. She felt it applied to her; and although she knew rationally that what she had done was not murder, it nevertheless felt as though she had violated a life. Perhaps linked with this feeling was one that associated the tanks to a man's violation of her own body, however much she had in some way been a willing party. Whatever the meaning of what she saw and felt (and no-one can ever be precise about a single image) sharing it with her counsellor helped, and Dora was gradually able to work through her experience sufficiently to feel her old self again.

It can be a surprise to a client that an abortion performed some years earlier still causes depression in the present. Anniversaries of an abortion, or of the time when a child might have been born had the pregnancy not been terminated, can be as significant as other anniversaries:

Edna constantly talked in her counselling sessions of pets and relatives dying, or of her fear of them dying. The community nurse did not wish to hazard a guess without more evidence, but being employed within a health service practice he had access to Edna's medical history. A glance at her notes confirmed his hunch that she had had an abortion some years before, and he tried to work with her with knowledge of this in mind, even though she never talked about it.

Guilt at having terminated a pregnancy can also lead to fears of being punished through being unable to conceive a second time. This is yet another reason (in addition to dependency needs referred to above) why one abortion may be followed by further pregnancy and the request for a second abortion, obviously proving fertility yet perpetuating a cycle of fear and uncertainty. With some women it is only the birth of a child to take the place of the one they have lost that puts an abortion to rest. But abortions and miscarriages are never forgotten and acknowledgement of their significance honours the loss.

Other outcomes to pregnancy can mean both a birth and a death at the same time. Stillbirth is clearly both; and although currently more rare in Western culture than once it was, giving a baby for adoption is a type of 'living death', which for the natural mother may lead to a lifetime's concern about the child who was hers; and for the child a lifetime's wondering about the circumstances that led to such a beginning. Clients who have been adopted, and clients who have long ago given their baby for adoption – whether or not they seek the other out through the permitted procedures –

suggest situations that clearly give rise to many of the different issues which this chapter has raised.

It is essential for professionals (doctors, nurses and clergy) to recognize too the significance of stillbirth in the care which they give to parents: allowing the dead baby to be seen and held, or photographed, encouraging the death to be talked about at the time, providing a tangible memento, naming the baby if so wished, and arranging for proper recognition of the death through a religious or secular funeral (see Case 1978; Kirkley-Best *et al.* 1982). In all these particular instances of loss (abortion, miscarriage, stillbirth and adoption) there may be clues to the nature of the relationship and the degree of loss in the words used to describe the foetus/baby. 'Foetus' and 'it' are cold and more distancing terms. 'He', 'she' and 'the baby' may indicate recognition of, or the wish for, a relationship and greater emotional involvement. 'The child' may refer to the unfulfilled fantasies of the child as he or she would have been in a few years time, or (looking back on such an event) as he or she might have been now.

When pregnancy goes to full term, with a successful delivery, there are again many different emotions. A mother has gained a baby, although she has lost part of herself; the actual baby in her arms replaces the fantasy baby whom she has thought about all during pregnancy. The difference between the ideal and the real, the demands of mothering, the sense of responsibility, even feelings about the smallest abnormality in a baby, and anxiety about being a good mother might contribute to post-natal depression. Here again talking and sharing mixed feelings, including the apparently negative emotions which a mother thinks she should not have, constitute a much more natural and normalizing approach than pathologizing and treating with powerful drugs or electro-convulsive therapy, which is the experience of some clients.

When their children have passed through the early dependent stages, and are becoming slowly more independent, parents have to learn about trust and dependency from a different perspective. Theirs is not normally a nonchalance which appears uncaring, nor an idealization of their children which fails to recognize pitfalls. Neither is it an intrusive or restrictive fussiness which fails to let their children experience the less pleasant effects of their actions. It is not easy to get the balance right, particularly in adolescence, where these issues are likely to be lived out with some forcefulness and angst on all sides. Since much of this is also about providing the right milieu for independence and autonomy, these issues are more fully discussed in the next chapter.

Trust and dependency enters into the learning and the working environment, and relationships outside the home at all levels, including that between a child or an adolescent and his or her teachers, or between employees and their employer, their manager, those they manage, and so on. In learning, too dependent an attitude can lead to swallowing whole what those in authority say; too much anxiety can lead to rejection, spitting out, tearing apart destructively what others try to teach and pass on. Although these again look like authority issues, more than dependency, the metaphors (such as 'swallowing' and 'spitting out') show how fundamental some difficulties may be in the learning process.

There was a time when work was very much tied up with dependency, even if the days are largely gone when someone can expect a job for life, and an employer who will be a benevolent provider in times of trouble and distress. People in current Western society show deep anxieties about loss of employment, which is so fluid. When politicians talk about the absence or presence of a 'feel-good factor' it is not too great a conceptual leap to issues about trust. In the process of growing up trust is encouraged in the promised goals of education and later in contracts of employment; when that trust is broken it may lead to a deep lack of faith in those who make promises and even in society itself as uncaring. That undermining of faith can easily lead to lack of faith in oneself. Where there is a split in society between those who have and those who have not, it is reminiscent of the basic split that can be experienced in infancy between the hungry baby and the mother who appears to withhold all the good things she has. Since Erikson links hope and drive as the two basic strengths of this first age, it is important to remember that people without work may not just lose hope that things can be different, but also their drive to change things. It is not surprising therefore that redundancy and unemployment can give rise to debilitating depression, to withdrawal into a frightened and fractured self, and all the attendant difficulties of moving out of that state. It is not just 'what I do' that has been taken away, but 'who I am' that has been questioned. Add to this living on benefits, or on a pension (apart from problems about the actual level of the payment), and it can be seen how dependency issues may be stirred up, encouraging some to sink into a dependency where their single expectation is to be looked after, while others feel guilty at being dependent, and blame themselves. Being without work (which for some people also happens when they retire) may make people feel even more helpless and infantilized, so losing hope that they can make an impact on, or contribution to, society.

> Frank had been unemployed for three years. His main preoccupation was getting a job; and this had become so central for him that he could not hear what anyone else was saying to him, unless they were giving him an opening to express his feelings. His manner reminded the counsellor of a hungry baby, for whom nothing else matters than being fed. Frank had no room for concern for others and their difficulties, even if they too were unemployed. Getting a job so dominated him that until that need was satisfied he could apparently not settle to any other activity, including relating to others at home. Frank's situation is probably not atypical of the effects of long-term unemployment. In fact he changed, at least partially, when he was encouraged to get involved as a voluntary helper. This gave him a sense of purpose and self-worth, which helped him to pay more attention to the needs of others outside himself, in turn helping himself more positively and less resentfully at job interviews.

In the second half of life there are a whole set of different issues, not normally faced before, such as having parents whose ageing can make them more dependent. There are, of course, differing cultural attitudes to care for elderly relatives, and expectations on filial responsibility. Earlier in this chapter issues about illness, ageing and the self were raised, to which it is important to add anxieties about having to be dependent upon others. In this reversal of roles, ruthless games can sometimes be played, including in caring institutions, in which older people are more infantilized by the younger generation than they are by their natural physical weakness. It is at this point in family relationships that the real ability of parents and their children to relate adult to adult is exposed and tested. There may be some reflection of these issues in even more frightening terms in the sadistic attacks which can take place on the defence-less old person by the young. These may be examples of the acting out of revenge which a younger generation might feel towards those who were once felt to be persecutory objects.

Some mental infirmities reflect psychotic states linked to deep problems with the issues raised in this chapter. Senile dementia, for example, can lead to fragmentation of thought, where fantasy appears confused with reality. Rayner reminds us that these fantasies are still symbolic and can best be under-stood when the symbols can be translated into present concerns – he provides some useful examples of this (1986: 259–60).

Some psychologists (e.g. Lowe 1972: 248) have suggested a number of psychological 'types' of old people, each one demonstrating a different reso-lution of the way they look back on their life. Most of these identified types reflect ways of dealing with basic issues about self and others. One type has been referred to above (p. 64–5) in describing a possible narcissistic reaction to ageing. Other types include the self-hating older person, who is despairing and pessimistic, who turns his or her hatred into self-contempt, and who has such a negative view of the past that death is looked forward to as a merciful release; or a different expression of hostility is seen in the older person whose anger is directed outwards, in criticism of others and in envy of the younger gener-ation, but who is fearful of death.

These reactions to ageing are very different from the psychologically mature older person, known by some gerontologists as the 'constructive' type. Such a person has high self-esteem and broad interests that were developed earlier in life, and remains self-aware, enjoying the sense of responsibility that is appro-priate to old age. He or she is eager to preserve personal integrity, and to enjoy a sense of tranquillity (like the dependent type), but (unlike the dependent type) remains aware of a sense of purpose and meaning in life, hoping for an even greater understanding of what life is all about.

Erikson writes of the eighth age as one of ego integrity, a phrase which has much in common with the truly ambivalent depressive position which Klein associates with more mature attitudes. Ego integrity comes from looking back over life, appreciating all that has gone well, finding pleasure in one's achieve-ments and in one's creativity and generativity, as well as the acceptance of those things that have gone wrong, and the recognition that these cannot be changed (concern without overbearing guilt). On balance the good things in life are felt to outweigh those inevitable experiences that have been bad.

Bereavement and dying naturally conclude this summary of ways in which trust and dependency issues affect different stages of life. Bereavement is part of the process of separation, which will involve different degrees of pain and intensity. The process of dying pushes at the limits of trust, and confidence in the self, whether or not people have a religious belief in another form of life after death. Care and counselling of the bereaved and of the dying has become a specialist area with its own large body of literature, and therefore needs particular study (see, for example, Kubler-Ross 1969; Speck 1978; Worden 1983; Raphael 1984; Parkes 1986; Lendrum and Syme 1992).

In a society where death is so often institutionalized and locked away, facing the dying and facing death itself is not surprisingly overloaded with fantasies of the most negative kind. Even direct experience of another's death (and that is not as common as it once was) cannot adequately prepare a person for his or her own, since it is almost impossible to conceptualize it, involving as it does the dissolution of the self (or of the self as we know it, depending upon one's religious views). Here we come full circle, back to the impossibility of being able to conceptualize pre-natal and postnatal experience. Rayner suggests that recognition of being mortal and finite (which does not really occur in most people until middle age) is frightening, but that it is also a relief, because the denial of mortality can be shed. Any kind of denial engenders inner stress, and being able to throw off denial releases some of the tension (Rayner 1986: 238–42).

The development of trust and the right handling of dependency is of course also an essential part of the therapeutic relationship, as much as it is in any relationship. Chapter 6 summarizes ways in which these issues form a natural sequence in therapy and counselling. These are particularly important issues at the start of therapy. The dependent, submissive client, on the one hand, or the mistrusting, distancing client, on the other, are not in the best position to make good use of therapy, but part of the skill of the therapist is to help create a trusting relationship, where the right degree of dependency can be fostered. As the difficulties associated with the themes examined in this chapter are to a greater or lesser extent worked through, clients can be supported in their development towards autonomy, and to mature working, social and intimate relationships.

AUTHORITY AND AUTONOMY

The second major set of themes with which a psychodynamic therapist or counsellor is invariably engaged takes its cue from that period of psycho-social development when an infant becomes capable of much greater coordination of muscles and brain. This leads in turn to greater mobility and dexterity, to speech and more precise communication with others, and to engaging more fully with other people and situations in the child's widening world. Like the first set of themes these issues, many of them to do with different aspects of control and becoming gradually more independent, are played out not only at this young age, which is sometimes identified as that of the toddler stage, but throughout life. Attitudes towards self and others over these important matters of doing, making, and acting, acquired in the early years, will be reinforced within the family in later childhood and adolescence, supported or challenged in school, and become a major influence on the way in which learning, work, and relationships with authority in particular, are faced and worked with in adult life.

Freud's early work tended to emphasize the anal aspects of this early period of development, and these certainly should not be forgotten. Graphic terms, such as 'messy', 'dirty', 'letting go' or 'holding in' clearly apply to attitudes and reactions to toilet training: but of course they apply to many other situations as well, where they are equally significant – for example, a messy room, or even a messy life; or the letting go of feelings as well as faeces. In developmental terms the second and third years of life bring immense changes, as an infant moves from relative helplessness to being able to move around, from being fed to feeding herself, from a few sounds to speaking her needs, from holding and hugging to taking things apart and putting them back together. As life proceeds the older child learns further skills, and faces the need to tackle new tasks: attitudes to these, as well as reactions from others to achievements and failures, may be influenced by and understood in the light of parental encouragement or restrictions in earlier years; and throughout adult life there are plenty of other opportunities and situations where early learning about authority and about being autonomous play a significant part.

This chapter therefore covers much more than Freud's apparently single focus upon anal eroticism and toilet training, and more too than Erikson's extension of the tasks of this second stage to 'muscular–anal' development. The language we commonly use (not just in psychodynamic discourse) about issues of control and autonomy does however frequently reflect these particular areas of child development and parenting, and the chapter will show how what have been described as anal characteristics (being ordered – or messy; holding back – or letting go; retention and spoiling or soiling) can also be applied to a range of other activities and interactions both in parent–child and in adult-to-adult relationships.

The themes of trust and dependency underpin the development of the 'self' and can lead to a positive or negative sense of 'who I am'. The earlier themes concern the essence of 'being'. The second set of themes around authority and autonomy are much more about 'doing' – 'what I can do' or 'what I should do' – and about the way people value themselves or feel valued by others on the basis of *what they do* (or do not do), rather than on the basis of *who they are*. This may seem an artificial division, because personal identity often includes what a person does as well as what they are like. But the person with a secure basic sense of self can change what they do without altering who they are; and the person who lives only for what they do, may be masking a weakened sense of who they are. Where people successfully handle the issues that arise in the context of this second theme the foundations are laid for self-esteem in terms of what might be achieved, for confident independence, and for the potentiality for the pleasure and creativity of self-expression. Negotiated less well, the same issues may lead a person instead to doubt, shame and inhibition.

The previous chapter showed how unwise it is to idealize early infancy as a time of bliss, without acknowledging the many other feelings present in a baby (and in those who care for her). It is tempting in contemplating older infants to see them as more capable, more wilful, more devious, and more understanding of the adult world than they actually are. We may forget how much there is to learn and absorb in the process of growing up. Children have to work hard to make sense of what is expected of them, of what words mean, of how things work, of what being in relationship to others might involve. It is not surprising that sometimes what parents and significant others say is misinterpreted or misunderstood by them. We hear children struggling to make sense of bewildering words by changing them into something that sounds familiar to them and which makes more sense to them: such as versions of phrases in the Christian *Lord's Prayer*, where 'Thy kingdom come' becomes 'Vikings will come' (there having been a project on Vikings at infant school); or 'Lead us not into temptation' is interpreted as 'Lead us not into Thames Station': the corrupted phrase is in each case more concrete for the child than the original unfamiliar adult concept.

Misunderstandings can easily arise also over adult expectations and 'rules'. Take an example from toilet training, which in our society is often given particular prominence as an indicator of 'being good' or being 'grown up'. A child learns that it is good to urinate and defecate on the pot, but he or she does not understand at first *why* it is good to perform in one receptacle, but not, for example, in a different place. If it is the pot that is significant for the adult, it might be (psychoanalysts suggest) that for a child it is her faeces that are more significant, and that they are precious, wherever you choose to deposit them. It may therefore be puzzling for a child to realize that not only is the pot a rather special sort of container, but to discover that when she has finished, these special offerings of hers are poured from the pot into a toilet, where they are then flushed away. Puzzlement may then become bafflement when the child is then told off for placing some other precious item (such as mother's necklace) in the toilet, which by now has become a particularly sacred place! Adults may smile at such mistakes, although sometimes it is we adults who become angry and punish a child, quite unjustifiably, for not knowing better. Children are then mystified, not understanding what it is they have done wrong, when they so much wished to please by doing the right thing.

It is scarcely surprising that it is difficult for a young child to comprehend in so short a time the complexities and subtleties of the rules of the adult game of life. As Lowe says, a child is sometimes 'damned if he does, damned if he doesn't' (1972: 9). It is a deeply puzzling world to be living in. Just when they feel most pleased with themselves, they may be scolded for their achievements; or what feels like an achievement at one time becomes a disaster at another. A child's energy and enthusiasm can be encouraged by being told 'there's a clever girl'; and then the same actions are suddenly curbed as being too disruptive – 'there'll only be trouble'. At other times a child may want to be more baby-like, and yet find herself forced to be active and to conform to 'being her age', just when it is that age she wishes temporarily to retreat from. So although some parents can be cruel and demanding, and crush the spirit of a growing child, it is not necessarily inadequate parenting that leads to inhibition or anxiety in the face of new tasks, new situations and new relationships. Some of the misunderstandings already described can have a similar effect.

Neither should we imagine that a child is ever only a passive recipient of adult wishes. The growing child and adolescent hopefully finds plenty of opportunity for exercising her own wishes, which sometimes leads to battles of will and, particularly in the most repressive families, to frustrations of freedom, as a child seeks to get something, or do something, which the parent will not allow. If confidence and autonomy can be facilitated, encouraged and rewarded in many families, in most it also has to some extent to be won.

This chapter therefore demonstrates how these issues around exercise of control, and autonomy, about 'doing' as well as 'being', about learning to live with, challenge and submit to authority figures, constitute different aspects of what is sometimes known in psychodynamic theory as the 'anal character'. In therapy and counselling, clients show various characteristics that are indicative of the significance of themes around authority and autonomy. These presenting issues are examined in some detail, with the principal indications best summarized as: rigidity (the uptight, controlled person); anxiety (about getting it wrong, or making a mess); the opposite characteristics of being disorganized, uncontrolled, 'letting it all out' indiscriminately; the need for clear answers; unquestioning adherence to authoritative ideas or figures; gratuitous challenging and antagonizing of others, who are not necessarily oppressive; and the ability to control and manage themselves and their relationships with others. Some of these difficulties may need considerable working through in themselves before counselling or therapy can make any progress in the initial concerns brought by the client: for example, where a client views the therapist as an authoritative oracle who has all the answers. Sometimes however the presenting issues are themselves directly related to the themes as they are explored below.

Fear of losing control

The emphasis upon anal functions and anal eroticism in psychoanalysis has tended to minimize the significance of other aspects of muscular development in infancy. These are many, including walking, grasping, playing with toys, speaking, feeding oneself, etc. It can also obscure the way in which all these developments introduce new ways of relating between parents and their children, as each learns to adapt to the consequences of a growing child's abilities. Most parents are of course delighted with their children's achievements, although there are bound to be mixed feelings: when a child learns to walk, nothing in the house is quite as safe as it was when she stayed where she had been put, and they were safely out of reach: watchfulness and a little anxiety goes hand-in-hand with pleasure at the child's first steps. Over-watchfulness on the other hand can convey over-concern, and hamper a child's confidence in moving around and exploring. When a baby begins to grasp a spoon and use it as a tool this is another important step; but her attempts at feeding will of course at first mean food everywhere but in her mouth, and the reaction of the parents to the resulting mess may again inhibit the child. Parental reactions to a child's advances provide important feedback on her initiatives.

These parental attitudes were of course present earlier, and will probably continue to be the same when other developments take place, as the child goes to school and into adolescence. A mother may therefore go by the rule book in providing feeds when the baby is young; a father may be disturbed by toys cluttering up the floor with his three-year-old, and by Doc Marten boots creating stumbling blocks with his teenagers; parents can show anxiety about a child's performance at school which resembles the pressure to produce results as a toddler. These responses about order and chaos, inevitable with growing children, run as deep as the first theme characteristics around trust and doubt, dependency or withdrawal. A parent's attitudes to the growing child were probably learned from his or her own parents, and will be passed on in turn to their children, although some parents make a determined effort to 'be different', knowing the stresses caused them in their upbringing by rigid parenting on the one hand or unboundaried parenting on the other.

The kind of authority exercised by parents is often clear from what clients tell of their past, in their memories of parental reactions and attitudes at many different points in childhood and adolescence. It may be difficult to glean much real information about a client's early feeding environment and the quality of the maternal provision because a client's memory does not reach back that far; but it is generally easier to gain considerable insight into the way parents have exercised their authority and responded to the child's initiatives, because these reactions have often stayed relatively the same throughout the client's childhood and adolescence; and may even be expressed in adult-to-adult relations between the generations. Some clients may have early memories which throw light on how they were parented, while others glean what it must have been like in other ways:

Gerry had great difficulty letting go of his feelings; he seemed afraid of being emotional. He could only express himself in a distant intellectualized fashion. He had a dramatic insight into his mother's probable attitudes to him as a baby when his sister had her first child. He had visited her home at the same time as their mother had done, and he listened with amazement to his mother telling his sister off, for not putting the newborn baby on the pot straightaway: 'You and your brother were put on the pot from the first day out of hospital.' Gerry was partly amused, but also partly relieved as he heard this, because he realized that it was not all his doing that he had become a person who had to be so ordered; and he was somewhat angry as he related this story to the counsellor, because he recognized that his mother's need to control potty training from 'day one' might have contributed to his problem about being spontaneous.

Henry initially came for counselling with problems with premature ejaculation. He found it very difficult to relax when making love. Although he 'let go' too soon, his tension also contributed to his difficulty. He recalled an early memory of walking in the country with his parents, and bursting to pee. He asked if he could go behind a bush, but his mother forbade it – he had to wait until he got home and do it in the right place. Not only did Henry find sex rather dirty, but he also recognized that whenever he was asked to produce results, whether in his academic work or in what he called 'sexual performance', he worried inordinately in case he did not do things the right way.

Other examples of parental rigidity, not necessarily related to toilet functions, show similar reasons for tight self-control:

Imogen was a quiet girl, who was very tense when trying to relate to others. She found it difficult to enjoy herself, and she particularly feared losing control when she was with a man, in case the early playful stages of the physical relationship got out of hand. She found it equally difficult to let go of her thoughts and feelings in therapy. The therapist's experience of being with Imogen was that she was constantly needing to draw Imogen out: in her counter-transference she found it difficult to play with words and ideas in the session. Imogen always seemed to be looking for some guidance as to what to say or do. In one session she told the therapist of a memory of a time in her early adolescence, which probably typified her parents' attitudes to her. It happened when she had some cousins to stay. The youngsters were all excited, and were bouncing up and down on the sofa, and when her parents came in they told Imogen off, but not her cousins. She felt very small and ashamed. It was a telling example to the therapist of how her parents' 'wet blanket' dampened getting too excited and letting off steam, and suggested that such attitudes probably pervaded her home, continuing to influence Imogen even when she had grown up and left it behind her.

These examples are all of people who had inhibitions about letting go; and in two instances any sign of spontaneity was missing in the therapy sessions as well. Each of them was afraid of what would happen if they lost control – perhaps worried about what they might spill out. Such characteristics can also be seen in clients who are very precise and exact, planning out what they want to say, perhaps with a written list of points they want to be sure to talk about; or in clients who speak in a measured way, detailing precise times and dates, as if each session is a minute-by-minute report of the last week. 'Getting it right' seems to dominate. Perhaps they too are afraid of letting something slip:

Joan was a really pessimistic woman, convinced that things would never work out for her. She really began to irritate her counsellor by the way she tried to express herself. She constantly introduced so many qualifications into each sentence that the counsellor almost forgot how the sentence had begun by the time she got to its end. 'I was pleased to be able to go to London – well not exactly pleased, but to go to London – well not to go to London, but to get away from Birmingham – it wasn't like a few years ago when I went to London . . .' Of course, by this time the thread was lost. Joan seemed so afraid of making a mistake in her choice of words, that the counsellor eventually put this to her, linking her dread of the things going wrong in the future to her fear that she was always getting it wrong in what she spoke of today.

Keith began every session by alluding back to the last. 'I'm sorry I said . . . I didn't mean . . .', etc. The counsellor eventually observed: 'You seem to leave here each time afraid that I have got you wrong.' It is also possible that in both these cases there was a lot of unexpressed anger in each of these clients, but their most obvious need was to try and make everything right in order to neutralize it.

Rights and wrongs, and particularly the words 'ought', 'must' and 'should', seem to feature highly in those who are held back by rigid self-control. It is even a relief when such a person can actually come late to a session (when normally the therapist would wonder why) without having to apologize:

Lionel was a very ordered and precise individual. It therefore felt as if it was a significant step forward when, after a missed session, he returned the next week, quite gleefully saying that he had hired a car for the day; and how much he had enjoyed sitting on a hill at the time of the session feeling that he could pay for the therapist's time but he did not have to attend! It was, of course, also an unconsciously aggressive act towards the therapist, who had been left worried about what had happened to someone who was normally so regular. But in this particular context it felt like a rather healthy 'one in the eye' for the therapist, as well as a bid to be independent, without having to feel guilty about it. Lionel could at one and the same time meet his obligation (he was of course still going to pay for the session), yet he could assert his freedom of choice. The therapist too needed to be free enough to see the positive side in this otherwise rebellious acting out.

Conscience and internalized parents

We may wonder why many adults, who have left their parental home behind them, still go on acting as if their parents were around, still the controlling figures they might have been in their childhood. In looking at the first theme of trust and dependency, I discussed the way a baby takes in (or internalizes) the experience of the nurturing parent, like an image or icon, which then becomes one important aspect of the self-image. This may be a good image, or a bad one, although continued exposure to good experience should lead to a more realistic self-image, one which is mainly good (without being idealized or omnipotent), with a few inevitable negative aspects to it as well (because no-one, thank goodness, is perfect). The growing child's inner world continues to act as a container for internalizing experience of the parents, including icons of the type of authority they represent. The key word here is 'represent', since the child's inexperience may make the perceived authority of a parent into something much more fearful than a parent intended. In this way internalized figures take on a life of their own, moulded by the child's perceptions. Although children are often highly intuitive, they do not have the breadth of knowledge and experience that an adult has. So, when something goes wrong for an adult, a balanced view would be to regret the mistake and to learn from it how to do better the next time. But when something goes wrong for a child, a child may exaggerate how 'bad' she has been, especially if a parent's anger at a mistake was sudden, forceful and frightening. While the parent's anger soon cools, and may even be quickly followed by a reparative hug, the outburst continues to echo in the child's mind like the echo of a warning shot across the bows. If the child is in turn angry with the parent, a parent's anger may be felt even more intensely, because the child attaches to it her own anger projected on to the parent.

A child will therefore cope with a parental rebuke in a variety of ways: she will probably learn not to repeat the offending behaviour; she may copy her parents in telling off her doll, a cuddly toy, or a younger sibling; she may get cross with a fantasy companion, thus disowning her own responsibility. In all these responses the critical parent is internalized, or becomes what is sometimes called an 'introject': the child becomes critical, of other objects and of herself. This introjection gradually takes up a permanent position within a child's mind, and forms (as Freud felt) the basis for the 'super-ego', or what might more popularly be called the 'conscience'.

To some extent this process is part of learning what is deemed right and what is deemed wrong in a particular family, in a particular subculture, and in society (or society as far as the growing child knows it). The equation of 'super-ego' and 'conscience' may be convenient, but perhaps a distinction needs to be made between the two terms, in that conscience is more aptly used of the relatively rational, conscious, self-observing aspect of a person, which enables self-control to be consciously exercised (what Thomas Aquinas called 'the mind making moral judgements'); 'super-ego' is better reserved for that aspect of reflection which is unconscious as well as conscious and which is often irrationally hostile to the self, so that a person might say, 'I feel very bad about myself, although I know I've done nothing really wrong.'

Other technical terms that have been used for this latter function in psychoanalytic literature throw further light on how people often experience this part of themselves. Fairbairn (1952), for example, prefers the terms 'internal saboteur' and 'anti-libidinal ego'. The former is an expression which therapists can readily adapt in their work with clients: 'It is as if something inside you sabotages you.' The second is less user-friendly, but refers to the way one side of the personality attacks the love-seeking side of the person. Klein's phrase 'the persecutory object' again graphically describes an internalized 'voice' (as people often hear it) which aggressively and sometimes destructively tortures the central self.

> Mandy was such a tortured person, always deeply anxious about whether she was doing the right thing. She had made some progress in her counselling, and as a reward for an event which had gone well she decided to treat herself to some new clothes. But when she walked out of the shop with them, she seemed to hear this voice inside her telling her off for spending the money, and asking her what she thought she would look like, 'all dressed up like that'. When the counsellor said to Mandy, 'It's almost as if one side of you is persecuting the other', she seized on the phrase: 'That's just it – that's exactly how it feels.' Her counsellor then wondered whether Mandy in any way recognized the voice. Mandy did not think for long, and soon responded that she knew that voice anywhere: it was just what her mother would say; even the tone of the voice was just like hers.

Bettelheim (1983) points out that the translators of Freud's works into English did him and psychoanalytic terminology an injustice by choosing to use Latin terms such as id, ego, super-ego. It may have been from a mistaken notion that such terms appeared more scientifically respectable. In the original German Freud's terms are personal, and should have been translated as the 'it', the 'I' and the 'over-I'. The last may be as ugly a phrase as the super-ego, but the other terms make more sense. They reflect everyday speech, as in the phrases, 'It wasn't me', 'It came over me', 'I don't know what took me over', 'I feel as if there's a little voice in me telling me how awful I am.' An alternative dynamic explanation is used in Transactional Analysis (Berne 1968) and is just as apt in psychodynamic counselling: 'It's as if there is a critical parent inside you getting at your child.' Or a different image: 'It feels as if you are at war with yourself.' All these phrases (I-myself; you-yourself; parent–child) illustrate the inner dialogue, or even the inner argument that so easily takes place.

In identifying the different aspects that appear to constitute the self, and in using terms for these internalized figures with which a client can identify, a counsellor provides support for the central self, the 'ego', or the 'I':

In Norma's case the images were taken from her own words. She was saying how restricted she felt in her digs. She could not play music late at night, because it disturbed people; but other people also disturbed her, because the walls were so thin. Her parents had been and still were protective of her, never allowing her any real freedom or independence, in case in some way or another she got hurt. What they said when she was with them continued to exert a strong influence upon her when she was living on her own. She always felt, for example, that she ought to be working. 'Working' was her only safe activity. She found it difficult to enjoy herself, which of course made it difficult for her too when she could hear the other people in her digs enjoying themselves. Her counsellor took Norma's words about her digs, and suggested that there were thin walls inside herself too; and that when she wanted to enjoy herself, she heard her parents saying inside her: 'Do be careful', 'You should be working', etc.

This internalized parental figure easily latches on for support to anyone who is in a position of authority. The internal saboteur finds an external ally when it needs it. Teachers, those in managerial positions, those who enforce law and order, clergy and counsellors – any of these may be perceived as critical and punitive even when they are not, and even when they have said or done little that could warrant such a perception. Counsellors and therapists particularly need to be careful that they do not present themselves in an authoritarian way because they will easily feed such notions; and they need to listen especially for any indication that this is the way their words or their ideas are being understood. Even observations that are intended to be facilitative can be taken as judgmental. Confrontation or challenge, which must always be used sensitively, is doubly difficult to get right with the client who sees the counsellor as a critical parent-figure.

Where this appears to be the case, a counsellor may look for an opportunity to link the feeling of being criticized, or the wish for an authoritative answer, to other significant authority figures past and present. If clients appear to have to defend themselves, particularly following a counsellor's intervention, the counsellor might observe: 'You appear to think I'm being critical of you – as if I was like your stepfather, who always picked on you'; or 'You know, you are very hard upon yourself, and I think you see me as treating you the same way.' It is essential to lessen the severity of a client's self-criticism, or anxiety about others being judgmental, if the way is to be opened up to work in therapy upon the client's most private thoughts and feelings, of which such a client is likely to feel guilty or ashamed.

Shame and guilt

In looking at the underside of narcissistic pride in Chapter 3, I referred to the sense of shame that may be present in the earliest months, describing this as lack of self-esteem. Erikson (1965) locates shame in the second-stage issue of autonomy, rather than as a counterpart to dependency issues. This apparent difference may be related to Erikson's association of shame with the inability to perform tasks, with feelings of incompetence, with failure to reach the aspirations and expectations set by others (or even by oneself), and with a self-image of being immature. All these are different occasions for shame than the despair which might be associated with narcissistic damage and the feeling of being ashamed about one's whole self. In both instances the feeling of shame may be completely crippling: it is what occasions it that is different. A further difference is that there is more hope for a fairly rapid recovery from a single failure to perform a task, than there is from that pervasive and basic lack of worth, or from a perpetual sense of not being able to do things well.

It seems sometimes that in common usage the terms 'shame' and 'guilt' are interchangeable, just as 'envy' and 'jealousy' may commonly be used as alternative expressions. In psychoanalytic terminology, however, envy and jealousy are quite distinct (see p. 75), and shame and guilt are used to describe quite different types of emotion. Precisely what are the differences is not consistent in the literature. Erikson makes it appear that guilt is a feature of later development (he associates it with the third stage), following Freud, who suggested that the capacity to experience guilt is one of the results of negotiation of the Oedipus complex (whether successfully negotiated or not). Shame, Erikson posits, results from failure to negotiate tasks involved in the muscular–anal stage of development. Therefore guilt is placed in the third stage, because it is a response more to what a person has done (Erikson places emphasis on 'initiative' as a virtue in his third age), whereas shame is related to that which the person has been unable to do.

The argument of this book is that it is unhelpful to link any of these emotions or psychological features to any particular age. Differences may be usefully defined, but only as long as it is recognized that guilt is also experienced at an early stage of development, particularly (as I have indicated) in Klein's association of guilt with oral–aggression and anal–aggression in infancy. Guilt may then refer to the anxiety experienced that we may have damaged the other; whereas in shame it is the self that feels damaged. Shame may arise from feelings of failure to achieve control, and from a sense of letting oneself down, or of letting others down. It is a kind of disappointment, sometimes very intense disappointment, rather than anger with oneself, the latter being more obvious at least in some expressions of guilt. Feelings of shame may be expressed in language that is reminiscent of anal images: 'I fouled it up . . . I made a mess of it . . .'. Indeed in this instance the anal stage provides a clear example of the distinction: a child who inadvertently messes in his pants rather than on the toilet may experience a sense of shame if he is told off – the opposite of the pleasure he feels when he does it in the right place. But if the same child *deliberately* messes his pants, perhaps as an angry protest, then when he is told off he is more likely to feel guilty. This anal language can also be used in the context of more obviously aggressive feelings, such as the wish to spoil or soil, to shit upon, as a token of angry defiance.

Ozzie gave an interesting example of the difference from another situation. In a nostalgic moment, he returned with a friend to their old secondary school to see their old classroom. They both climbed over the fence, and were wandering around the outside of the building when the caretaker caught them. Ozzie felt very guilty at having been caught trespassing, but his friend simply walked up to the caretaker, and started to chat, man to man, about their reason for being there. The caretaker quietened down, and accepted what the friend had said. Ozzie, however, felt ashamed at having felt so guilty, and of not being as 'cock-sure' (as he put it) as his friend had been in that situation. It is incidental perhaps, but Ozzie had regularly wetted the bed until way into his teens, and he also felt very ashamed about that.

Perhaps it is the client's tone of voice and facial expression that is the clearest indication of these different feelings, with shame being the more depressed and despairing in its expression. Shame is often communicated non-verbally, with the head down, and gaze averted, enacting the phrase used in some cultures about shame: 'loss of face'. In such a situation a counsellor's choice of language is important: 'I think you're worried that I may be disappointed in you', is more relevant to the situation than 'You may feel that I'm angry with you'.

It is an interesting question of whether people are generally more ready to acknowledge something about which they feel guilty, than something of which they feel ashamed. Shame seems to cut deeper than guilt, as in this example, where Petula described her view of the difference:

> She told her therapist that she did not feel guilty if she told white lies. The therapist thought that in some way she *was* concerned about this, and asked what sort of lies she meant. She explained that if people asked about herself, she could never let on to them that she was really unhappy and discontented; she led them to believe that she was on top of everything, and that she got on well with others. This was not the case at all, but Petula knew that she would feel ashamed if she was seen as less than perfect in other people's eyes. She preferred to tolerate the unease of telling what she called white lies than experience the shame she would otherwise bring upon herself.

It is obviously important to help a client to talk about the trigger for his or her feelings, but this can only be done when it is clear that the counsellor is not apportioning blame, or meting out criticism. Some people use denial or projection to avoid facing their feelings of shame and guilt: 'It wasn't me . . . it was the drink in me'; 'I wasn't myself'; 'It was their fault'; 'It was the devil in me'; 'I blame my parents'. It is of course possible that others, such as parents, might in some way be to blame, and in some instances it is important to be able to allow those feelings to be expressed: I think here particularly of working with survivors of abuse of different kinds, where if anyone experiences shame it should of course be the perpetrator, but it is all too often the survivor. It is not sufficient, as some psychoanalytic practice has done, to link such experiences of shame to the fantasy wishes of the survivor. Proper attribution of where responsibility really lies is necessary when there is obvious evidence of abuse or neglect. At the same time a fully objective stance requires us to accept that those who have damaged others are often themselves damaged, and that 'the sins of the fathers are visited upon the children', generation after generation. Therefore in some cases to blame is unproductive, whether it be self-blame, or the accusation of others. Perhaps one of the main differences between shame and guilt is that guilt can be appropriate, whereas shame never is. Justifiable guilt involves accepting responsibility for oneself, or for a part of oneself, albeit a part a client might prefer to disown.

Conditional love

A system of rewards and punishments often seems to accompany the process of growing up. It is difficult to know whether parents change from giving unconditional love towards a baby, to a rather less tolerant love as a child grows older, consonant with the need to introduce their child to family norms and social realities. Do parents therefore become more conditional in the love they express, and more ready to show displeasure as well as affection? I suspect that the same type of love (which of course can be clinging, fickle, deep or shallow) applies throughout child-rearing, so that a generous parent is always so, from feeding the baby through to selfless support of the adolescent; or that a parent who shows conditional love similarly expects children to conform in order to gain their affection, as much in the early weeks as well as in later years. The notion of conditional love that is communicated to young children will be lived out, although then internalized, in adult life. It is seen in the phrase, 'I will only be loved if . . .', or 'I will not be loved unless . . .'.

> Queenie showed the effects of this type of upbringing. Life was not going well – mainly, it has to be said, because her own very severe conscience (as Queenie described it) pulled her up for every little fault she detected in herself. She openly declared that there was no such thing as unconditional love – you had to work for it. She felt an inordinate need to please her parents; and from what Queenie said of her, it appeared that her mother needed her children to be successful in order to feel good enough herself as a parent. In one session Queenie declared, 'No one would really love me if they knew me – only God.' Queenie's faith was important to her, not least because God was the only one who she believed fully accepted her. But after this session she visited the parental home and told her parents that she was seeing a therapist, something which up to that point she had been too ashamed to tell them. To Queenie's surprise, her mother responded by saying that she didn't mind, and that she still loved her. As the therapist observed in the following session, her mother's words still had a slight tinge of conditional love to them ('I love you, despite your seeing a therapist') but Queenie had found a sort of expression of unconditional love at home. What she had experienced earlier in her life in relation to her parents' love might not apply any more; but such a strong internalized mother image still needed many more months of the type of reassurance shown to Queenie more recently by her mother before it could replace the more negative view she so often had of herself.

'Unconditional love' is a phrase that is used in some therapeutic literature to describe one of the necessary conditions for counselling. It is of course a major element in the therapeutic relationship, but if it is necessary it is not always sufficient. When the internalized conditional parent, who has been around in the client's conscious and unconscious mind for many years, continues to exercise a powerful force, it is difficult for a client like Queenie to recognize, or believe in, the therapist's unconditional regard. The therapist may need to help her see what she does to herself, in the way her ability to accept herself is also conditional, as well as to discover with her where these powerful constructs may have come from.

Obsessional rituals and perfectionism

One form of internalized 'conditional regard' can be seen at work in obsessional rituals, and even more commonly in perfectionism. In these instances perfectionists really only feel secure, temporarily free from anxiety and at one with themselves when what they have been doing or making has been completed 'without any blemish'; or obsessional people only feel safe from some unknown and unnamed dread when they have performed certain rituals properly. For example, perfectionism may involve having to make sure that a piece of writing has no obvious errors, or no alterations – some people have to start again as soon as they have crossed something out on paper; or a room must be kept in order, with nothing out of place. In the case of rituals, in order to feel acceptable (sometimes to God, but just as often to oneself) certain actions have to be performed, perhaps in a particular sequence, or so many times, or both. Only then does the person feel relatively calm and at peace with him- or herself. It is as though the conscience has been calmed, the super-ego assuaged, or perhaps the internalized parent satisfied. Obsessional symptoms may take the form of checking, of compulsive actions like repeated hand washing, or the repetition of certain words and phrases in the right order.

Freud (1907) observed how religious practices sometimes fall into this category: they serve the same purpose of warding off anxiety. Nevertheless some rituals serve a more positive purpose, assisting psychological change: rites of passage are perhaps the best examples. Other rituals may be used to deny experience, and to prevent change. Mitchell (1982) presents a case study where the ritual use of prayer is used as a massive denial of death:

> Valerie (as she is called in the article) was a popular high-school girl who suddenly fell ill. It was difficult to diagnose her condition, but her doctors had little hope of saving her life. In desperation they gave her drugs which had very uncomfortable side-effects. The hospital chaplain who visited Valerie found her mother and father in constant attendance, never leaving her side. The community in her home town were whipped up into a campaign of hope by friends and the local press, and her church congregation was praying for her recovery. They were convinced that if only they and she had enough faith she would come through. The pastor of her home church, despite his misgivings about the hysterical reaction, colluded with the community's wish for a vigil of prayer. Valerie's father also seemed to collude with his wife's need to maintain their watch over

Valerie's bedside, while the doctors' use of drugs also seemed to be a denial, which father secretly regretted, seeing the discomfort his daughter was experiencing. It was not until the chaplain was able to visit Valerie alone (her parents being fast asleep in the room) that she was able to learn from Valerie that she felt she was having to put an act on for her parents and her community back home, and that she wished more often than she could admit that she would be left alone. Even after Valerie's death, her mother arranged a funeral that was more a celebration of resurrection than a true expression of the pain and grief which had been present throughout the whole situation, yet denied by nearly everyone.

The case is also a fascinating example of how an immature religious faith can take over a whole community. By contrast there are commendatory rituals in religious practice that give permission for the dying person to let go ('Go forth upon your journey from this world . . .'). The significance of control over dying is examined again at the end of this chapter.

In the case of Valerie's parents and the community around them it is relatively straightforward to see that their anxiety is about the power of death. What might the anxiety be about in private rituals, such as those which Freud observed in his paper? It is perhaps that same persecutory anxiety which is associated with the first theme of trust and dependency, although in the context of obsessional behaviour it takes a particular form, as if actions of one sort or another can set that anxiety to rest. Sometimes the anxiety masks guilt – and it is often guilt or a similar feeling of discomfort that is experienced when the person does not perform the rituals satisfactorily. Sometimes it appears that what is being kept at bay is the expression of strong desires, such as sexual or aggressive feelings, of which the person feels afraid, as well as the feared punishment for having such feelings in the first place.

Matters of belief are not necessarily brought to therapists or counsellors as being problem areas, except where there is guilt over transgression of moral rules, failure to perform rituals at the right time, or doubt about matters of faith. There is a type of religious faith (and indeed of political ideology) which has strong connections with the theme of this chapter, seen for example in beliefs in a rigidly authoritarian God or political system, in inflexible moral thinking and in the control of belief systems through dogmatic creeds. This is often accompanied by the expectation that as long as faith and ethical codes are followed to the letter, then the faithful will be numbered amongst the elect. Such strongly authoritarian thinking also includes severe criticism of those who do not believe, or those who appear to act immorally, and that criticism is sometimes expressed in sadistic ideas about, and threats of, eternal punishment. Other indications of a religion which is fixated on issues of control include ritualistic actions accompanied by obsessional thinking, mindless repetition of prayers, self-righteous discipline of the reading of holy books, compulsive attendance at services to assuage guilt, absolute and often literal authority vested in the priests and other religious leaders, and masochistic self-punishment by a sadistic super-ego. (For a fuller description of the way in which authority issues can be of value, but also inhibit the development of belief systems, see Jacobs 1993a.)

Roger was a devout Catholic, who intellectually put himself on the liberal wing of the church, but he could not shake himself free from the legalistic religious discipline which his schooling had imparted to him. This education probably only confirmed the right-wing authoritarian views he got at home from his mother. Despite the forgiveness he received through confession, and the reassurance he was given by priests to whom he spoke, Roger worried inordinately about minor sins, which he could see were scarcely sins at all, such as having one small drink of alcohol as a night-cap. He could not receive communion following these occasions, because he felt so bad. Like other obsessional difficulties it was very difficult to shift this pattern of thinking. Roger knew he was worrying unnecessarily, but he could not get beyond listing these worries in his counselling. It was as if 'free association' might give rise to thoughts and feelings which he would express, and which would then make him feel even worse.

It has to be said that in many cases, outside as well as within unhealthy religious practices, it is very difficult to shift obsessional rituals through using psychodynamic techniques alone, unless the client is both ready to move beyond his or her preoccupation with the rituals in order to explore other experiences and other feelings and thoughts, and is able to experiment with postponing or relinquishing such rituals. It is difficult to get beneath the rituals, which are mainly successful in defending the person against ideas that they cannot contemplate: that they are only 'mainly' successful is perhaps the reason why the obsessional person seeks help; it is as if they know something is not right. But because the rituals are more than 50 per cent successful, it is still dangerous to contemplate dropping or altering them. Such clients are preoccupied with their actions, however inconvenient they find them, and their wish to give them up is accompanied by considerable reservation. For therapy or counselling to work at all, symptoms need to be experienced as alien, something a person wishes to change. Where the symptoms serve a useful purpose, it may be too hard to give them up, let alone look at what they might mean.

The same difficulty applies to working with other behaviours that have a similar repetitive, compulsive and addictive quality to them, such as alcohol and drug dependency, eating disorders, etc. It is difficult to ignore the symptoms, sometimes because they can carry risk of damage to the client's body or even life; but even when the behaviours are less severe, such clients set great store by them, and find it difficult to move beyond their preoccupation with them. That does not mean that a psychodynamic therapist has to give up the attempt to look at the meaning of these presenting issues, and at other aspects in the client's life, but it may be that it is only some changes in these other areas of the client's internal and external relationships that will lead to a position where it becomes possible to consider tackling and changing the more obvious presenting difficulties.

Sylvie had been seeing a therapist for a year, during which she related well to her, and had talked about many aspects of her life other than her presenting issue, which was a fastidious and obsessional concern with the number of calories she was consuming every time she ate. She was not strictly anorexic, but there were signs that her preoccupation with food might lead that way, if it was not alleviated. Therapy went well in some respects, inasmuch as Sylvie was able to reflect upon a large number of different issues past and present, although her behaviour relating to food showed no sign of shifting. What puzzled her was that whenever she went on holiday, all the worries about food completely disappeared, only to return the moment she returned home, when the internal debate about how much to eat resumed. Her husband had commented on how much she changed when she was away, almost as if she was two different people. After one rather longer holiday than usual Sylvie started the first session back by saying how wonderful things had been, and how relieved she was by not worrying about food. She enthused about the holiday, and how lovely it was not to wear a watch (which she was not wearing either in the session); and what a contrast this was to being at home, always having to keep an eye on the time, because of this or that engagement, including returning to therapy. In her more relaxed state the therapy moved some-what faster than usual – food no longer dominated the session. Instead the therapist followed up a remark Sylvie had made about what life was like when she was a child, with her mother constantly carping about tidi-ness, and the children always having to be ready for meals that were served at the same time every day, exactly on the hour. Sylvie concluded her vivid description of an obsessional parent with the words, 'You could set your clock by my mother.' Her earlier remark about how nice it was not to wear a watch made much real sense at this point. It was as if on holi-day she could shed her internalized mother, whereas at home, and at work, Sylvie got into these continuous, tiring arguments within herself, as to whether she should eat this or that, about how many calories she was permitted to take in, whether she had done this right at work, and whether she was doing what others wanted, etc. It was as if her mother's voice constantly argued with her own. It was only when she could shed all her responsibilities on holiday that she found a place where she could be herself, and enjoy being herself, doing whatever she wanted, without having to count the cost. This link was not of course a point of immedi-ate change for Sylvie: psychodynamic therapists do not expect miracles from good interpretations! But it was a breakthrough moment when some of the reasons for her obsessional worrying began to fall into place for the therapist, and for Sylvie too. Sylvie went on to describe many other ways in which her mother ordered their lives as children, of which she had never before spoken so clearly. 'I'm sure I've turned out just like my mother', she said. 'I'm not so sure', answered the therapist; 'I can see a healthy part of you that tries to argue against the mother inside you, and which on holiday really shuts her up; but at other times I can also see that it's a real battle to find yourself.'

These situations are made even more complicated because psychodynamic thinking suggests that rituals or addictive behaviours, that in many ways are defences against anxiety, sometimes express the very conflicts that the person tries to repress. Rituals can be a way therefore of warding off and yet at the same time acting out repressed wishes. This may be another reason why they cannot be easily relinquished. They perform a number of functions:

> Ted had to wash his genitals very thoroughly after masturbating and he worried because his penis felt so sore that he thought he may have damaged his potency. He then had to masturbate again to see if everything was all right; and this then involved more washing – and so on: a dreadful vicious circle, which dominated Ted's thoughts and behaviour. Although he denied feeling guilty about masturbating, it is possible to see a parallel between masturbation and washing his genitals – both of which gave him erotic pleasure, as well as leading to fear and guilt over the way he handled himself.

It is also the case with phobias, which according to a dynamic explanation similarly often ward off sexual or aggressive feelings that cannot be admitted to consciousness, that a psychodynamic approach needs to incorporate cognitive–behavioural methods to help modify the symptoms. This may be necessary as a prelude to a wider exploration of the underlying issues, as when an agoraphobic person needs help in coming out of the house for therapy. In cases of single symptom presentations (at least as perceived by those clients who deny that anything else is wrong) management of the symptoms through behavioural modification may be the only treatment suitable, and some change may be achieved, even if there is no insight into causes or other personal issues:

> Umberto worried about every choice he had to make, in case he got it wrong. It was not easy to shift this obsessional pattern, although the counsellor achieved some success with one particular symptom. Umberto needed to check all the calculations involved in his work at least five times. The counsellor persuaded him first to check only four times; then three times; and finally to make the calculation just twice (a very reasonable check), leaving it there if the results were consistent both times. Although it may have been coincidental, this change appeared to influence other areas of Umberto's life, because having achieved this small change, he became less apprehensive about other decisions, although he still sought further appointments with the counsellor whenever there were particularly crucial choices that had to be made.

With some clients this modification of rituals might be used alongside ongoing attempts to uncover unconscious feelings and ideas, together with any guilt and shame that might be attached to them. This is possible when the client is ready to talk more freely about other things that come to mind:

> When she was on her own Vivienne went through a ritual at bedtime, checking all the doors and drawers in her room, lest there was a man hiding there. It seemed an intractable symptom, and there was no shifting of it through behavioural modification. Vivienne was easy with the therapist, and spoke freely about herself and her relationships. She had been able to tell the counsellor of an incestuous suggestion made by her father when her mother was away. But talking about this, and

understanding the link to looking for a man in her room, made no difference to the ritual. The therapist was not too concerned about the lack of
movement on the issues, since the focus in therapy was more on the difficulty Vivienne experienced in giving up a boyfriend, whom she was
'forced' to share with other women. This was linked to the situation arising at home with her father and temporarily absent mother, and not to
the ritual itself. In fact the checking ceased soon after Vivienne was able
to break her relationship with the boyfriend, who she now knew was
sleeping around with the other women. Nevertheless the therapist was far
from sure that the ritual would not return (since therapy had to stop about
the same time) if Vivienne were to form another relationship that had
similar (oedipal) complications.

Perfectionism is a milder form of this obsessive behaviour. It is also a more
common presentation, and one which is accessible to a psychodynamic
approach, without the need for such active intervention as may be necessary
with obsessional–compulsive disorders or phobic states. Although checking
may be involved in perfectionism, the obsessional element is not expressed so
clearly in a definite ritual. The perfectionist similarly needs to feel blameless,
and although often anxious about the judgement of others, they are normally
their own most severe critic. The following example demonstrates perfectionism where it is often found, in the work setting; and at the same time it illustrates anal characteristics, which appear to be related to a number of these
presenting issues:

Wallace was a young doctor who had failed a professional membership
examination, when a recent separation from his wife had interfered with
his studies. It soon emerged that one of the reasons she had left him was
because he constantly complained about her untidiness about the home.
Many other features emerged in the counselling. Wallace had himself
become (as he put it) quite 'lazy' in his work. He had lost the capacity for
'hard slog' which had seen him through his training, and he felt guilty
about that. He found himself irritated by one of his medical partners
whom he described as a perfectionist; so he condemned perfectionism in
his work partner, as well as the absence of it in his marital partner. As he
described his background it appeared that both his parents had felt failures
compared to their own siblings, and that they had put all their aspirations
into their son, expecting him to be brilliant. Wallace's father was continuously afraid of 'doom striking' – particularly lest he fall ill and could not
keep the family. This must also have communicated itself to his son, perhaps contributing to his wish to become someone who cures illness. His
father worked in quality-control and hated his job, but he was doing a job
which perhaps expressed some of his own desires for perfection. The father
went to the toilet at least five times a day to empty his bowels, and at the
age of eleven Wallace was admitted to hospital with severe constipation.
He still felt very angry at the humiliation of the enemas and other treatment: he thought he should at that time have seen a child psychotherapist, and not a physician. In some ways he hated the medical profession,
but he had as it were identified with his aggressors and had become a

doctor (if you can't beat them, join them!). During his training Wallace realized how much he feared illness in himself, just as his father did, and how depressed he became when the patients did not respond to treatment. He felt that the life of a physician was 'purgatory' and himself recognized how close this term was to his being 'purged' when in hospital as a child. He was constantly struggling with a lifetime's identification with 'perfection' against anxiety, and had lately reacted against this.

Controlling and being controlled: the passive character

A common expectation at the beginning of any therapy relationship is that the therapist will understand the reasons for the client's state of mind, and will tell the client what to do. This is in itself no indication of passivity on the client's part, but simply a belief that like other experts – lawyers, doctors, or teachers – therapists will pronounce once they have heard the facts. Many clients learn that the therapeutic approach (at least in the psychodynamic, integrative and humanistic traditions) is not one of instruction, and that the particular expertise of the therapist and counsellor involves a very different approach both to factual knowledge and to advice and guidance.

There are some clients whose initial expectations about the expertise of the therapist come not from ignorance, but from a trait in their character. They seem to live by what others say, and indeed for them pleasing others is high on their agenda. They are constantly seeking advice and approval. They continue to want the counsellor to tell them what to do, to answer their questions for them, and to show them the way ahead. Counsellors and therapists may of course collude with such a role, especially if they basically want to be seen this way.

It may be that these passive clients are anxious to trust their therapist's judgements, in case something goes wrong. They prefer the security of doing little from their own initiative, or of someone else being able to carry the can. It is as if the normal uncertainties of life and ordinary levels of risk are too dangerous.

> Yuri visited the family planning clinic and asked the counsellor a series of questions about the effectiveness of the contraceptive pill. He had chosen a subject upon which an almost 100 per cent guarantee could be given, as long as the pill is taken as prescribed. This led Yuri to ask another series of questions about abortion. The counsellor at first answered these questions, since giving guidance was natural in this setting; but she then realised that there was something else behind them; and instead of answering them she asked Yuri whether these questions were important to him because of the new relationship he was in. Yuri nodded, and went on to describe two areas of his life where he felt uncertain: first he was unsure whether he and his girlfriend were right for each other; and second he did not know whether he was making the right choice over a change of job. The counsellor observed that in his initial question Yuri wanted 100 per cent guarantees. He agreed: 'But life's not like that, is it?' This led

on to other worries, including his anxiety about engaging in a sexual relationship; and in turn to feelings of failure to meet the high expectations he always felt his father had for him.

A counsellor may collude with the passive client by giving too many answers, as well as by taking over initiative and control in the session. Clients cannot always be protected from themselves – new counsellors can feel particularly anxious about the welfare of their clients, as if they, the counsellors, had ultimate responsibility for them. Like growing children and adventurous adults clients must be allowed to make the mistakes, some of which are inevitable, and most of which are far from disastrous. While being alert to potential actions that might be damaging to self or others, in truth most counsellors and therapists only see clients once a week, and cannot keep an eye on them during the six days between sessions. Like the toddler who moves away from the parent, but only as far as feels safe, before running back to check all is well, clients need to be able to put some distance between themselves and the counsellor, and in the week between try out new initiatives, in their thinking, their feeling, and their relationships, as far as feels safe for them to do so, returning the next session to check out their thoughts and actions, and to review their options further. This is particularly important when working with young people, who often have many different choices to make within a relatively short period of time. Gone are the days when the early psychoanalysts advised their patients not to take important decisions while in therapy.

Zena was still a student, and her parents gave her everything that she wanted. Nevertheless she still experienced a lack of trust on their part. Instead of allowing her to have her own money and to budget for herself, they had told her just to ask whenever she needed more. She experienced her parents as being too possessive, and she used the phrase that she felt 'tied to their apron strings'. She felt much more independent when she was able to negotiate with them to be paid a lump sum at the beginning of term, which was no greater than her fellow-students had, and when she determined to try to live within that budget. Likewise in her counselling she eventually asked for appointments once a fortnight, and then once a month. This seemed a reasonable request, since she wanted to test out her independence there too, if only gradually. With all clients, but particularly with passive clients, a counsellor or therapist must acknowledge and affirm their need to be independent, and weigh this against any advantages there may be in encouraging them to stay in therapy.

There is implicit in this suggestion the need to distinguish between the dependent client and the passive client. The client who is extremely distressed may need to be provided with the security of reassurance or gentle management – this relates more to the theme of trust and dependency, and to the therapist as a nurturing figure in the transference. Such a client is not the same as the passive, anxious client, who dare not try out his or her autonomy, and who in the transference looks upon the therapist as the authoritative or authoritarian parent. The counsellor in the next example was acutely aware of the dilemma:

Alan was in a real panic. He had recently, and rather suddenly, had doubts about his sexuality, and was afraid that he might be gay. He wanted the counsellor to tell him that he wasn't. These appeared to be anxieties which had come out of the blue, with no precedence – in other respects it would not have occurred to Alan to doubt his heterosexual orientation. As he related recent events, it turned out that the previous weekend Alan had had a stand-up row with his father over the way his father had treated his mother. Grievances nursed over the years were unleashed. Father was taken aback. This challenge to the principal authority figure in Alan's life appeared to have brought on anxieties about retaliation from the father, and becoming submissive to another man. Much of this was related to themes more appropriate to the next chapter, but also concerned feelings of neglect that Alan had experienced from father's distant manner (as he thought his mother had too). The counsellor (a man) could fairly easily have given straightforward reassurance to Alan about his sexual orientation, especially since Alan had made his hitherto heterosexual preferences clear. But he felt that if he were to do so he would be putting himself in an authoritarian and superior position, and that Alan might later feel similar anxiety that he had needed a man to tell him what he knew for himself, or even that he needed a man to 'comfort' him. As the counsellor thought about how to resolve this dilemma he decided it would be better to share it openly with Alan: 'I could tell you that you are not gay, and that might reassure you, but I think you might then feel anxious about me becoming a man who tells you what to do. You do want a man, you want your father, and you want him to be closer to you. I think that makes you draw the conclusion that you must be gay.'

The way in which authority is exercised in various institutions in society may encourage the passive character. It is easy, for example, for someone in a strongly hierarchical organization to become a cog in the machine, to receive orders, and to do as he or she is told. Alternatively lack of stimulation may also lead to passivity, such as in the person who is made redundant, and in whom all self-confidence evaporates. The passivity which sometimes accompanies being in work or even out of work may tempt the counsellor to assume the role of the 'manager'. When there have been tight controls on such clients, or when their sense of security within a tight structure or ordered life is replaced by the anxiety of having few or no parameters, a counsellor can provide containment, but without at the same time becoming a replacement for the limiting authority figures the client has relied upon in the past.

The passive personality also finds it difficult to stand up for him- or herself against dominant others, or to exercise legitimate authority over other people:

Brian, a student teacher, found it impossible to control his classes, so much so that near-riots were taking place. As he told this to the counsellor, Brian was laughing and clearly covering up his own anxiety about the situation. But it also felt as if he was getting some pleasure from seeing the children play up, something he would never himself have dared do with his teachers or with his parents. He had decided that teaching wasn't for him, although his father had felt it a good and safe job, and he did not wish to let his father down. Since Brian was religious, he said he had prayed about it all to God, and God had said, 'Go ahead, do a different job.' In fact this seemed a sensible decision, but it was obvious Brian had needed to refer to his God's authority to carry it out, since it was only his God who could over-rule his father! When the counsellor observed the different ways in which the problems about authority figures were causing difficulty, Brian asked the counsellor: 'Could you repeat all that? I'd like to be able to write that down!' It may have been that the counsellor had said it too obscurely, but it seemed more likely that Brian wanted to put the counsellor's authority on record, rather than use what had been said to make something of it for himself. 'Tablets of stone', thought the counsellor.

In this example, Brian's control of the children was made more difficult because there was a part of him that identified with, and wished to express, through them, his own repressed high spirits. In the next example, the anxiety about exerting control seemed related to some fear of damaging others:

Colin was the manager of a large office, who had achieved his position through efficiency and his ability to charm those who worked for him, and by his gentle nature and example. But he had problems with the occasional employee who took advantage of his quiet manner. In those cases Colin could not bring himself to administer a rebuke or a warning. He told the counsellor that he was afraid of hurting people. He related this anxiety at what he called having to play 'the heavy father' to an earlier time in his life when he had felt extremely worried. His best friend had died as a result of a heart attack when they were playing a rough adolescent game of football, around the same time that his father suffered considerable ill health following a series of heart attacks. Here issues about exercising authority and control seem to be connected with rivalry and competition.

The way in which people exercise authority over others will often be influenced by the way in which they were themselves controlled and managed when they were young, in the family, and at school. Some of those who have been held back and put down by authoritarian regimes at home or elsewhere continue to be passive: others, of course, identify with their authority figures and become controlling, authoritarian, rigid people themselves, who cannot allow their hold over others to be relaxed.

The passive-aggressive personality

Another common personality seen in therapy is known as 'passive-aggressive' – a term which does not mean swinging between passivity and aggression, but rather someone who expresses his or her aggression passively. The passive-aggressive person is encountered in a number of ways. Two of the most common presentations are the 'yes . . . but' character; and the person who seems very passive and submissive and yet provokes considerable anger in other people – and then has a disarming way of appearing quite 'innocent', wondering why there is all this fuss. It is as if the angry feelings in the passive person have been projected into others, who then find themselves more and more irritated, and unable to 'pin' it anywhere. In psychoanalytic terms this is another example of projective identification taking place in those who are made angry:

> Darryl was asked to go to the university counselling service because he was not handing in work as requested. His tutor described Darryl in his phone call to the service as pleasant enough, but told the counsellor that he could never get anything out of him either by way of work or by way of explanation. He added that Darryl had insisted upon standing up all the way through any interview, making the tutor feel that Darryl was a rather submissive character. When the counsellor met him, Darryl had no hesitation about sitting down, and she formed a quite different impression: of a confident young man, who took perverse pride in boasting how little work he did, and who obviously led an active life in all other respects at university. He also mentioned how he had refused to sit down when seeing his tutor. As the session went on the counsellor suggested (in a clearly challenging way) that Darryl was actually quite angry with the tutor for expecting him to work, and that he enjoyed standing up, watching the tutor squirm in his chair. He seemed to want to impress people by turning on its head the idea that you earn praise for working hard. He got admiration from his friends for getting away with it. Darryl seemed to appreciate the way the counsellor had spoken so frankly, and felt the counsellor had hit the nail on the head. He opened up considerably about his parents' aspirations for him, but also about his feeling that he would never be as well respected as his father was in his career. He agreed to meet again. Within a few weeks he was working so hard that the tutor jokingly said to the counsellor, 'What did you say to him that I didn't?'

There may have been some splitting here, between male tutor and female counsellor, and beneath the humour this tutor may have been left with some feelings of failure where the counsellor had been successful. Father–mother–son dynamics may have been played out in the two helpers. Passive-aggressive clients can split authority figures, turning one against the other, getting them to do their dirty work for them, while they stand on the touch line and watch them fight, in the same way as a child learns how useful it can be to run to one parent with a complaint about the other. Handling such potential splits, particularly over the questioning of the authority of the other helper, means that the 'good parent' helper, while providing some security and comfort, must not be drawn into an alliance against the other 'bad parent' helper. Such splitting differs from more primitive splitting (p. 68) because here the passive-aggressive client uses one authority figure to get at another with whom he or she feels angry.

Another expression of passive-aggression is 'withholding', not through shame or fear of letting go (see below), but to convey discontent. A client who misses a session, who comes late, or who unusually has nothing to say, *might* be holding back angry feelings towards the counsellor for something which occurred in a previous session.

> Emma came very late two sessions running. On the first occasion and late in the same session she told of an incident where a man had exposed himself to her at a party. In talking of this incident, she got very upset, and the counsellor, because he had no-one in the session following, let the session go on for longer. He hoped (or at least this was his conscious motive) that by helping her express her feelings, this might help make the incident less upsetting for her. Emma arrived late the next week too, and this time she was reluctant to say anything. The counsellor suggested to her that she might not want to talk about the things which were so upsetting to her last week. His remark had some truth in it, but he did not fully realize what he was saying, nor that this interpretation had applied as much in the previous session as well. After a difficult session Emma eventually said that she was very angry with the counsellor for giving her more time the previous week. It was *then* that she hadn't wanted to say any more about the incident. Instead the counsellor had been somewhat like a voyeur, encouraging her to expose feelings she had deliberately wanted to keep to the minimum. She had come late the previous session, because she felt ashamed, and wanted to flee as soon as she had mentioned the incident; she had got her timing all worked out. But this session she had come late because she felt so angry.

The 'yes . . . but' client is easily recognizable through the frustration experienced in the counter-transference by the therapist or counsellor, as each successive intervention (and often more actively, each suggestion) is greeted with the response, 'Yes . . ., but on the other hand . . .', and is effectively rubbished by the client. Tempting though it may be to indulge in argument with the passive-aggressive client, the client will continue to see argument as an attack and will probably continue to defend themselves in the same way. The empathic response is to be preferred: 'You sound as if there really is no way out . . . that must be pretty frustrating' (or, 'My ineffective suggestions might make you feel rather angry with me'). While the 'yes . . . but' may indicate a client who cannot express their anger and frustration in any other way (it is the therapist who feels it instead), there may of course be other reasons for such a response, such as somewhat obsessional difficulty about being committed to any view or action because they might make the wrong choice ('shall I, shan't I'); or an anxiety about commitment leading them closer to situations which they fear. Again here the empathic response is better than trying (in desperation!) to push a solution on to the client.

The rebel

The rebellious type of person, who always seems to get into scrapes with authority, and who may even be in other relationships which are strained and hostile, is not typical of the average counsellor's caseload, unless he or she is referred for counselling as part of a disciplinary process. Counselling may be viewed by those who manage an institution as a means of exerting some sort of control on the difficult employee or student, or law-breaker; and counselling will probably in such circumstances, at least initially, also be experienced as a means of social control by the reluctant client.

While always bearing in mind that today's rebel may tomorrow be recognized as yesterday's innovator, some acting out of aggression may be the necessary result of earlier unconscious repression, or of family or societal suppression. Giant statements (in words or in action) may have to be made in order to gain a little freedom:

> Fulton's very traditional, narrow-minded, conventional family would be very shocked when he told them that he was gay. He smiled as he said it, making it clear that it was also going to give him considerable pleasure to see how disconcerted his father would be. The 'shock, horror' aspect to his wish to come out was also apparent when his college tutor rang his counsellor: 'I hear you've got something surprising to tell me about Fulton.' The counsellor refused to be drawn into the game: 'If it's what I think it is, he can tell you himself', she replied, telling Fulton about the call and her reply, of course, when they next met.

The most obvious presentations of rebelliousness are either in adolescents, or when adult clients refer back to their adolescence, or even need to live through a feature of adolescence which they never experienced at the time. Battles of will, representing a natural need to assert independence, occur of course in infancy – from feeding at the breast onwards. But they are associated most perhaps with the adolescent years. Rebelliousness is a natural part of this growing up and growing away. Winnicott writes well about this particular period of the maturational process in two papers (1965a: 79–87; 1971: 138–50), particularly in terms of the parental experience of this turbulent time:

> If you do all you can to promote personal growth in your offspring you will need to be able to deal with startling results. If your children find themselves at all they will not be contented to find anything but the whole of themselves, and that will include the aggression and destructive elements in themselves as well as the elements that can be labelled loving.
> (1971: 143)

This rebelliousness is part of the adolescent's need to push away from parents, both as love-objects (see next chapter) and as authority figures. Taking the latter as particularly related to this chapter, a young person and his or her parents are often involved in boundary disputes: the adolescent wants independence, while the parents want to retain their sense of authority. Winnicott, using metaphor as a powerful means of describing the process, writes:

> If the child is to become an adult then this move is achieved over the dead body of an adult . . . [W]here there is the challenge of the growing boy or girl, there let an adult meet the challenge. And it will not necessarily be nice.
> (1971: 145, 150)

In the same paper he stresses the importance of parents surviving: 'there will be this long tussle which you will need to survive' (1971: 143). They can help the process 'only a little: the best they can do is to *survive*, to survive intact, and without changing colour, without relinquishment of any important principle' (1971: 145, Winnicott's italics). Which principles might actually be 'important' and which might be outdated tradition he does not question. What is felt to be inviolable principle in one culture (for example, obedience to parental plans for marriage) may be totally oppressive in another. It must be remembered, as in all the expressions of the themes related in this book, that cultural variations exist. Independence from parents is a typically Western concept, and in some societies would be regarded as a sign of extremely discourteous, if not disturbed, relationships. In a private communication Laiqa Elahi writes:

> It may be because the western concept of gradual 'healthy' separation and autonomy from parents to live an independent self-directive life is so peculiar, not encouraged and often blocked by parents, that when separation does occur it is often in a pathological way . . . One is then faced with an ultimatum, personal freedom or family belonging. If this is the price one has to pay in pursuit of personal happiness it is no wonder people comply without question or challenge, or risk the severing of all family relationships.

Western, white, middle-class psychodynamic values need testing against the norms of personal development and family dynamics in other cultures. It may still be true that the critical, hostile parent who does not permit any independence, or the over-indulgent parent who puts no limits on the teenager's testing of the boundaries, each in their own way prevent the adolescent achieving maturity. Winnicott gets closer to the difficulty of knowing what it is right to be firm about and where to give way when he argues that a young person must be allowed to be immature, as long as adults do not abdicate responsibility (1971: 146). All this of course applies to the therapist working with the creativity and the destructiveness of the rebellious spirit (recognized across cultures in many world myths as two sides of the same coin – Shiva, Janus, etc.). It is also an important question to ask of all therapy, whether it is basically anarchic, or whether indeed it is concerned with persuading people to conform as part of the process of socialization.

Where parents are in conflict with each other (in one sense perhaps trying to kill each other off), or where one or both parents are weakened by physical or mental ill health, it may be more difficult or impossible to challenge them, for fear that the challenge will in one way or another finish them off. Indeed where adolescent rebellion coincides fortuitously with the separation or divorce of parents, or the death of a parent, this can leave indelible marks of self-blame:

> Greta had found it very hard to express any independence openly in her teens, not only because her father was strong-willed, but also because her mother had suffered a severe heart attack. Open rebellion carried with it the fear that either her own actions, or her father's reactions, might

damage her mother. The therapist wondered at one point how Greta had felt after she had criticized him, although Greta's response was more confident than the therapist expected: that it was 'OK – I pay you to take it!' Some clients however are equally concerned lest any bid for autonomy and independence on their part may in some way cause their therapist damage or hurt.

Losing control

We need to distinguish between creative attacks that are part of the process of personal (and indeed of societal) development, and the pure destructiveness of vandalism and cruelty, that is more associated with hate and envy (see Chapter 3) than with battles over independence. Where there is absence of love and trust then aggression can become ruthless. It is also important to distinguish between destructive feelings and behaviour, as part of what might be called, following Winnicott, the 'anti-social' character, and the explosive release of feelings. These may on occasion also prove destructive, because they have been held back for a long time, and the effect of their release in prospect or in actuality may indeed be terrifying. In relating issues of control to the expression of anger and of other emotions, we often see an explosiveness which is not unlike a volcano blowing its top. Emotions are held back, like faeces have to be held back when learning self-control, and burst out when the limits of endurance and tolerance are passed.

It is ironical, of course, that those who hold back feelings for fear of the damage they may cause eventually let them go with such force that some hurt can be occasioned to others, or some damage to themselves. People who fear their anger tend to bottle it up, but inevitably have to let it go every now and again. Suppression is not an effective defence: it seldom works for long. Depression is sometimes caused by angry feelings being held back (perhaps knowingly, but more often unconsciously repressed) and then turned back on the self. Constant irritability frequently indicates such held-back anger. When a client can explode at the therapist or counsellor and learns that the outburst does not spoil the relationship between them, this is a major step forward. Therapy has ultimately to help the client learn that in other situations where people may not be as accepting as the therapist, feelings have to be expressed more appropriately: the freedom just to 'let it out' in therapy is not necessarily acceptable or wise in other settings. Therapy also needs to explore the factors that provoke such strong feelings, in order to look at cause as well as effect. This combination, of trying (where it is possible) to reduce the impact of frustrating circumstances, and of allowing and yet containing the force of feelings thus evoked, can be combined with rehearsing ways of expression, that will both honour the client's feelings, as well as meet his or her concern and respect for others.

Hedda was referred to a therapist in desperation by a psychiatrist who did not know what else to do. She acted out continuously, getting herself into all kinds of trouble, effectively ensuring that she got the attention of all the mental health services in the area, and making everyone very angry. At the time of this example she had been through many ups and downs with the therapist, but fortunately the therapist remained a constant figure for Hedda throughout. Much of the work to date had been around issues of trust. There was still clearly a long way to go, but there were signs of a potential breakthrough to a different way of acting when Hedda began to express her seething anger towards the therapist. She blamed the therapist for changing her, so that she no longer acted impulsively, but instead found herself thinking first about any wish to create mayhem. The result of thinking was that the moment passed, but she was still left feeling frustrated; and because she was seen by those around her as behaving better, she got far less of their attention. Hedda spoke her mind in no uncertain terms. At the very end of the session Hedda said, 'I think I may have hurt you by saying all that.' The therapist's reply was a good one: 'Well, you shocked me by saying it, but I'm perfectly all right, and I'll see you next week.' Referring to the shock (which it had been) she let Hedda know that she had made a real impact upon her: there was no way in which what Hedda said and felt was going to be ignored, as happened so often when she kept things to herself; at the same time the therapist made it clear that she was not *hurt*, and that what Hedda had said had not spoiled their relationship.

The pleasure of control: sadism and masochism

Sadism is a good example of how impossible it is to place the causes of behaviour in one single stage of human development. For example, sadism is often closely associated with sex, and therefore would appear to be better located in third-stage issues. Yet Melanie Klein (p. 75) uses the word in connection with first-stage issues (oral–sadistic fantasies) and second-stage issues (anal–sadistic fantasies). The reason for placing sado-masochism at this point is that it is partly about issues of control: controlling another person, and achieving heightened sexual pleasure by being dominant; or being controlled, and receiving heightened sexual pleasure through being dominated.

This is a complex area which, like some other presenting problems, requires special study. (In working with alternative sexual behaviours see for example Rosen 1979; Bancroft 1983; Lieblum and Rosen 1989.) Sado-masochism may not basically be about sex, because as Rycroft (1972) writes, it is not clear whether the pleasure obtained by the sadistic person is due to the enjoyment of the suffering of others, or to the sense of power and control over others. Alfred Adler's view (1922) was that it was power that was the basic drive, rather than sexuality as Freud posited, and that it was the inferiority complex rather than the Oedipus complex that was the determining factor in neurosis. Without repeating those old arguments, it is clearly important to recognize that while sadism may be linked to sexual pleasure, it is also a form of aggression, which varies from the socially acceptable sado-masochistic sexual practices to inhumane treatment of children (including political acts such as torture). (I recognize, of course, that S-M and other sexual variants may not be generally practised, and may raise appropriate questions about the degree of acceptable pain in sexual relationships however willingly invited; but I describe those practices as socially acceptable because in a liberal society they are not illegal and are accepted by quite a number of people who are not themselves turned on by any of them.)

Except in particular settings (such as forensic psychotherapy) counsellors will rarely see clients whose sadistic behaviour causes difficulty for the client: it is more likely to be others who are troubled by those who present themselves for counselling or therapy. Where there are indications of the acting out of sadistic fantasies (whether in the client or as described in others by the client), especially with minors or unwilling partners, the counsellor should consult the social services child protection team in the case of child abuse, or a forensic psychiatrist or psychologist in the case of unacceptable behaviour towards other adults. Evidence of cruelty to animals (whether in the past as a child or currently as an adult), and pleasure from the idea of acting out sadistic fantasies, as well as more obvious signs of such actions, indicate that the client or others are at risk, and must be taken seriously. This does not mean a counsellor should avoid talking about these issues with the client who expresses them, since closer questioning of such fantasies and of any instances of their being acted out is not only important for the assessment of risk, but also to give verbal expression to them (Prins 1975, 1995). It is the same with suicidal threats or anxieties, where talking openly about such feelings does not encourage acting out, and may even help to prevent it.

Sadistic thoughts rather than sadistic behaviour are more likely to distress a client – thoughts that have never been acted upon, but which cause debilitating guilt or shame. Here again a therapist can help the client, first by assurance that the expression of such thoughts and feelings is not the same as acting upon them; and second by relating the presence and pressure of such ideas either to other aspects of the present relationship in which they are experienced, or to earlier relationships.

Sadistic ideas may represent a deep wish to get back at someone who has made the client suffer (what is known as the *law of talion*: an eye for an eye). Revenge is a powerful drive, which mirrors negative experience in the same way as caring for others mirrors nurturing experience (Jacobs 1991). One component of sadism may be the wish to turn the tables on past oppressors, and compensate either for intense feelings of inferiority, or for the pain of being severely hurt and punished. The drive to attack women, for instance through indecent exposure, through denigration, through rape, through domestic abuse etc., is probably indicative of a deep fear of women, or an indirect fear of men; each gender in its own way is experienced as a threat, not just to the masculinity of the offender, but sometimes to his very being. The object of the sadistic attack is often someone who is perceived as physically weaker, and therefore easier to control. Women who have been subjected to this type of attack may similarly need the opportunity in therapy to vent their own feelings of revenge, which could well take an understandably sadistic form.

Masochism is at the other end of this particular spectrum, although it is a serious mistake to see those who are subject to undesired sadistic attacks as being 'unconsciously masochistic'. It is not unusual to find that women living with abusive partners also had abusive parents, and indeed find themselves entering a series of such abusive relationships (Walker 1990: 145–71). It is simplistic to see these patterns as indicative of a masochistic wish, and to suggest that such women simply provoke such behaviour: these types of explanation are themselves denigrating of the motives of such women in staying in such relationships. One element may be the powerful pull towards a mirror image of the father (or the mother – Freud suggested that women can find partners whose most negative features mirror the negative features of their mothers: 'Many women who have chosen their husband on the model of their father . . . nevertheless repeat towards him . . . their bad relations with their mother' (1931: 377). Another element in this choice may be the wish to repair past damage by making a relationship that can work better. A further aspect may be that it is the very vulnerability of such women that attracts men who need to dominate.

Masochism is seen rather in the satisfaction that comes from being dominated; or in the pleasure (strange though it seems in happier moments) in being self-critical and self-denigrating – the ongoing equivalent of self-flagellation and the hair-shirt in mediaeval piety. It is not unusual to find that the 'martyr' touch has its own pay-off: the fantasy, for example, that others are being made to worry about you, a fantasy which in itself contains the sadistic flip-side of the masochistic personality. Masochism may also be anger turned back on the self rather than expressed outwardly, held back perhaps because of guilt about anger being sadistic. Sexual pleasure linked to masochism may indicate guilt about sexuality, which has to be punished at the same time as it is being enjoyed. Masochistic thinking may also be linked to the child's struggle to make sense of painful experience. If parents have been abusive towards a child, relating more obviously through physical and verbal punishment than through affection and encouragement, until the child learns otherwise, this is all a child can understand about 'love': love which such parents tell the child they feel: 'I'm only saying this because I love you; I know this hurts, but I am doing this for your own good.'

We have to add to this topsy-turvy picture the difficulty of knowing what is culturally acceptable and what is not – questions that were raised in Chapter 1 and again above. 'Spare the rod and spoil the child' was socially acceptable in Britain until relatively recently. I once heard an anthropologist speak of her experiences researching Buddhism in a Japanese monastery. During meditation she found herself subjected to heavy slaps across her back. At first she thought she was being punished for doing it wrong, but she discovered that the 'beating' was a sign of encouragement and affirmation. She had to explain to the master that as a Westerner it had the opposite effect on her, and fortunately they passed her over for the rest of her stay. If, in that context, beating was a sign of the master's pleasure, it is not difficult to imagine a child (who in the early years knows no other culture) attempting to incorporate negative experiences into a more positive framework. We can see how in the days of frequent enemas, such uncomfortable intrusion of the child's body could lead to anal masochism; or how, when beatings and other primitive practices in the British public school system made Golding's *Lord of the Flies* look like an Enid Blyton story, this could lead to fantastic sexual practices in men in the upper echelons of society. For some children being punished or abused may be the only time when they have had any sort of relationship with their parents, so that the perverted expression of love becomes better than no love at all.

Furthermore, the child's own anger, which is not expressed openly because of fear of retaliation by the adults, is turned back upon the self, willingly accepting another's anger. The child, or the child in the adult, gets it all back to front. Masochistic tendencies may therefore be the result of learning about relationships 'through the looking glass'; or, given the relationship between the Duchess and her baby, perhaps *Alice in Wonderland* would be the better reference:

> Speak roughly to your little boy,
> > And beat him when he sneezes;
> He only does it to annoy,
> > Because he knows it teases.

Work and play: the rigid personality

The development of autonomy and independence comes about in childhood as a result of many factors – increased dexterity, verbalization, testing out boundaries with parents, and undertaking different tasks. Many of these occur through play, and it is play which provides the opportunity to learn about objects and about people (playing with substitute people like dolls, toy soldiers, etc.). Play lays down the foundations for learning at school later, and for continued exploration of different areas (of place and people) in adult life. It is also a way of expressing internal development, and not surprisingly is used to effect this not only in schools, but also in child therapy. In work with adults there are other forms of play which are considered briefly below.

Children who are restricted in their freedom to experiment, who are suppressed in their enthusiasm and in their curiosity by lack of trust or by threats, will find it difficult to use play in this way. For them it may sometimes be school work that acts as a substitute for play, although without the spontaneous element books and school work can sometimes become too serious, and too isolating. In adults the repression they experienced in childhood may show itself in their rigid attitudes, their inability to let go of their creative and expressive feelings, and their difficulty finding any real pleasure in play. For some of them work becomes their obsession; for others it is hobbies, or even sport that can take on a similar mantle, so that whatever their interest, it occupies the person's whole life, excluding other ways of expression and different types of relatedness. Whether it is having to order everything, or collect everything, or do everything to perfection, the fun seems missing.

Perhaps this can sometimes be understood in relation to the earlier theme – as if work, or a pastime, fills a void, even becoming a way of trying to pass time. For others it may be more related to the later theme of competition. In some it will be related to the general characteristics of this theme, of being unable to let go of feelings, of being unable to tolerate imperfection or disorder, or of needing to please external or internal authority figures.

Ida initially came for counselling because of the difficulties she experienced breaking away from the influence of her parents, although it became apparent that she also had problems in her work. She was so particular about all she did that she was always behind schedule, she felt exhausted, and wanted to give up her job and return to living in the parental home. Her parents had protected her when she was a child: against making mistakes; from other children by not letting her go out to play; from climbing trees in the garden, and from doing anything which could lead to her getting hurt, or (it seemed just as important) from getting her clothes muddy or torn. Over the weeks of counselling Ida became less obsessional in her work. She was able to take short-cuts, and that helped her bring schedules up to date. She surprised herself with her accuracy, which was as great as when she had taken so much time going over her work. She was pleased for a short time, and she felt much better. But now she had time on her hands, and felt depressed and listless when she was not working. She felt guilty that she was no longer taking work back to her flat for the evening and at weekends. The counsellor began to explore what it was that made it difficult to take up other interests, to meet other people, etc., in her spare time. It seemed that again she feared making mistakes, appearing foolish or getting hurt. Play and other relaxing activities also demanded the same high standards. Other people who played sports (Ida quite liked tennis) demanded only the best. It took a long time before she was prepared to risk looking foolish, and before she found real pleasure in playing. And when she discovered some of the excitement in these other areas of her life, she appreciated aspects of her work as being even more interesting.

Work and play in therapy

Counselling and psychotherapy are serious-minded occupations, and require much hard work – in terms of emotional wear-and-tear, as well as some keen thinking. This applies to both client and therapist. Yet both client and therapist ideally need to relax into the work: that was one of the reasons that Freud introduced the couch for his patients, to encourage their free association, that was matched by the therapist's free-floating attention. And although there is much that is hard and painful, both therapist and client can benefit in the work from a certain type of playing both in mind and imagination. This happens for both parties as clients feel less anxious (and therapists therefore also less anxious when with them). Either external situations that trouble them, or the therapeutic setting itself, become less threatening. Humour also often indicates that the therapeutic relationship is relaxing, and that the client is beginning to feel more at ease about the whole business of self-reflection.

There are of course many clients who in the beginning are too weighed down by their problems to consider anything like therapeutic play; but there are some clients who continue to make heavy weather of their problems and who become fixated upon their symptoms. They may find it impossible to play with ideas, images and associations. The free associative method which is important to the psychodynamic approach is an attempt to give expression to the different concerns, whether obvious and hidden, whether easy to talk about or usually censored, which are buzzing around the client's conscious and unconscious mind. Clients who find this difficult may be afraid of what they will reveal to themselves about themselves. Another important aspect of the psychodynamic approach therefore is being able to work with these anxious defences (Jacobs 1988, ch. 5).

Similarly there are counsellors and therapists who are too concerned about getting everything right and therefore unable to allow free play with their intuition, their imagination and their thinking. Yet it is playing, such as playing with words, images and ideas, together with the judicious use of hunches and shots in the dark, that are just as important a factor in good therapy as the need to use careful evidence in making interventions. Frequently it is the off-the-cuff remark that the client remembers the next week, or reports back at a later point in therapy as being significant, and not the well-thought-out and well-rounded psychoanalytic interpretation!

The work of therapy combines the working alliance, which includes thinking and a type of play, with the spontaneous relationship between therapist and client, some of which arises through the transference and counter-transference (Jacobs 1988: ch. 6). The working alliance is equivalent to the latency mode (see Chapter 1), in which for a while the turbulence of emotions and the irrationality of fantasies are temporarily held in check, so that a relatively cool and thoughtful look can be taken at what has been said, and what has been experienced, and what it might reflect or might mean. It is in the latency mode that tentative explanations can be put forward for testing. Where the transference to the therapist or internal anxieties and fantasies in therapist or client become too intense, it is much more difficult to work in this relatively rational way. Probably the most productive counselling consists of a backward and forward movement between catharsis of feeling and expression of fantasy on the one hand, and the working alliance on the other. In this latter state both partners in the enterprise unpack that which emerges in the former state and together try to understand its significance.

Since learning is much more difficult when a person is in a highly emotional state, there are occasions when a counsellor or therapist has to wait until strong feelings have been expressed and have begun to settle before he or she can say anything that a client is likely to hear or to reason. It is rarely any use making a studied interpretation when a client is distraught or furious. Empathy, warmth, acceptance, accurate reflection and sometimes even gentle advice are more appropriate when the client is in full flood. Clients sometimes wish they could have seen their therapist at the time of great distress, and feel frustrated by having to wait for the next session before they can express their feelings: 'You would understand much more if you could have seen how I was then.' While the fixed appointment appears then to be a disadvantage to the client, not only is the secure boundary important for the development of trust and the management of dependency issues, but it is also helpful as a model of learning to hold on to feelings in order to express them and process them later. A counsellor's interventions are of a different nature at the point of extreme stress in the client. It is at quieter times, when the ups and downs have levelled out somewhat, that the reflective interpretation comes into its own:

There are some occasions where emotional factors are so strong that it appears to be impossible for a client to make use of the counselling at all. Jean very much wanted help, and wished to unburden herself of a number of things that were troubling her about her behaviour, but found great difficulty in telling the counsellor about them. Fortunately she was able to tell the counsellor that she felt very nervous before coming, that she could not sleep the night before, and that she had been physically sick on leaving some sessions. Gentle empathic calmness and acceptance on the counsellor's part appeared to do nothing to help her to feel at ease; neither did interpretation of her feelings of anxious shame, and her possible fear of the counsellor's reaction if she were to voice her concerns more openly. In the end, at least with Jean, it seemed it was the silence of the counsellor – unhurried and unruffled – that appeared to help her to break through her reticence.

This working alliance between therapist and client depends upon being able to work through authority issues, to the point where the client becomes less worried about the counsellor being critical or punitive, and is able to show feelings and talk openly. Clients begin to take their own initiatives in therapy, and suggest their own understanding, as they start to accept the encouragement that their own authority and expertise is as important as the therapist's. On the other side, counsellors and therapists need to take account of their own counter-transference feelings, particularly those which tempt them to take on the role of the dominant, knowledgeable, over-ordered, authoritative and judgmental parent. As Hartung (1979: 184) suggests, therapists need to have worked through all these issues themselves if they are going to be able to demonstrate the generative mode of middle adulthood. Hartung's ideas refer to Erikson's seventh age, with its developmental tasks of generativity and creativity. The broader view that this book takes of the Erikson stages suggests that generativity requires the benefits that come through successful resolution of authority and autonomy issues. A counsellor, like a good teacher or parent, can provide a model which helps change a client's reactive patterns:

Ken panicked whenever he was faced with a learning task that he could not immediately grasp. He really needed time to think, but he could not relax enough to allow himself such space. Unless he was getting something down on paper, he felt anxious, and began to fear that he would never complete his task on time. These work issues were reflected in his counselling, where his counsellor was also aware of being under pressure: Ken dropped clear hints that he was wondering when the counsellor was going to make some constructive suggestion. The counsellor shared this sense of urgency with him, but in a calm and unhurried voice trying to indicate through her whole manner that she and he both needed time if they were ever going to be able to produce results.

Another aspect of the work of counselling that is closely related to authority and autonomy issues is the freedom which a counsellor or therapist needs to allow the client to develop in their own way. I need not repeat the warning in Chapter 2, or the examples in this chapter about how subjective and culturally determined psychological models of development and definitions of maturity are. In our search for answers such models may have acquired an authority beyond anything their authors intended. Parents, teachers, and other authority figures share with the counsellors and therapists the temptation to mould the child or the client, through looking for certain responses, in encouraging certain attitudes, and through setting boundaries which all in their own ways can restrict the unique direction in which any one individual needs to move. This is especially so when counsellors and therapists are caught up in the need to produce results, or to show their effectiveness in response to targets set by their employing authorities. Counsellors and therapists who are too keen to be successful parents or productive workers risk turning out clones, instead of allowing individuals the opportunity to create or recreate themselves.

Winnicott stresses the importance of a mother providing the environment in which a baby does her own growing. He also underlines the need for someone to be there while children (and clients) play: 'Responsible persons must be available when children play; but this does not mean that the responsible person need enter into the children's playing' (1971: 50); or, we might add, it does not mean that counsellors need to tell the client what to play or the aim of their play. Parents who are always trying to help their children to make or do things that are useful, or to play according to the rules, not only act unnecessarily (children soon develop their own system of rules for games which can be more exact than an adult's); they also stifle growth.

It is obvious how different attitudes to work and play can stifle or promote autonomy, and with it the Erikson seventh-age strengths of creativity and generativity. A therapist's solutions are not necessarily a client's solutions. The patterns a counsellor sees may not fit their client's situations. The comfortable, white, middle-class counsellor or therapist (and there are a good many of them) particularly needs to learn from those who do not easily fit into stereotypical societal norms and assumptions, and who themselves have much to teach those who may be tempted to see themselves as the rescuers.

Authority and autonomy through the life cycle

This chapter has discussed various presenting issues that arise within the context of this major theme of authority and autonomy, including issues of control, of rigidity in oneself or towards others (authoritarianism), perfectionism, the expression of anger and loss of control with emotions generally, obsessional behaviours and attitudes, conditional love, internalized authority figures (conscience or super-ego), etc. In developmental terms the theme represents moving outwards from a more confident sense of an inner central self to explore the potentiality, the power and pleasure not only of body and mind, but of the interaction with others, including those who are authority figures. All this is with a view to becoming more independent and autonomous, and at the same time creative and generative.

This movement takes place from birth onward, and we should not forget that birth is one of a number of involuntary occasions in which the body leads, and the person (in this case mother and baby) has to follow. There are many more such occasions in life, as we have to come to terms with bodily changes, initially changes which extend our horizons and bring new opportunities (such as in adolescence), but later which diminish possibilities (such as in old age). I return below to see how this is also true of dying itself. There are some changes over which we have no control, including those in our own bodies.

Yet even a young baby possesses considerable power to bring mother to her beck and call, although the response to this will depend upon the openness of the mother to the demands of the baby both in terms of her own feelings, and in terms of the 'rules' of childcare which her particular society has laid down. In the middle of the twentieth century Truby King, and the strict notion of four-hourly feeds, whatever the baby's needs or demands, is one example of the way in which rigid ideas entered into childcare. The danger of all books on childcare, and indeed books on developmental psychology, is their tendency to lay down what is right and wrong in child-rearing and personality development. This again is not necessarily what their authors intend, but parents who want to do their job well, and students who want to pass their exams, tend to take what they read as gospel.

Parents who find their lives taken over by a baby, and who are unable to accept the mini-chaos temporarily caused to timetables and social plans, may find it hard to reconcile themselves to letting go of their ordered lifestyle. In the toddler stage there is more opportunity to order life, as older children learn how to accept frustration and accommodate themselves to the rest of family life. Nevertheless the child's wish for experiment and freedom also requires parents who are happy enough to accept a floor littered with toys and other domestic articles, who can enjoy the bathroom carpet and walls being soaked at bath time, and who are proud of the advances made by their child, however inconvenient these may be at certain times. Challenges to parental control, and the way these are handled, together with the patience in answering all those questions 'Why?', set the foundation for initiative and exploration as the child grows through school and into the adult world. The way in which the rules of family and societal life are enforced and explained also lay the foundation for belief in others and the world (as Erikson says of the second stage) as basically fair and just. At the same time parents should not be pressurizing the child to achieve beyond what he or she is capable of and wants to do.

The inter-relationship of the stages in Erikson's model means that one of the strengths of the last stage – renunciation – is also a necessary concomitant in working with issues of autonomy in growing children and young adults. Parenthood is an extended period of gradually letting go of the child through successive developmental points. This depends upon the parents' ability to relinquish control at a gradual pace, in tune with what a child and adolescent wants, and also what the child can take: passing over authority depends not just upon the ability to relinquish power and responsibility, but also upon the ability of the child and the adolescent to take it; or in working situations upon the experience and confidence of the adult. A mother who has felt satisfaction in meeting the dependent needs of her baby will be ready to let her or him take the first steps (literally) towards autonomy; a father who has felt the right balance between allowing freedom and exercising necessary restraint will be more confident in allowing the adolescent to discover what might work best for him- or herself. Yet if parenting does not cease to be a preoccupation (as Winnicott terms the early months) and so becomes a total occupation, this may lead to difficulties for mothers or fathers (less likely perhaps for men, who tend to use their work as their total occupation):

> Lucy was an only child who had had to work very hard at school in order to satisfy her parents. She was not all that clever, but she had been able to make up for the disappointment about her progress by working equally hard in her spare time to help her parents with their corner shop business. When she married and had children of her own she was determined not to put them through what she herself had experienced: her children were indeed her pride, and they grew up as well-adjusted, healthy, normal teenagers. When they left home Lucy became very depressed. She might have expected to be pleased that she had brought them up so free from the pressures she had had on herself when she was young. But she had not recognized until this point that in doing so much for her children she had also been totally occupied in 'working hard' to achieve this end. With their going she had no longer got anyone to work hard for: this had become for her, over the years of their childhood and adolescence, the only way she knew of feeling that she was acceptable.

Going to school is a further (and major) step towards autonomy, although it also involves walking straight into a new set of authority issues. The school years are a very formative period which, when they work well, equip young people for work and life as an adult. The amount of basic learning to be acquired is immense – verbal, literary and numeracy skills, as well as physical, manual and technical skills. For some children, their evident success at school opens up new horizons, and may separate them more than usual from their family or their culture, especially when they come from families of poor educational background, or from closed religious or racial backgrounds. There may of course be severe authority and control issues which hold them back. Others, who for one reason or another fail to succeed, may be left with a different form of low self-esteem than is encountered over issues of trust and dependency; they cannot believe themselves capable of performing certain tasks, although in other areas of their life they know themselves to be more confident and capable.

This period of learning in childhood and adolescence (referred to in Chapter 1 as latency) or the activity of learning in adult life (which involves the need to engage in the latency mode) needs to be relatively untroubled by issues of authority and control. It is obviously essential that those who teach possess both authority in their subject, and skill in their communication, that enable them to engender knowledge and expertise in those who learn. At the same time those who teach need to be able to provide the confidence to those who learn that it is all right to make mistakes in the course of learning; that it is important to order information, as well as to play with ideas; and that it is productive to give free rein to thought and imagination. Problems over issues of authority and lack of confidence in their developing autonomy may lead to learners finding it impossible to start a piece of work, or unable to complete it and hand it in, because it then has to be marked, and marks bring back memories of failure. Others think they have to get every fact and word correct. This type of perfectionism tries to obviate all criticism from teachers. Some adolescent and adult learners even fear to ask their tutors for guidance, thinking they will incur displeasure. How different is this inhibition from what was once a thirst for understanding as they began to ask their parents the many questions with which the wider world presented them:

> Mary came to the university counsellor as a desperate last measure since she was about to fail her exams. She had not worked for almost a year. Although initially there had been some adolescent acting out of rebellion against her strict home and school which had led to non-attendance at lectures, the situation had got out of hand because she was afraid to approach her tutors to ask for help in catching up. She feared that they would tell her she was lazy, just like her father had told her in the past. The counsellor pointed out that if she wanted to repeat the year, she would have to see her tutor – was it still fear of her tutor's criticism that prevented her from asking? Had she felt afraid of coming to see the counsellor too in case she also told her she was being lazy? Mary decided she had to see her tutor, and returned the following week to say that in fact her tutor had been most understanding! But now she had to tell her parents. Her counsellor wondered whether Mary really carried an outdated view of her father's criticism within her, and whether even he would be as severe as she imagined. Perhaps she had even fostered his criticism by presenting herself as a naughty child who expected punishment, rather than as a young adult who had a mind of her own?

Problem solving which is tackled with rigid perfectionism, and sometimes with an over-strict sense of the need for order, may suffice at the simpler stages of learning, but sooner or later (particularly in higher education) such self-imposed expectations become impossible to meet. The person who sees everything in black-and-white terms, or who has to be certain before passing an opinion, often fails to see other dimensions, or is afraid to express any opinion at all. Caution likewise prevents the imaginative leap which often lies at the heart of intellectual and even scientific discoveries. The student cannot see the wood for the trees. At later stages of learning it is necessary to learn to tolerate confusion, particularly about the interpretation of facts. The wish for certainty can sometimes foreclose the search for more information and further thinking, which may ultimately bring about a more comprehensive solution.

School phobia may also be the result of such fears: children may try to opt out of the situation if they are afraid of putting up a weak performance; or that their teacher will shame them by criticism or punishment; or when they feel that they are not as good as their peers. Some may have experienced critical or even sadistic teachers (particularly those in the older generation), but students like Mary in the last example can feel this concern, even when their teachers and tutors have always shown themselves tolerant of mistakes and understanding of difficulties. Other children or older students may wish to please their teacher, and parents too, so that working hard becomes an end in itself and not a means to an end. Typical of such is the workaholic, the person who can never relax: like Sir Jasper in Wycherley's play *The Country Wife*, who says to his wife that he must 'go to my pleasure, which is business, while you go to your business, which is pleasure'.

While there are some who learn in order to appease authority figures, there are others who reject learning as a way of expressing their reaction against the authority of the teacher or of the institution. This may also be a rebellion against parents who have sent them to school when they did not wish to leave home, or against parents who are felt to be pressurizing them to go on to further or higher education when they wish to get a job and become more independent. Others may use opportunities for conflict with authority as a way of testing out boundaries in the institution, which they have been unable to test out at home, where discipline has either been over-lax or repressive:

> Naomi had got behind with her work, and saw her school counsellor when she thought that she was going to fail her first set of public exams. It soon became clear that Naomi was terrified of her father, and that she had chosen to specialize in certain subjects because he insisted. Her elder brother, who had been at the school before her, had been a rebel and a constant source of worry to her parents and to his teachers. She could not bring herself to ask her teachers for more help, saying she had wanted to do it all for herself. The counsellor was not sure at first whether Naomi was in fact sabotaging her chances as a passive rebellion against her father. She was obviously trying to achieve some measure of independence, by doing things herself, although it was an inappropriate time to choose to do this. The counsellor felt confirmed in this view because after a few sessions in which Naomi initially kept asking the counsellor to provide answers, to ring her father, etc., she then seemed in a hurry to leave sessions early. This may have shown Naomi's need to feel independent of an adult, who even if she was caring was nonetheless still an authority figure; or it may have been because her counsellor was unable to give her the clear-cut answers she had come to expect from a father who always knew his own mind.

Teachers (including those who teach or supervise counselling and therapy) need to have mastered their own authority problems in order to be both firm and yet flexible, including in the way they maintain boundaries. As already suggested, some teachers, and some institutions, reinforce their authority through psychological rigidity and punishment, rather than through persuasion and encouragement. Even where a child's home has provided a good enough facilitating environment, the sadistic or over-critical teacher, who inevitably becomes a parent-substitute, can equally plant a strong negativism in the child, and reinforce the super-ego, often prejudicing a child's view of all that is associated with education and learning. Where both parents and teachers are cold or critical, the task of achieving confidence and self-esteem becomes doubly difficult. There are of course many teachers both at school and in continuing adult education who provide a different model of the accepting and caring parent figure, and who can modify the harshness of the child's experience.

The adult learner, whose efforts have been devalued or derided in the family or at school, for whom learning has become associated with demoralization, and who has consequently dismissed learning as irrelevant or impossible, may find retraining or the learning of new skills in adult life just like going back to school, and associate the new opportunities with unhappy or unsuccessful experiences. Retraining cannot be considered positively, since it is linked too much with parent or teacher expectation; or with lack of interest from parents; or with feelings of inferiority towards peers or siblings who learned more rapidly. Anything which smacks of education might therefore be resisted, or taken up only half-heartedly, when it might be that retraining or learning about new areas of life is not just essential, but positively rewarding. In working in the current situation, a counsellor or therapist may want to look into attitudes formed by previous learning settings:

> Omar's father was a semi-skilled mechanic who took great pride in the academic success through university of Omar's two elder brothers. As neither of them showed much manual dexterity, and Omar did, Omar became the son who shared his father's interest in rebuilding cars and other practical tasks. There was no reason to think Omar was not also bright, but his father had often said to him, 'Of course you're like me, you won't go as far as they have, but you'll be good at my sort of work.' This identification with his father was very satisfying at the time, since a child will enjoy being close to father; but it also overshadowed Omar in later life, when he discovered his own intellectual ability, and went to university by way of a college for mature students. Exams terrified him, because he could not get it out of his head that he was treading on territory that had been reserved for his brothers.

In distinguishing types of adolescence Marcia describes what he calls the 'foreclosed adolescent' (1975). Such a young person's identity is determined by parents or by peers. He or she does things because someone else says so, or because others do. This type of adolescent tends to be authoritarian, less able to evaluate critically, and can easily lose identity both in the crowd and to the crowd. Black-and-white attitudes predominate. Religious faith may also be used to foreclose the real questioning of values and beliefs that might be expected in adolescents:

> Paul was actively searching for 'the meaning of life', but when he came to see a counsellor he was caught between the wish to belong to a dogmatic Christian group on the one hand, and to be 'one of the boys' who had a good time on the other. His parents were very protective: they did not let him stay out at night, and had always refused him a bicycle in case he hurt himself. Seeking counselling might have been a chance to work through wishes to belong to groups representing the first two types, and to move into the moratorium area below; but Paul wanted the counsellor to tell him the answers, and was not yet mature enough to use the time to work things out for himself.

Such young people cannot allow themselves to experience immaturity, which Winnicott describes (at this age) as being healthy: 'Immaturity is an essential element of health at adolescence . . . in this is constrained the most exciting features of creative thought, new and fresh feeling, ideas for new living' (1971: 146). When such young people are asked to complete the phrase 'I am . . .', they use such descriptions as 'I am a daughter, a niece, my father's son (like Omar above), my neighbour's neighbour.' They are still, at least in their self-perception, someone else's possession.

Therapists and counsellors are readily perceived as parental figures, by young and older clients alike. In working with young people counsellors often find them anxious about needing adult help, and reluctant to accept it for any longer than is immediately necessary. 'I want to solve this myself' is a sign of health, indicating a natural wish to be independent. Acknowledging this wish (especially where the indications are of a normal developmental crisis rather than a more serious disturbance) is much more appropriate than with adults in whom their anxiety about being dependent may lead to a type of defensive independence. Young people are on the whole more adaptable, and often find quite brief counselling sufficient for the moment, preferring to arrange with the counsellor 'to come back if I need to' – thereby ensuring for themselves a safety net, seldom needed, like the toddler's parent, within reach to run back to if necessary.

An important aspect of achieving personal autonomy in a young person includes the need for economic independence, which a job and a salary can provide. The workplace provides a focus for many of the issues related to this theme, some of which have already been referred to in examples in this chapter.

Reference has also been made briefly to the effects arising from unemployment, redundancy and early retirement. Those without work and those who unsuccessfully seek it may have reason to see the world as unfair and unjust. Being without anything to do (and *doing* is a strong feature of this set of issues) those without work can perceive themselves as incompetent, as criticized by the family at home for failing to provide for them, and by society at large which is always ready to blame the unemployed rather than the system. It may be difficult to meet others, particularly those who are still in work, because of feelings of inferiority and 'loss of face'. Deprived of the opportunity to be productive, and to take pride in their work, it is little wonder that the unemployed and even the retired can feel inferior; those who adapt better are those who develop ways of expressing their need to be creative and productive outside work, or in alternatives to paid work. The more a person has invested in their work in order to ensure their self-esteem (particularly the workaholic, or the obsessional achiever) the harder redundancy or retirement is likely to be.

For others no work, or less work, gives them the chance to learn new skills, adopt new interests, to play and to use time in a far from passive way. Reappraisal of their life may be particularly valuable (but perhaps also particularly difficult) when they have been influenced by family and school to overachieve, and when work has been at the expense of 'play'. In their desire to please parents, teachers, supervisors and bosses they have been unable to find independent satisfaction for themselves. There may be many who look back from their new position of relative freedom to their previous full-time occupation, and see how much it depleted the rest of life; and how being an employee is to risk becoming over-conformist; or, as Erikson puts it: 'a thoughtless slave of [human] technology and of those who are in a position to exploit it' (1965: 252):

> Ruth feared this even before she started work. She had not made any job applications for over a year, since leaving university. She became depressed because of her passivity: and the counsellor was tempted to drop hints about the value of getting something to do to occupy her (as Ruth's mother was described as saying). That would not have helped, because Ruth felt she was a disappointment to her mother, and her mother's hints only made Ruth angry. Instead the counsellor took up Ruth's reluctance to seek work, which seemed based on her feeling that being in work meant becoming part of the system, and that she would only be an insignificant cog in a machine. Her father's legalistic attitude, schooling which had suppressed individual expression, and her underlying anxiety that she was not up to competing with men combined to reinforce her inactivity. She said she preferred the freedom of not being in work, although it appeared that she was rejecting opportunities to use her own qualifications in a way that could lead to eventual seniority, and the chance of exercising authority towards others in a less restrictive way. Despite being apparently anti-authority, one of the features of the relationship between the counsellor and Ruth was her constant attempt to get the counsellor to give her answers, which was reflected in his counter-transference feeling of wanting to kick her into action.

A further aspect of work is the question of mastery and control. This is put forward by Rayner, who suggests that some occupations require mastery of anxiety about the nature of the work involved, especially where that work involves coping with basic emotions. For instance, 'a dustman has to master his disgust, a spiderman vertigo, and a teacher has to master class discipline' (Rayner 1986: 166). Therapists and counsellors have to master their own anxieties for the work they do (Jacobs 1993b: ch. 4) – particularly about their own human nature and needs, which if not judiciously used can lead to abuse of the client. Two of the most difficult areas for counsellors and therapists to master, that are in line with the themes in this chapter, are first their inability to help by *doing* something, and second the refusal to exercise the type of authority that the client imagines and hopes will automatically change things:

> Sue was training as a counsellor, and she was obviously anxious to do well in her practical work in order to pass her placement. In addition, like many a beginner, she took her work home with her, worrying about her clients' welfare between sessions, trying to plan ahead for all eventualities in her wish to help them in the time available to her. She was not helped by having parents who had expressed disappointment that she had not used her considerable intelligence and qualifications to go for a more prestigious career, but had instead chosen a course which did not hold out any easy prospect of 'success', at least in her parents' eyes. Her supervisor

recognized how important it was to model a new type of parenting, through the careful use of his authoritative position.

Turning to another feature of the theme, as expressed in attitudes to work, where one or both partners in a relationship live for their career alone; or one or both cannot relax at home, but always have to be busy about the house, then issues around work may interfere with the intimacy of such a couple. These different expressions of rigidity of attitude in one or both partners prevent the couple relaxing with each other, including in their freedom to explore and experiment with each other, discovering more about each other not just sexually, but in the total relationship.

There are other issues linked to the theme of authority and autonomy that are at the centre of many relationships. Living together means learning to live with another person's norms, values and 'rules'. Often these are unwritten, and unexpressed, especially in the early period of establishing a relationship. Cutting across another's norms and rules, or not conforming oneself to expected patterns of behaviour learned in a partner's family of origin, can lead to resentment, open criticism, or even to one partner laying down the law to the other. In the critical–submissive partnership, ways of living and making decisions cannot be openly questioned or shared. One partner becomes (or is felt to be) the authoritarian parent, while the other initially tries hard to please and conform, until they come to the end of their tether and rebel or collapse (explode or implode). Decisions about money, about the home, about the management of children and about the expectations of wider families on both sides can all become a battleground for two people when each needs to prove to the other his or her independence or dominance. Where authority issues interfere with a relationship, conflicts and disagreements become occasions for fighting old parent–child battles about freedom and autonomy. Even minor matters can become excuses for one partner to try to impress their authority on the other.

Another aspect in the relationship may be the wish to please: one partner may always feel inadequate in the eyes of the other, sometimes because of their own expectations, not always because of their partner's. They make strenuous efforts to feel good enough as a bread-winner, as a home-maker, as a lover, or even as a parent responsible for what feels like the other's children. Sex, for example, becomes both a demand and a performance, where results such as the partner's orgasm predominate over mutual enjoyment. As in so many of the examples in this chapter, *doing* becomes more important than *being*.

The process of ageing has its own associations to this major theme. It is interesting to reflect how many people do not feel sufficiently internally free of parental expectations until their thirties. By the forties external physical signs of ageing are more obvious, although increasing freedom with children becoming more independent still holds the prospect of further development of interests. Despite beauty products, fitness centres and even plastic surgery, it is impossible to control the march of time, and those who are control freaks may find themselves fighting a losing battle against their bodies, raising perhaps some of the narcissistic issues discussed in Chapter 3 (pp. 64–5).

Resignation is seen by Erikson as a positive strength of old age, with despair being its opposite when resignation is not possible. Although ageing and retirement (especially to those for whom either are premature) may appear to involve further losses and limitations in terms of physical strength and stamina, a definite working role, a definite structure to the working day and week, and reduced income, much of course in the end depends on attitudes and not upon externals. One particular psychological type identified in old age (Lowe 1972: 248) is reminiscent of the anal character: the old person who is fearful of old age, retirement and infirmity, and who defensively remains or becomes compulsively active, rigidly self-sufficient and over-controlled.

Yet this rather bleak picture neglects the advantages and new strengths which old age also brings to those who can accept the limitations, and who can enjoy the new opportunities which retirement presents, as long as they have the financial means and the physical health to take advantage of them. Such people show perhaps the greatest development of personal autonomy. It can also be rewarding for those who are now senior workers and senior members of the family to watch younger people, whom they have trained and guided, taking over their responsibilities. Where older people are respected for their experience, wisdom and judgement, there can be satisfaction at being in the background in a 'consultative' capacity, knowing that their experience of life and work is valued by the generations that follow them.

Restructuring of time enables old and new interests to be pursued, and for the mind to be kept active – memory, for instance, appears to function better when there is continuing mental activity. Tolerance is frequently a quality which is acquired in old age, with older people often feeling less threatened by the young than the middle-aged 'parental' generation are. Aware too of the shortness of remaining life, it probably makes more sense to enjoy relationships while they last, and to let go some of the rigidities and certainties of the past.

A final example of the way in which control and letting go are seen is at the very end of a life, in the way in which in some instances it appears that those who are dying almost appear to choose the point at which they die. So while death is in one sense a stage of life over which we have no ultimate control, dying, like so much growing, is also a psychosomatic process. Someone who still has needs to be met can control their failing body sufficiently long to fulfil their dying wish; or may abandon hope and rapidly decline. Dying is so much harder when there is still unfinished business, or when there are open wounds, unrealized hopes, memories needing to be relived and reworked:

Teresa had an advanced cancer, and the doctors told her, when she asked them, that she had only a few months at most to live. Despite being confined to her bed, Teresa worked from home to help other cancer victims whom she heard or read about, writing them letters of comfort. She herself received great support from her husband. Her one regret was that her eldest son would not visit her. He lived some distance away, but she knew that the real reason for his not visiting her was that he could not face seeing her in this condition. Despite requests from others in the family he did not appear. Teresa was still alive, though much less active, a year after the last date which her doctors had given her for her survival. At last her son came to see her, and he stayed a few hours. Within a week she had died. It appeared that she had waited until then, when she had been able to say her good-bye, and was then able to let herself go.

With the confidence in the core self that comes from working through issues of trust, to the confidence in one's abilities that can come from working through issues around autonomy, the growing child, adolescent and adult is better equipped to handle the third major set of issues. The themes cluster around aspects of competition and cooperation, and concern different kinds of relating, from the wider social networks to the intimate partnerships of equals. While these relationships clearly also involve trust and authority issues, there are further elements to their dynamics to which in the next chapter I now turn.

COOPERATION AND COMPETITION

The ongoing resolution of matters about trust, and the differing degrees to which people have worked through issues of authority and autonomy, profoundly influence the type of relationships which they form whether they are intimate partnerships or friendships, at work or in other social and societal groups. But relationships consist of more than trust, and more than the balance of authority and autonomy. The two key words in the third theme reflect two further aspects of relationships, particularly whether relationships incorporate parity and equality, or whether they are fraught with rivalry and competitiveness. If the first theme revolved around issues of dependency, and the second around issues of independence, the third is essentially about interdependence. As such it has much to offer in assessing the quality of relationships between parent and child, between sexual partners, between friends, in working teams and social units, as well as in gender attitudes, racial harmony and political situations.

This theme takes its cue from psychoanalytic writing about three-person relationships (triads) rather than the two-person relationships (dyads) which are more typical of mother-and-baby or parent-and-child with the key issues about dependency and authority. Whereas the relationship in the first theme can be described as partly about symbiosis, and the relationship in the second as partly about separateness, the third is more about complementarity: about togetherness with the acceptance of difference. The features accompanying this theme perhaps also represent the potentiality for a type of wholeness in relationships in which we see others as complete persons, and not either as providers of care on the one hand or of rules on the other; instead they are people who have their own needs, to whom we may give, from whom we may receive, and with whom we may share, in acts of love, of friendship and of social cooperation: at least, all this may happen when the different aspects of cooperation and competition are satisfactorily negotiated, developmentally and currently, in the past as well as in the present.

Relationship problems in adult clients related to this theme are probably the most commonly presented ones, at least initially, with difficulties over control and autonomy running second. Modern psychoanalytic writing has tended to concentrate on the first year of life and the problems related to it, but it was with many of the issues with which this chapter deals that Freud's initial investigations began. Those who write extensively about the earliest period of life acknowledge that what this chapter will later address as oedipal issues cannot be bypassed, even when deeper disturbances are clearly present. Guntrip (1968: 278–9) writes that 'the first few years of analysis' will be concerned with the oedipal period! If that is the case, it is clear that this theme, linked as it is to oedipal material, is also going to predominate in the much shorter times involved in most counselling and in some psychotherapy.

Psychoanalytic theory particularly highlights sex and sexuality as central to this theme. In developmental terms this chapter reflects the way adult clients re-experience questions, anxieties and pleasures that first arose for them as children, as they encountered physical differences in gender, and as they explored birth and sex and relationships in the family. Oedipus, castration anxiety, penis envy, and the differences between men and women are all central ideas within psychoanalytic thought (about which there is plenty of disagreement). This chapter discusses these ideas in relation to the issues clients can present in therapy and counselling.

Male and female: masculine and feminine

If it would be retrograde to describe the politics of sexual relations as 'the battle of the sexes', issues about gender are of vital importance in our world. The challenge to patriarchal dominance in politics, at work and in the home and family means that there are many issues presented explicitly or implicitly in counselling and therapy, about being a man or being a woman, in society, at work and in intimate relations. Modern Western society has undergone a revolution in gender expectations which is bound to go on having an impact on women and men alike.

At the same time, at a more basic level (such as, for example, sex and reproduction) ordinary sexual differences fascinate, repel and attract. Indeed, with the possible exception of the colour of a person's skin, gender identification is probably the initial reaction to any meeting – whether of strangers passing in the street, or introductions to a family or the workplace. 'Is it a boy, or a girl?' is perhaps the most frequently asked question in a pregnancy or following a birth. In some cultures the gender of the newborn child is of crucial economic importance (girls are a greater financial burden, for example), but such attitudes are not confined, as might be thought, to the Oriental or African societies:

Ursula was one of two girls, who were rejected by their father because he wanted boys. As far as he was concerned, they could be left when he separated from their mother, and largely ignored in their growing up. When Ursula herself had two boys she found her father showed more interest in her and her family, as if she had provided him with the sons his former wife had failed to. Although this came both as a surprise and a reward to Ursula, it was quite clear from the way she described herself, that bearing two boys was about the only really positive thing she had done. In much of the rest of her life she felt a failure. Some of this might be attributed to her mother's 'perfect' example of motherhood, with which Ursula felt she could not possibly compete. But it was also to do with her deep-seated feelings from childhood that she and her sister were never good enough for her father. In psychoanalytic terms, indeed, one might almost say that (for her father) she was born imperfect, lacking what she needed to be her father's son.

A psychodynamic view values post-Freudian psychoanalytic theory since it extends the nature of human relatedness beyond Freud's rather drive-based model. Those who followed him took up particular aspects of his work, about relating to objects, so that in object-relations theory it is the wish to relate that is stressed rather than the need to discharge instinctual drives. Nevertheless sexual and reproductive drives remain powerful in the human species, however much the veneer of civilization may have curbed and directed sexual energies in other directions. The physical features that distinguish boys and girls, men and women are significant to us all. Sexual similarity or difference is one of a number of rapidly exchanged signals when people first meet or make contact, even if these initial reactions generally make way for a meeting with the person as a person, and not as just as a sex-object. Nevertheless, that the other is a man or a woman continues to influence any interaction. As I discuss further later in this chapter (pp. 177–88), some clients react quite differently to being with men or being with women, and these initial reactions may run deep enough to make the gender of the counsellor or therapist of real significance to them.

Sexuality is signalled (or hidden when there is shame) by the way men and women dress; certainly the wish to display attractiveness should not be mistaken as a seductive ploy, but the way in which people present themselves does tell others about their own sense of body-image. There is of course more to being male and female than physical difference and body-image. Indeed it is important to distinguish between the terms 'male and female', which describe primary genital and other secondary physical characteristics with which we are born, and are only in rare cases changed, and the terms 'masculine and feminine', which describe supposed psychological characteristics and gender roles. A further distinction concerns sexual orientation, which may be heterosexual, bisexual or homosexual. Thus a male client may present with sexual difficulties within a heterosexual partnership, in which anxieties about being stereotypically 'feminine' seem to play a part:

Vernon suffered from secondary impotence (i.e. he was occasionally impotent in sexual intercourse with his female partner). At college he had been laughed at by a particularly 'macho' group of friends, who played a lot of sport, and thought that Vernon's love of poetry and the theatre meant that he was effeminate. For a time Vernon decided to try and join these so-called friends by becoming a member of their sports club, and going for long training sessions with them. In fact his anxieties around sex were related much more to unexpressed anger with his partner, and when he began to express these, and recovered his confidence in his sexuality, he felt able to give up his attempts to be a tough rugby player, realizing that this was not at all his scene. His sense of being a male became rooted both in sexual confidence, and in a conviction that love of the arts need not in the least be regarded as either feminine or masculine.

Freud twice quoted a phrase of Napoleon's: 'Anatomy is destiny.' It is a quotation that has sometimes been turned against him by others who have questioned his views about men and women. What we find in Freud concerning this subject is an inevitable contradiction – inevitable because he wrote so much over so long a time and concerning such a wide range of topics. On the one hand he makes it clear that psychologically there is no reason to identify any differences between men and women. To equate men with being active, aggressive and independent, for example, and women with being passive, intuitive and sensitive, has no real basis in psychology, only in social convention. We see Freud touching here, as he does elsewhere, on the social construction of gender: 'all human individuals, as a result of their bisexual disposition and of cross-inheritance, combine in themselves both masculine and feminine characteristics, so that pure masculinity and femininity remain theoretical constructions of uncertain content' (1925b: 342). He also recognized the way social customs can force women into passive situations (1933: 149). On the other hand Freud also argues that psychological development in boys and girls, while in common through the first two stages (oral and anal), divides at the phallic stage, because boys and girls engage with the Oedipus complex in different ways. Freud suggests this leads to psychological differences in adult men and women, and he observes that women are not as harsh in their moral judgements as men. This is probably an accurate observation (at least in the society in which he was working), one that is confirmed by Gilligan in her development of Kohlberg's study of moral development (see pp. 35–6). Freud's reasoning may be questionable, that women have not developed as strong a super-ego as men because they have never really left the oedipal stage behind them as boys do; but the point is well made, that there may be some psychological differences related to gender.

Freud's understanding of male and female sexuality, and much of his writing upon the psychological development of women, has of course come under attack, partly from feminist writers. As this chapter shows, feminist thought is not monolithic, and there are, as in any intellectual discourse, various opinions about how far Freud got it right or got it wrong. Popular feminist thought has moved from at one time appearing to make men and women precisely the same, to identifying the possibility of different ways of being and relating. I have already made some reference to these differences in Chapter 2. We have to be very careful about sweeping generalizations, such as those found in Lowe, that boys are intrusive and girls inclusive (1972: 92). However, those who write from the feminist psychoanalytic perspective posit significant differences not just in society's views of men and women, but in the different way in which mothers relate to their sons and their daughters. They suggest that there may be something distinctive about the female psyche, that, for example, 'while the basic feminine sense of self is connected to the world, the basic masculine self is separate' (Chodorow 1978: 162).

There are some important differences in the way men and women theorists have approached these matters. I have alluded in Chapter 2 to the criticism by feminist psychologists of the way in which many male writers, including Freud, seem to have taken male development as the norm, and anything different in female development as a deviation from the norm. These critics have attached greater force to the way in which society has contributed to gender roles, and argued that differences are neither innate nor unchangeable. Values and attitudes in Western society changed so rapidly through the twentieth century that it is impossible to predict what directions the debate about psychological differences between men and women will take. What is clear is that counsellors and therapists must recognize the false dichotomy between masculine and feminine that is prevalent generally in society, and therefore in many of their clients, seen either in their attitudes or more likely in the attitudes to which those clients were subject in growing up. Clients (but also counsellors and therapists) have been presented in the home, in the media, at school, and perhaps also in their religion, if that has been a significant feature in their background, with images and models of men and women, which will have influenced their own view of themselves.

Working with men and women in therapy may involve helping them to develop other ways of being; for example, to help women caught in submissive or intertwined relationships to develop separateness; or to enable men who fear closeness or homosexuality, for example, to develop their capacity for relatedness with other men as well as with women. Jung (1953) expresses similar ideas to those found in Freud's view of psychological as well as physical bisexuality, although Jung uses different terms: men need to acknowledge and find greater expression for the 'anima' (female principle) within them, and women for the 'animus' (or male principle) that is within them. Jung's ideas are perhaps open to criticism, as equating masculine and feminine qualities with animus and anima, although his intention is far from that. Whichever way we look at these complex issues, it can be simply stated that counsellors and therapists need to recognize that all the psychological qualities that constitute the full emotional and interpersonal life are capable of being developed in men and women clients. Each client, irrespective of gender, ideally needs to find the capacity to be active and passive, rational and intuitive, assertive and sensitive, and to be able to be close to and separate from others of his or her own and the opposite gender. These are not rival qualities, but complementary.

The politics of sexual difference

In considering the relationships between people as equals, it is essential to recognize and honour difference. Psychoanalytic thought has often appeared to equate difference with deviance from the norm. But we have to question what normality is, and whether what psychoanalysis has done (although it is common to psychology generally) is to devote so much attention to deviations from the norm, that it has not stopped long enough to study the norm, or to question whether there is a norm at all. Chodorow observes, for example, that in looking at the possible reasons for homosexual development, psychoanalysis has never given a satisfactory explanation of heterosexual development, and why it should be the way it is:

> . . . heterosexuality has been assumed, its origins and vicissitudes have not been described: psychoanalysis does not have a developmental account of 'normal' heterosexuality (which is, of course a wide variety of heterosexualities) that compares in richness and specificity to accounts we have of the development of the various homosexualities and what are called perversions.
>
> (1994: 34)

No wonder gay therapists have asked the same questions of heterosexuals, as have been asked of them: 'When did you first realize you were heterosexual, etc.' These are serious questions for those who study psycho-sexual development to address, not just questions that might be asked to highlight bias and prejudice.

It can indeed be said of much psychoanalytic theory around sexuality, sexual orientation and about gender relations, that it is contentious. What we often find is that Freud's *observations* are perceptive, but that the *explanations* of those observations are not as complete as they could be; and sometimes they have been understood (at least by those less familiar with them) as dogmatic, literal statements. Freud can be both self-effacing about his lack of understanding and the need for confirmation of his ideas before they can be considered of any value (1925b: 332); but at other times he can be forceful in his descriptions, as in this example from the same paper, of what he thinks a girl feels when she realizes she has not got a penis: 'She makes her judgement and her decision in a flash. She has seen it and knows that she is without it and wants to have it' (1925b: 336)!

One of the difficulties of using psychodynamic theory is that its terms are sometimes used literally, sometimes symbolically, and sometimes as a confusing mixture of both. Thus when Freud writes about the fear of castration in a man (or a little boy) or penis envy in a woman (or a little girl), he adduces these ideas partly from symbolic communications from his patients. At times he translates them into what may appear to be very narrow concepts, unless we in turn translate those terms back into their symbolical meaning. Freud also takes as his raw material both events which patients report, and their fantasies and dreams. Again this leads to confusion (especially so over reports of childhood abuse, another contentious subject that I take up later in this chapter) – confusion which is reflected in the contemporary debates that take place about these vital matters.

The question of genital difference is a case in point. Children are clearly interested in their bodies, in their parents' bodies, and in the bodies of their siblings and peers. Children ask questions, such as where babies come from and how they are born; and if they have some strange ideas about that, involving the stomach and food, and the rectum as the birth channel, these ideas are not so strange when parents speak of a new baby as being in mother's tummy, and defecation is the major form of expulsion. Children are equally interested in and puzzled by sexual differences, and we might imagine how a little boy (without the knowledge that an older child has) might react to discovering that his mother, his sister or girl friend does not like him have a penis; or how a little girl reacts to seeing her father's, or her brother's, or a boy's penis. We do not even have to imagine it, because children tell us, especially when they are not made to feel ashamed of interest in their bodies. The following comments were made in a child observation by a trainee therapist learning about child development. He was observing a girl, who was at the time nearly three years old:

> She had watched her father in the toilet, and now wants a willy of her own. When taken to the doctor she asked him if he had a willy, and was greatly reassured to hear that he had. She expressed a desire to urinate standing up, like father does.
>
> A boy, a friend of the same age came to see her. 'He has a willy', she told her mother, and she wanted one also. She was only cheered up when mother told her that when she was grown up she would have breasts, which he would not have.
>
> A week later the little girl wanted to see the male observer's big toe. 'She pulled up her sweater to show me her stomach in an effort to get me to show her my big toe.' Later that day there was an episode when the little girl encouraged a friend who is a boy to 'shoot people with his gun'.

The first two paragraphs are clear – there is no symbolism there. Freud may even be thought to be right at this stage: 'she has seen it and wants to have it'. But what is the third paragraph about? Is it purely about big toes and guns? Or is this symbolic communication, so that in either case of the incidents with the big toe and the gun, or both, is it possible to say that the little girl's actions are connected with her fascination with the penis? Clearly some readers may feel it is right to make the connection. Others might only prefer to accept the evidence of what is obvious, less impressed by the possibility of symbolic communication, although it is that symbolic communication which is so important in psychodynamic counselling and therapy.

If we take this little girl's interest one step further we enter the field of speculation, although there may be evidence to support it. Might, for example, this child go on to ask the question 'why'? 'Why has he got a penis? Why have I not got one?' Psychoanalytic observation suggests these questions are asked, and psychoanalytic theory suggests some answers. One explanation (for the girl) is that she once had a penis, but that it has been taken away; and one possible fantasy (for the boy) is that if she has lost hers, then he might lose his too. Alternatively, such explanation or fantasies may arise not so much from within the child, as from the threats used by parents: we may wonder, for example, what the effect was on her son when a mother noticed him handling his penis and said: 'Do that again and I'll call the doctor to cut it off.' Whether or not she meant that as symbolic message, she said it, and it must have sounded a horrifying possibility. If this seems an isolated incident, I recall a group of young mothers discussing this example in an adult education class, and recognizing a parallel in a local expression several of them playfully used with both their sons and daughters: 'If you're naughty I'll cut your tail off.' It was an expression that had been used by their mothers to them, and which they used with their children without thinking that it might cause them any anxiety. We do not know, of course, how their children understood such words, or whether different children might have reacted differently. It is possible that the only tail they could identify was a boy's penis.

I do not underestimate the symbolic significance of genital differences; but for the moment it is useful to stay with the literal meanings. While it is unlikely that every child has these kind of thoughts, and it is equally possible that other children may have different bizarre explanations about the circumstances around genital differences, some adult clients show clear evidence of penis envy (as this whole issue is conceptualized in psychoanalytic thought). The two examples that follow include a male client and a female client. It is important not to forget that literal penis envy is probably more obvious in boys and men (centring round the size or length of the penis) than it is in women; and that if at times symbols appear to relate to the penis, sometimes the penis itself has symbolic significance, as I shortly explain:

> Winston greatly admired his father, whom he described as a 'big man' in his business. His father was looked upon fondly by everyone, but was frequently denigrated by Winston's mother as not being assertive enough of his own rights. Winston wanted to be like his father and rise to the top of the same profession, but he could never follow through the opportunities which might have led to this. The only time he had ever criticized his father was when he had given him a wallet, because it was a plastic one, and not like the large leather one his father possessed. Winston threw it through a closed window in his temper. It seemed to symbolize his own feeling of inferiority. Winston treated his wife as inferior too, as if she embodied the inferior side of himself. He constantly drew attention to her mistakes, denigrating her (as mother had done father). He was deferential to his male therapist, although he spoke of relations to other authority figures as often fraught: he was frequently angry at their power over him. He usually made such situations worse by lashing out at them in a manner which reminded the counsellor of the way a child can hit out at an adult – ferociously but ineffectively.
>
> In his dreams Winston would sometimes see himself as a woman in the presence of others whom he would identify as gay men, whom he had met socially, and who at the time of his therapy were also looked down upon in society. The therapist drew upon the implication of this imagery to illustrate how Winston felt inferior (like a woman in society), and that he felt weak and powerless in his transactions with other men. In his dreams he 'castrated' himself, becoming a woman and submitting to other men. Winston was thrilled one day when he was able to stand up to the driver of a huge lorry who had forced him off his pedal bike, even though inside himself he felt like running away.

The imagery used throughout this example (lorry/bike, man/woman, leather/plastic wallet) appears to link symbolically to the terms 'penis envy', or 'penis inferiority'. This thought occurred to the therapist, although he did not put it into words. But it appeared to be confirmed when the therapist drew Winston's attention to his envy of his father's wallet. Winston responded with his own association to this, that he remembered once seeing his father's penis, and thinking how big it was compared to his.

Yvonne had come for counselling because she was unable to enjoy sexual intercourse with her husband. Much that she said pointed to her wish to be a man, although she did not use so open an expression. She said that she liked 'to wear the trousers', and did not permit her husband to take the initiative in sex. She was very excited by pin-ups of women, and could only allow penetration if she was on top of her husband. She preferred watching him masturbate, or bringing herself to a climax with a vibrator (her own penis). She was turned on by reading letters in male magazines about men's erections. Furthermore, she enjoyed rifle-shooting, and she once cornered an instructor at the shooting range and told him what a 'lovely cock' he had, although having excited him she would not let him have sex with her. Although Yvonne never acknowledged that she envied the penis, she often expressed envy of her brother, who was very successful in his career, and who she felt was her parents' favourite. She also envied men all the privileges they had; but what was interesting was that she was as opposed to the feminist movement as if she had been the most chauvinist type of man.

We do of course live in a culture which has absorbed much Freudian thinking and mythology: 'He is no more a person now but a whole climate of opinion', Auden (1976) wrote of Freud. We must always allow for some clients using these Freudian images either because they have learned them from their milieu, or because that is what they think a therapist expects to hear. Even if this is the case, the symbolism can become an effective way of reflecting upon the wider context of a client's relationships; and on occasion the imagery may even need to be taken rather more literally in its own right.

As we pursue this symbolic path, we come to realize that in other ways Freud's thinking was too narrow. For example, while he has much to say about the significance of the penis envy in women and castration anxiety in men for the psycho-sexual development of men and women, he says nothing comparable about the significance of the womb, or breasts for both women and men. Karen Horney observes that there are young boys who express the wish to have breasts or who wish they could bear children (Rubins 1978: 149). There are also suggestions in post-Freudian thinking that each gender wishes to rediscover early feelings of completeness and unity, and that this is represented by the desire to possess the opposite sex, of which the breast or the penis is a part-object symbolization (see, for example, the French psychoanalyst Lacan, who in one sense has rediscovered Freud, though with much greater symbolic meaning).

Another expression that is used in current psychoanalytic discourse is 'phallus', which originally meant the penis as an organ, but is used in a new way to mean the penis as a symbol of power. Thus it is possible to speak of a 'phallic woman' or the 'phallic mother', as a woman or as a mother who exercises power over the child, a power which the child wishes to possess, and of which the child feels envy. The equation of breast and penis in Kleinian thought similarly uses both part-objects as symbolic of each other, but also as symbolic of the powerful mother, who can give and can destroy. A man's fear of a woman's vagina, that she may use it to cut off his penis (*vagina dentata* – with teeth!) may then be a 'spill over' (as Segal puts it, 1992: 45) from fears of the damage that could be done by the mother, or a projection of the fear of damaging the mother by biting the nipple.

In classical times the phallus represented both the erect penis and the ruling power. We may therefore consider the absolute appropriateness of penis envy if it is translated not just into individual symbolism (the baby and the phallic mother) but into the way in which women, in particular in society and in the family, should be enabled to seek equality with men, who through the patriarchal organization and assumptions of society and its institutions have dominated those whom men have called 'the second sex'. In working with individuals, therapists and counsellors need to be aware of the actual oppression of the engines of society, as well as the real economic and political issues that may have bearing, presently as well as in the past on oppression within the family. Freud clearly recognized these pressures, and even if some of his assumptions about women are limited by the political and cultural climate in which he lived, he breaks sufficiently free of it to assert that marriage, for example, as practised in his society, was damaging to a woman's mental health. He is especially critical of the double standards that allow men a different sexual morality (1908: 47).

The external world, including politics and society, is as important in its effect on the psyche as internal processes. Some writers, such as Winnicott, see engagement with the wider world as the ultimate in personal maturity, where the adult is able 'to identify with the environment, and take part in the establishment, maintenance and alteration of the environment' (1965a: 102). Samuels observes that Jung too appears to have thought that those who had become individuated through analysis would have a decisive effect on the world scene. Combining Jungian, Freudian and Kleinian ideas about maturity in a composite definition, Samuels appears to question whether by itself analysis achieves this object: 'The person who, via analysis conforms to the reality principle, has achieved ego mastery, become genital, or reached the depressive position, is often represented as belonging to an élite that is . . . less susceptible to the group psychological pressures of the social and political world that they inhabit' (1993: 55). Samuels himself believes particular attention has to be paid to political development of the individual, although until the individual has acquired a sufficient sense of personal power, those wider issues are not capable of being contemplated.

On this wider scale, the individualism of much therapy and counselling, and the private nature of many counsellors and therapists, does not give much hope of their taking on political issues as a necessary adjunct to their work with individuals. There are some signs that this is happening, but changing the system is a daunting task. As Seidler writes, 'the connections between the inner and the outer world are more direct but also more difficult'; therapy can 'help us to treasure individuality while keeping sight of the importance of transforming relations of power and subordination'. He observes that therapy has the potential to deepen our sense of injustice' but at the same time 'it limits our sense of politics as we learn to expect less from political changes', and 'take responsibility for our emotional lives' (1991: 191).

Oedipus myth and Oedipus complex

Freud made it clear that he believed that there are four cornerstones to psychoanalytic theory: unconscious mental processes, repression and resistance, infantile sexuality and the Oedipus complex. As long as we extend the notion of infantile sexuality to include the wish to make loving relationships with others (over and above the erotic pleasure of the body in oral, anal and genital stimulation) these four concepts are equally important to a modern psychodynamic approach.

The Oedipus complex is not the same as the Oedipus myth, but it takes its cue from Sophocles's tragedy, which Freud recognized as so moving, because 'everyone in the audience was once a budding Oedipus in fantasy and each recoils in horror from the dream fulfilment here transplanted into reality' (Masson 1985: 272). In effect what happened to Oedipus is what happens if relationships in the family (or with trusted figures) go wrong, as when there is abuse, whether it is sexual, physical or emotional. It is this rejection and abuse, so the story runs, which Oedipus initially suffered as a baby, which perhaps lies at the heart of all the tragic circumstances – incest and murder – that followed in his life. Even then, the myth is far from straightforward, because there is also a sense in which all the principal characters in it were trying to avoid incest and murder, just as in many families the wish of both parents and children is to be able to relate lovingly without sex and violence. In this section I concentrate upon the relationship between child and parent, and not on the adolescent or adult client, although they will feature as I develop the oedipal theme in the sections that follow. There we shall see how actual abuse or abusive attitudes affect adult survivors, and how abuse can be perpetrated by members of a child's family, by grandparents, parents or siblings, as well as by teachers, clergy, care staff, or even (but much less rarely) strangers.

The dramatic story of Oedipus is a massive and tragic example of what can go wrong in family relationships. Human relationships will always contain some elements that are symbolized in the Oedipus myth, but in healthy development the extremes of that story do not occur. The Oedipus complex certainly lives up to its name, because it contains many possibilities of resolution. It includes normal development (even if there is wide variety in what is 'normal'). Where it culminates in a satisfactory resolution (more or less, and perhaps for most of the time) adults can relate to their sexual partner as man/woman to woman/man (I include gay and lesbian partnerships here), without the earlier child–parent relationship distorting the present.

We may think we know the Oedipus story well: Oedipus killed his father and married his mother, and then blinded himself when he discovered what he had done. But the original is much richer than that: Laius and Jocasta, the rulers of the city-state of Thebes, were expecting their first child, but were told by the oracle at Delphi that their son would grow up to murder his father and marry his mother. Because they feared both incest and patricide (they too wanted to avoid what they knew to be wrong), Laius ordered a servant to take the baby to a mountain side and leave him to be devoured by wild animals. Bettelheim observes the significance of this abandonment: 'Oedipus acted as he did because his parents completely rejected him as an infant' (1983: 22–3). But fate was not to be thwarted, because the servant instead softened and gave the baby to a shepherd from a neighbouring state. The shepherd took the baby to Corinth, where the rulers Polybus and Meropé were childless. They adopted the child as their own son and Oedipus grew up believing Polybus and Meropé were his real parents.

A chance remark at court sent Oedipus to the oracle at Delphi to question his origins, and the oracle informed him too that he was destined to kill his father and marry his mother. Believing Polybus and Meropé to be his real parents, Oedipus vowed not to return to Corinth, because he too wished to avoid such heinous crimes, unaware of course that he was much safer in Corinth than anywhere else. On his travels he got involved in a brawl with a nobleman and killed him, not knowing either that it was Laius or that Laius was his father. Further on his travels he came upon Thebes, a city racked by plague and famine, and there he rid the city of the malign influence of the sphinx by solving its riddle: what is it that in the beginning of life goes on four legs, in mid-life on two and at the end on three? The answer is 'man'. As a reward Oedipus was offered the widowed Jocasta in marriage, and he became the ruler of Thebes.

A few years passed, and another plague overwhelmed the city: the oracle suggested that it was because the death of Laius had gone unavenged. Oedipus resolved to find the murderer, and set about calling witnesses who might help him get at the truth. Sophocles's drama resembles a piece of early Freudian psychoanalysis (or perhaps analysis resembles the play!) as Oedipus pursues the truth, but cannot see it when it is staring him in the eyes. He finds relief when he learns that Polybus has died a natural death, and is soon again in anguish when the same messenger tells him that he is not Polybus's natural son. Jocasta recognizes the truth first, that she has married and borne children by her long-forgotten son. When Oedipus discovers her body, where in remorse she has hanged herself, he blinds himself with the pins of her brooches. Bettelheim observes that he does this as much for failing in knowledge (not seeing) as for the crimes themselves: 'Oedipus acted out his metaphorical blindness – his blindness to what the oracle had meant, based on his lack of knowledge of himself – by depriving himself of his eyesight' (1993: 23).

There are many different levels upon which any myth can be interpreted. Bettelheim observes how much rejection and lack of knowledge lie at the centre of it, although at the same time we may feel rather sorry for Oedipus who had the fates stacked against him. What Freud found telling in the myth is the idea that in every child there is a desire for closeness with the first love object, a desire which at first is met in the intimacy of the mother–baby relationship. As the child grows older mother and child have to separate, a complex process in which both child and parent try to find the right balance between love and intimacy, without becoming over-close, sexual, or incestuous. As I shall shortly show, Oedipus's fate may be repeated either when either or both parents reject the child's love and sexuality, or when either emotionally or sexually over-stimulates the child. In successful resolution of this stage children learn that their love and their innocent sexuality are accepted. Through a positive relationship to both parents they identify with them both, and form a good enough but not over-close relationship with them both. A child can then begin the process of growing away from parental ties, so that later in adult life he or she can form intimate relationships of her or his own outside the family, based upon identification with the parents and with their relationship with each other. Such identification often includes negative as well as positive features.

Early psychoanalytic writing placed the Oedipus complex at the age of about four or five. That timing was based on the idea that in the oral and anal stages of development a child's relationships are essentially dyadic. The theme of trust and dependency concentrates upon the maternal side of the parent–child interplay (even if other women, and fathers, may play a part in the mothering), a one-to-one dyadic relationship. The theme of authority has much that is paternal about it, even though mothers as well as fathers are authority figures (Samuels (1993: 133–5), for example, writes about 'the father of whatever sex'). Fathers are traditionally seen as authoritarian figures, although it is often mothers who carry the bulk of the responsibility, sometimes as a threat invoking the name of the father, who is absent at work, and even sometimes absent emotionally at home. These may be called one-by-one relationships, still in essence dyadic. In both these stages (so more traditional theory runs) it is felt that the child relates to mother or to father, but not to mother-and-father as a couple.

By the time the third stage is reached (I stay here with the standard Freudian view), one-to-one and one-by-one relationships broaden out, so that there is a recognition that the parents have their own relationship. Similarly siblings are related to more fully. In play, within and outside the home, children begin to interact properly with each other, not just playing singly in each other's company, or using each other as objects to be manipulated as part of the play. Three-person relationships have now become significant, and with the recognition of three persons there are new conflicts about who goes with whom, and who gets left out. Two's company, three's a crowd.

So runs the early Freudian view. It goes on to suggest that children have fantasies of killing off the parent of the same gender, and having the other parent all to themselves. Children do not constantly dwell on their desire to marry one parent and kill off the other, but those ideas are present in dreams and nightmares, as well as in innocent expressions of affection, like the six-year-old boy who said, 'If anything happens to Daddy, *I'll* marry you, Mummy'; or the eight-year-old girl who said to her mother, 'I'll never find anyone as good as Daddy to marry.' There are inevitably rages when a child wishes one of the parents dead, but such thoughts are normally soothed by bed-time. There are bound to be times when a child feels jealous of the parents' relationship, and comes into their bed, not just to share their closeness as before, but also to separate them, so that the child can have either of them to themselves. Children and adults are not normally conscious of any wish for sex with their parents, although as Jocasta says in the original play, 'many a man hath dreamt as much'. They learn that their wish for intimacy has limits set on it by both parents; they recognize their parents' own intimacy; and, encouraged by social factors such as going to school and so beginning to leave the home, children take further steps towards separating from mother and father.

Later Freudian thinking (aided by Kleinian theory that places the Oedipus complex in the first year, not the fourth or fifth year) is broader, and indeed is consonant with the position of this book, that these themes and issues can be seen at every point of development. The three-person relationship can be used as both a literal and metaphorical idea, as, for example, when we acknowledge the presence of the father in the early months of life, acting as a natural force against the baby's intense wish for mother: 'fathers are also felt to come between the baby and the breast, separating them and destroying phantasies of fusion with an internal and external mother/breast' (Segal 1992: 49); or in the way in which a mother, in weaning her child, comes between her child and her breast, the mother acting as a third force. Taking the number three as a potentially significant one, we can see how three-person, or three-object situations arise throughout life: such as the parent who comes between a child and her faeces, taking them away from her; or in the struggle implicit in Freud's model of personality structure between ego, id and super-ego (the latter perhaps coming between the first two). Nor should oedipal anxieties be confined to infancy. At adolescence sons, daughters and parents often do not quite know how to manage intimate feelings which previously had been expressed naturally, such as a hug or a kiss, since each is in some way conscious of the sexuality of the other. In adult life, triangular relationships are a common feature.

There is further complexity about oedipal issues which cannot be ignored, especially in any discussion of gender or sexual orientation. The traditional Freudian view about the development of infantile sexuality is that boys and girls follow a common path of psychological development up to the Oedipus stage, but then negotiate the Oedipus complex in quite distinct ways. Both boys and girls start life literally attached, and after birth emotionally attached, to mother. It is probably with her that they relate most closely in their early years, and it is probably with her that they mostly wish to share their love. Boys have to make a transition from directing their love towards mother in childhood, to sexual intimacy with other women from adolescence onwards. The woman to whom the young man is later attracted often has some psychological resemblance to his mother. Father plays a significant role, because in the oedipal stage he represents the barrier to a close relationship with mother. She is his possession (or appears to be his, especially in a patriarchal society where men are seen as owning women!), as well as a model for how the young man would like to be. Freud also believed that boys wish for a close relationship with father, and that mother comes between son and husband. In this triangular situation a boy wishes to push mother away, and get closer to father, in order to do so identifying with mother. It can be seen that this is all more complicated than the simple 'kill father, marry mother' formula as it has been popularly understood.

The path is not a smooth one for boys, even if at first it appears relatively easy given that (for most of them) their love object in adult life is the same gender as mother. It is generally supposed that it is an even harder path for girls, and at first glance it appears to be so. Their first love object, their mother, is a homosexual attachment, and they need to move from this to heterosexual love. But father is a temporary love object, because girls have to make yet another shift away from father towards other men. Such a double shift may appear to carry with it a greater risk of problems than a single shift of object. It is suggested by Freud that this leads to a different resolution of the Oedipus complex: the significance of fathers for boys is that they drive boys out of the Oedipus complex; but in the case of girls, fathers take them into it, and they never completely leave it.

Yet these differences in oedipal paths occur earlier than the standard idea of an oedipal stage. A number of feminist writers, who are also psychotherapists (e.g. E. Belotti 1975) have described, as Freud himself suggested, how mothers tend to nurture their daughters less generously than their sons. However, they also observe how mothers identify more with their baby daughters than their sons (Chodorow 1989: 47–50). If there is truth in these observations, it may mean that it is less easy for a girl to detach herself from mother from whom she still wants more. Men often fail to recognize that women want mothering as much as men do; there are often problems because a man takes a woman's wish for comfort as a sexual sign, and not as an expression of her wish for him to nurture her. In the following example, the young woman was still attached to a mother-substitute, not yet ready to integrate the sexual into her relationship with her partner:

> Zoë did not know how to cope with her partner's wish for sex. As long as he was caring, did things for her, bought her presents, and was kindly towards her, the relationship went well. But when he wanted to sleep with her, not only did she feel anxious and refuse him, but she turned to her close girl friend for sex. As long as her partner was maternal Zoë appeared to be happy; as soon as he wanted to be 'male', she was driven back to a homosexual love object, and to her need for a mother figure alone.

It is the greater difficulty of detachment for a girl from the same gender mother that helps us to understand what is probably a greater tempestuousness in adolescence in a mother–daughter relationship than we are likely to find in mother–son or father–daughter relations. Since a heterosexual young woman has to make such a major change, from a female to a male love-object, and not just a change of person in her object choice, she needs more assertiveness if her wish for separateness is to overcome her wish to remain attached. Even then many mother–daughter relationships remain very close. Chodorow confidently comments on how 'a woman is pre-occupied with her mother as an internal image and object and that this intrapsychic pre-occupation helps shape her love relationships (and much else about her intrapsychic and interpersonal life), are near-universal clinical observations' (1994: 83).

The more extensively the Oedipus complex is considered, the less straightforward it is to suggest that one or other gender has an easier or more difficult time of it. It used to be thought, and in some places is still said with some vehemence, that successful resolution of the Oedipus complex led to heterosexual object choice; and that homosexuality represents the negative Oedipus complex, where love for the parent of the opposite gender has not occurred as it 'should' have: a boy, for example, has over-identified with his mother, or has to be literally submissive to father in the oedipal struggle; or that a girl has not been able to separate from her original homo-erotic love for her mother. Such views in psychodynamic thinking are now reckoned to be simplistic, partly because the gay and lesbian community has rightly challenged straight psychologists and psychoanalysts on such questions, and partly because the variations in development are given fuller recognition. Chodorow refers to the work of Kenneth Lewes, in which he takes classical theory apart, especially for boys. She observes the complication that even in heterosexual development a boy's identification with his father can only take place if father is also a love object:

> Lewes suggests that the origins of normal heterosexuality in the Oedipus complex are much more complicated than Freud and those that follow him believed. He describes twelve different possible oedipal constellations for the boy: depending upon whether his attachment is anaclitic [someone unlike self] or narcissistic [someone like self], whether he takes himself or his father or his mother as object, whether this mother is phallic or castrated, whether he identifies with father or (phallic or castrated) mother, and whether his own sexual stance is passive or active. Six of these constellations are heterosexual but only one . . . is 'normal'.
>
> (Chodorow 1994: 43)

The passage illustrates what variations we need as therapists to recognize in the negotiation of oedipal issues. The need to leave parents to their own relationship, and to form intimate, sexual partnerships of one's own is a common task for many people, although we also have to acknowledge that some people choose to remain single. The Oedipus myth, in differing degrees of intensity, echoes normal as well as abnormal development. Each person undergoes their own Oedipus complex, so that as Chodorow urges at the conclusion of her short book re-examining these matters: 'We must investigate individually how any person's sexual orientation and organization, erotic fantasy, and practices arise from anatomy, from cultural valuation and construction, from intrapsychic solutions to conflict, from family experience and from gender identity. All these will enter the individual case of how any woman or man loves' (1994: 91).

Difficulties arise when the issues around sexuality and the limits of its expression are made more obvious, less natural, and more bewildering than they already are, through the action of parents and others acting them out: when, as the following sections show, a child or young person feels that one parent's attention takes precedence over feelings for the other parent; when the parents' relationship is so bad that the child is terrified of the wish to split them; when sexual feelings for the child are expressed or acted upon directly or indirectly by the parent; when death or separation takes one parent away; or when a child feels her or his love and sexuality is rejected. At those times elements of the Oedipus myth are repeated, inevitably affecting intimate relationships later in adult life. As Chodorow writes: 'How women and men love will be heavily influenced, though not determined, by their navigation through the relationships and fantasies of early childhood, and this is the terrain that we think of as more typically psychoanalytic' (1994: 82).

Heterosexuality and homosexuality

More recent signs of the recognition of the diversity of sexual relationships are a welcome return to an attitude in Freud towards sexuality which was less hide-bound than many of his followers. His attitude to homosexuality, for example, was that while it might be a variation from normal sexual orientation, it was not psychologically abnormal. As I have described, for Freud bisexuality is the common path of development until the oedipal stage, and it is only then that the developmental process splits into different paths for boys and girls, with different consequences in terms of the eventual sexual object. Freud clearly labels homosexual love as an *inversion*, and not a *perversion*, the latter label being attached more freely by him to certain sexual practices such as exhibitionism and voyeurism. Inversion is the only distinguishing mark of the homosexual, who in other respects need not be psychologically impaired, and may even be 'distinguished by specially high intellectual development and ethical culture' (1905: 49). In other words, a person's sexual orientation, whether gay, lesbian, bisexual or straight, is not in itself an indication of his or her psychological health: counsellors and therapists will have gay and straight clients who present a whole range of issues. This is particularly important to remember, since working with a client population tends to a rather biased view of what the general population is like. Gay relationships may be presented as problematic, but this does not mean that all gay relationships are; and of course there are plenty of heterosexual relationships which are equally difficult. It is also important to recognize important distinctions between, as well as different issues for, gay men and lesbians, and not to treat them as identical. Simon observes furthermore that much liberal heterosexual thinking assumes that a gay or lesbian couple will function as a heterosexual couple. This they may do, but 'a gay couple's description of their behaviours which might not fit with the therapist's ideals may provoke discomfort, impatience and disapproval in the therapist and a retreat to more stereotypical beliefs about lesbian, gay and bisexual "psychology" ' (1996: 106).

Simon goes on to suggest the importance of contextualizing a gay or lesbian couple within the experience of their own gay or lesbian community. We also have to recognize that where a society's, or a community's, or an organization's attitudes to gay men and lesbians (or indeed to any particular section of the society, such as Black people or those with disability) is antipathetic, this causes distress. Gay and lesbian groups have rightly rejected the type of classification of their difficulties in psychiatry, behavioural therapy and psychoanalysis which has in the past labelled homosexuals as psychologically damaged. But in psychoanalytic circles, particularly in some of the more conservative societies, there still appear to be difficulties about accepting gay or lesbian candidates for training, as if in some way they are deficient in their psychological development. Psychoanalytic writing is as yet thin on the affirmation of homosexuality as a valid sexual orientation. Ratigan

(1996), writing from a psychodynamic perspective, cites some positive approaches, including Lewes (1988) on male homosexuality (referred to above) and O'Connor and Ryan (1993) on lesbianism and psychoanalysis. Davies and Neal (1996) have assembled a collection of essays from a variety of theoretical perspectives that challenge the views of all therapists on gay and lesbian issues, and promise further volumes extending the subject (Davies and Neal, in press).

With the changing climate of opinion, clinical presentations about being gay or lesbian are far less common than they once were, particularly in young people in the 1970s at the turn of the tide of public opinion. A number of young people, aware of homosexual feelings and attraction to the same gender, presented at that time as confused in their sexual identity, afraid of parental reaction, unsure of whether they wished to be gay or straight, and unclear as to how to express their sexuality. These issues are sometimes still present, and may continue to be seen where older clients face up to a sexual orientation which they have perhaps suppressed from earlier in their life, when it was unacceptable for them to adopt any other path than the socially dictated one of heterosexual marriage.

In terms of the development of sexual aims (the persons to whom we wish to express our sexual feelings) we need constantly to remember the Freudian schema, that bisexuality is part of normal development, and that indeed homosexual attachment is a normal part of the development of the mother–daughter, father–son relation. Homosexual expression of sexuality may even be a fairly normal feature in childhood and early adolescence, without in any way dictating eventual sexual object choice. Loving, idealizing and sexual feelings are often directed initially to peers of the same gender (known in old magazines and books about school life as a 'crush'). These feelings are sometimes acted out in early adolescence. It is often helpful to reassure the anxious teenager on this point, without in any way dictating their sexual preference. A young person is free (external and internal psychological pressures notwithstanding) to develop as they wish:

Alex (now a young man) recalled that at his single-sex school he and other boys in their early teens had played fantasy games of who was going to marry whom amongst the other boys. Like other boys of that age, they would also compare the size of their penis and growth of their pubic hair. None of this was felt to be either abnormal nor necessarily homosexual at the time, nor did it worry Alex now, despite more recent anxieties about his sexuality. At that time he had felt fine.

When there were more single-sex schools than now, same-sex relationships not only acted as a mirror to a developing young person, but also represented a rather better known, and therefore safer way of relating sexually than as yet did (or could!) the opposite sex. Co-education in most schools has changed much of the anxiety about relating to the opposite sex. There are still attractions, of course, to same gender as well as opposite gender peers, and to older students and staff: some things do not change. Attraction to older adolescents or adults of the same gender sometimes takes the form of admiration of someone who represents the man, or the woman, whom the young person wants to be like, this person often demonstrating physical or personal characteristics which the younger or less confident person would like to possess. We also need to remember that sexual identity – like other aspects of identity – is still plastic throughout adolescence, especially when there has been little or no sexual experience. It is often only by asking sensitively about the fantasies which people use when they masturbate, or when they get sexually excited, that a counsellor is given a sense of where the client's dominant sexual orientation appears to lie.

Barry, a student at university who had not yet had any sexual experience, found himself gazing at other young men who were well-built, good looking, and 'macho' in their relationships with others. The more he looked at these men, the more he feared that he was gay, although the thought of sex with a man turned him right off, and when asked his fantasies when masturbating they were obviously only about women. In the course of counselling, these sexual anxieties were relatively quickly settled as Barry went on to look at other aspects of himself. He described how he swung between thinking himself 'top dog' (as he had been at home and at his school) and a 'right little shit' (which he had sometimes felt at home, but more often felt now he was at university). In comparing himself with the men he looked at, he felt the 'bottom dog' – a passive somewhat anal image, and in the animal world a female position. So he felt cowed by these men whom he admired. There was a sense in which he wished he was inside them, or they inside him – which of course might have given rise to his homosexual anxiety (buggery can be a form of dominance used in war, when the victor humiliates the vanquished). There was another element, because Barry also wished to be hugged by some of the men he admired, which might have been a way of latching on to some of their strength, and perhaps an indication of a wish to make up for a less than adequate relationship with his father. Given that in some cultures, such as the British, hugging by men can be considered threatening, and its absence a sign of homophobia, it was little wonder that Barry felt confused about what his different feelings meant.

Earlier in this chapter the false dichotomy between masculine and feminine has been observed. This dichotomy is just as false when applied to sexual orientation, and the sexual positions which people adopt, despite the populist stereotypes of gay men as camp, and lesbians as butch. Counsellors and therapists need to be especially aware that they are not caught up in such stereotypical reactions or attitudes. It is often other factors, that are described throughout these major themes, which are relevant in helping a person reflect on their sexual orientation, and the expression of their sexuality in relationships. Trust and dependency issues, questions of power and authority, autonomy and independence, parental attitudes, and societal pressures, personal experiences and private fantasies – all these contribute to the way any one individual works out his or her sexuality. Sometimes over-concentration upon sexuality itself masks the essential issues which actually make a person feel inadequate:

Clive had visited many gay clubs in search of a permanent relationship. When he came for counselling he was depressed and disillusioned, since his experience over the last year had consisted of one date after another, in which he had been picked up for a night, and then dropped. In his counselling Clive began to recognize how submissive he was in these relationships, but he also realized that this submissiveness, as well as his difficulty in taking initiatives, applied just as much to his relationships with women, to whom he had been unable to relate, for that very reason. What was at issue were these inter-personal difficulties, and not his sexual orientation.

Despite over 100 years passing since Freud realized the importance of sexuality in the issues presented to a therapist, sex in both its heterosexual and homosexual expression is only just beginning to emerge from the closet. With the lid of repression and oppression in society lifted, psychodynamic therapists and counsellors are increasingly having to re-examine their attitudes, knowing that in following Freud they are seeking to understand one of the most basic forces in human relationships. Heterosexual relationships are complex enough, but in the gay and lesbian communities there is a wide variety of lifestyles, as if in throwing off the yoke of heterosexuality, gays, lesbians and bisexuals have found an opportunity to experiment with restructuring sexual relationships. We need further research and experience in these matters: but bearing in mind the dangers of impressionistic judgements made from the narrow sample represented by client groups, it is possible that in some respects gay men have more in common with heterosexual men (e.g. men tend to be more promiscuous than women) than they have with lesbians: lesbian relationships, for example, generally seem more stable, as heterosexual women are more stable than men in theirs.

The seducing parent

It is ironical that psychoanalysis, historically so eager to identify its roots and its developments as being true to Freud, should have resulted in attitudes towards two important aspects of sexual behaviour which are so antithetical to Freud. Homosexuality is one such area. The other is the experience in childhood of sexual abuse, where the psychoanalytic record has been generally a troubled and troubling one for many decades, even if there are more positive signs now that views are changing. The basic psychoanalytic position has been that much that is related by adults as sexual abuse in childhood is in fact a screen memory based on the fantasy wish of the child for a sexual relationship with the parent, combined with the experience of erotic stimulation that inevitably comes with baby and childcare, such as in washing and powdering of the genitals. The blame for this view is sometimes laid at Freud's door, and his retraction of his theory of infantile sexual seduction (Masson 1984). I and others have argued that this is an exaggerated criticism of Freud (Jacobs 1992: 101–7). Those arguments should be considered briefly here, because this is another of those complex areas in which mistakes can so easily be made, in understanding theory, as well as in therapeutic practice.

Freud's earliest explanation for the symptoms which he witnessed in many of his patients of hysterical conversion (where a limb, or one of the five senses, is numbed, paralysed or in some way affected physically due to emotional tensions), was that they had been traumatized by parental sexual seduction. He then realized that such an explanation was too general, and could not explain every neurotic presentation. He therefore added a further explanation, that of the child's fantasy of sexual seduction. This is still too limited an explanation of neurotic symptoms, but nonetheless it is important to recognize that this was an additional explanation, not an alternative one. There is plenty of evidence to show that throughout the rest of his life and writing Freud retained his belief in the actual seduction of some patients, citing it as an important factor in a number of his cases, while the explanation of the fantasy of seduction occurs as a major factor in others.

We now know that Freud's original explanation, preferring actual abuse over the fantasy, was very close to the truth. The number of actual instances of child abuse are considerable. It is as if the repressive censorship imposed by society on the memories of individuals has been lifted and it has become possible for a large number of survivors to speak about the abuse they suffered. They are now more widely believed, whereas for too many years followers of Freud, and other health professionals, have dismissed such memories as fantasies. There are of course some who now claim that recovered memories are false memories, including some who defend themselves, despite successful legal prosecutions against them, by saying that memories have been implanted by unscrupulous therapists.

On the other hand, there are also therapists and counsellors who, having recognized this issue, now see it everywhere. They prematurely suggest the possibility to clients whenever they hear of difficulties that sometimes can be linked to the experience of childhood abuse – such as eating disorders. It is as if they, like Freud at the beginning of his career, have only one explanation. There are others who accept a client's blank memories in childhood years as incontrovertible evidence of the repression of abusive experiences. Alongside these doubtful diagnoses, there are many apparently genuine examples of memories of childhood sexual abuse, and even more examples of childhood physical and emotional abuse, which arise spontaneously without any suggestion being made to the client, and in some cases are later confirmed from external sources. Therapists and counsellors can cite many examples in their adult patients, and social and family workers many examples in the children they work with, where it is not fantasy, but rather a clear memory or clear evidence of actual abuse. It no longer surprises those in the caring professions when such material is included as a presenting issue, or emerges later in therapy, as it becomes safer to recall or recount such dreadful events.

We have then today, as much as in Freud's thinking in his early years of practice, a struggle to comprehend the dimensions of these issues: to know when clients are speaking about actual events, or when they may have unconscious reasons for believing themselves to have been abused. We can no longer dismiss these accounts as examples of sexual precociousness, or label clients as sexually provocative. Those who have had their own sexual boundaries invaded as children may sometimes be deeply defended against anything erotic; or may themselves not know how to manage erotic boundaries in their own behaviour:

> Doreen came for counselling after an interview for a job, in which the man interviewing had tried to date her. She had refused him, and he, in turn, declined to give her the job. The initial session gave Doreen the chance of expressing her feelings, and calmed her furious tears. In the next session Doreen said she felt better and she began to talk about other relationships with men. She had noticed how often men tried to pick her up – in pubs and elsewhere. She felt she must be giving off some signs to them. She was sitting in her chair in the counselling room in what might be called a provocative fashion, in a short skirt with her legs wide – and in the presence of a male counsellor who could not help but take notice of these apparently sexual signals being made to him as well. But as Doreen went on she talked about her father's sexual advances when she was in her teens, sitting next to her and stroking her breasts while watching television. Doreen managed to control the situation by sitting in another part of the room and resisting his invitations to come and sit with him. But she deeply regretted that she had to lose out on the closeness which in her pre-adolescence years she had always enjoyed with her father. The counsellor pointed out how she may indeed have felt she wanted to impress the interviewer and other men, but was very upset when they inappropriately asked her out; in her interview this meant she had lost the job she wanted; just as her father's approaches were inappropriate to their relationship, and turning him down meant that she lost out there too. His lack of sexual boundaries were perhaps still unconsciously being played out in her manner with men.

The dilemma of wishing for a close relationship, and yet either needing to stay clear of sexual implications, or getting involved promiscuously but not able to tolerate a close relationship, appears time and again. Later relationships go wrong, it appears, as a result of past damaging experiences:

> Erica could not allow herself to get too close to men: she preferred a series of casual sexual relationships. She had once had to resist her stepfather when he made it clear that he wanted to come into her bed when her mother was away. On protesting to him she was told, 'But you're not my real daughter.' This added a deep personal wound to his sexual threat. Erica tended to get caught up in relationships where she was 'the second woman'.

Other examples could be given (though they are less frequently encountered) of men who have been seduced by a close female relation, in whom there appear similar difficulties. Women do abuse, both boys and girls, although it is possible that the tabu on mother–son sexual relations is stronger than the father–daughter tabu. It is more often a man who invades the boundaries, whether father, stepfather, grandfather, brother or half-brother.

> Fiona's father had married a second time when she was still small and she acquired a new 'mother', as well as a stepbrother ten years her senior. She

idolized the brother (perhaps as a substitute for her rather distant father), and was content just to sit at his feet and enjoy being in his presence. When she was twelve he suddenly left home to join the army, and she was heart-broken. Two years later she received a further blow when he married. He and his wife came to stay, and when everyone was out except herself and her brother, she cuddled up to him for comfort, but the closeness led to sex. Fiona felt so guilty afterwards that she could not speak to her stepbrother, and she had not done so since. She was unable to let men near her (except on the stage, since she enjoyed amateur dramatics). She could only be friends with those men she described as 'older and married . . . on a sisterly basis'. It was ironic that these were the men with whom she felt safe, since they also represented the one man with whom a sisterly relationship had gone wrong. It was, as in so much that goes wrong in relationships, as if she was trying to find a relationship, close in character to the one that had gone wrong, where she could put it right.

The therapist working with Fiona tried to remain sensitive to her wish to end her isolation from men, but also to her fear of letting any man get too close. As a man himself he tried to demonstrate to her that he could be trusted, so that she could learn to trust in turn her sexual and loving feelings for men, without fear that her feelings would provoke an invasion of her body. She tended to see men as the ones who had designs on her, and found it difficult to acknowledge her own desires. Her anger with the stepbrother gave way to feelings of the love she still had for him. In this case therapy had to finish before it was clear whether the issues could be resolved, but the therapist felt that Fiona made some progress towards talking about intimacy, and towards the expression of her love (including her affection for the therapist) without it turning into an inappropriate sexual relationship.

There are many examples where clients have been abused sexually even earlier in their lives than the clients reported in the examples above. Working with survivors of child sexual abuse is an area of work which requires specialist training and specialist supervision, with a considerable literature that supports the understanding of the dynamics of the different relationships and the therapeutic task. The following books either draw upon a psychoanalytic or psychodynamic model, or consider the issues of sexual and physical abuse, multiple personality, and recovered memories from a variety of perspectives; and point more extensively to other relevant literature: Walker (1992); Davies and Frawley (1994); Jacobs (1994); Scharff and Scharff (1994); Mollon (1996); Walker and Antony-Black (in press).

With so much emphasis rightly being given to actual sexual abuse, we should not forget another section of the client population where the sexual intimacy was not physically expressed, but emotionally was just as seductive to the child – and just as difficult to know how to respond to, since it involved intimacy without the threat of physical intrusion. These are those instances where parents use their children as confidantes, revealing to them the secrets of their sexual relations, or their sexual frustration or dissatisfaction with their partner; or where the parent–child relationship is emotionally over-close. In these instances a child may find the apparent level of trust and attention attractive, but is also aware of a threat, since such a situation appears to drive out the other parent, or other siblings. These are seductive relationships too, in which the child is presented with tempting rewards, but can feel equally guilty or frightened, especially when the opportunity comes for them in adult life to make their own intimate partnerships.

Some clients have parents who had their own difficulties about sexuality and have conveyed the impression that sex is something to be ashamed of or guilty about. They do this in what they say, such as those who simultaneously stimulate and put off their children by making them their confidantes in sexual matters; or by what they do – such as switching off the television whenever sexuality or nudity is shown.

> Gill received such mixed messages from her home. Her mother confided in her that she found sex distasteful and painful; while her father, though not physically touching her, related so closely to her that Gill herself normally avoided any young man who might present a sexual threat. Her closest friend was a young gay man, who represented for her a safe way of relating to a man without the usual sexual complications. Only when she had drunk too much at parties did Gill become aware of any sexual desire in herself for the opposite sex.

Triangular relationships

A child's fantasy wishes, which include thoughts of having the undivided attention of one or other of the parents, can get acted out when either parent gives substance to the child's fantasy, for example, by using the child as an ally against his or her partner. Where a child becomes a confidante (sometimes from an early age), perhaps being inappropriately told intimate details about the parents' relationship, he or she may feel very confused. The child may feel excited at being given such privileged information, the details of which feed the voyeuristic wishes of the child. At the same time a child may feel guilty (or even disgusted) by what they hear or in some other way witness. Freud suggested that the primal scene of the parents' bed was both fascinating and frightening to the child. Perhaps it is this voyeuristic fantasy that the tabloid newspapers feed upon in us when they divulge juicy gossip about famous people, who are significant popular transference figures.

Children and adolescents are not slow, given the opportunity, and not fully realizing the troubles it might cause, to exploit the differences between the parents, sometimes playing off one against the other, sometimes trying to achieve closeness with one to the exclusion of the other. Should the parents separate, or a parent die, then a child or young person may experience particular guilt at seeming to have brought this about, or at having in some way contributed to the situation. The Oedipus tragedy may to some degree be played out again. John Le Carré writes of what a child can feel in *Tinker, Tailor, Soldier, Spy,* and has since (in a television profile) identified the experience of the young boy in that novel as his own:

Most of all he blamed himself for the break-up of his parents' marriage, which he should have seen coming and taken steps to prevent. He even wondered whether he was more directly responsible, whether for instance he was abnormally wicked or divisive or slothful and that his bad character had wrought the rift.

(1974: 15)

We might add, since this passage is set in a school, that unresolved oedipal problems in a child's home can also make school attendance difficult, particularly where the state of the parental relationship causes anxiety about losing mother or father while away from home.

Novels, films and plays often revolve around triangular situations, showing us perhaps, as Freud said of *Oedipus Rex*, that what moves us in the arts is seeing our own struggles played out: these three-person relationships – usually two women and one man, or two men and one woman – present us with unresolved issues that we too have known in our own childhood and adult experience. There can be very few adult relationships where there has not been at some time the hint of a triangular situation, sometimes involving the parent–parent–child relationship, sometimes in the fantasy or fact of one or both partners being caught up in an affair. Whether or not these fantasies are acted out, counsellors and therapists will find considerable evidence of unresolved oedipal problems. Indeed it is perhaps in the nature of the Oedipus complex that it can never be fully worked through.

Triangular relationships seldom consist of one triangle alone – the apex of each triangle can also be the apex of another. Systems theory similarly would want to look for the interconnecting threads that mean that when part of one relationship alters, other relationships are similarly affected. It is a kind of cat's cradle, a web of connections. Herbie's situation illustrates this well:

Herbie was a mild-mannered man, married to a woman who was something of a tyrant. He was pushed around by her, always feeling unable to make his own decisions. The relationship survived for some years, as long as Herbie was willing to take on this role. Then his mother died. The death of a parent sometimes leads to a radical shake-up in the balance of the relationships in the next generation. Herbie's mother had been a fairly timid and distant person, perhaps a figure with whom he had closely identified. Now Herbie 'found himself involved' (as he put it, as though he was purely the passive recipient of the situation) with a woman who was herself engulfed by her husband. Her situation aroused anger in Herbie towards her husband. He identified how she felt as also being true of his own relationship (and perhaps of his mother's too?). They started an affair, which after a few months was discovered by her husband, who forbade his wife to see Herbie. This she refused to do, trying to seduce Herbie away from his wife, yet at the same time taking fright whenever he seemed prepared to take such a step. Then she distanced herself from Herbie.

Herbie began to feel guilty, but also very angry with this woman, and he described in counselling how he felt just as he did when a child, with his mother being distant, and father making life hell for him. His father would express violent jealousy of mother's affection for Herbie, although Herbie himself never felt that mother had dared express her feelings towards her son. He was therefore angry with the woman's husband for being like his father; and with her for never being brave enough to follow her feelings through. He also felt angry with his wife for being so tyrannical. We see in his marriage an inverted oedipal resolution where Herbie has identified with his mother, and married someone rather more like his father. In his affair he was attempting to set that situation right by choosing a woman more like his mother. But, as can often happen, it was a false solution, with the second woman reinforcing the negative side of his mother, and simply compounding the problem. In despair Herbie left them both, and chose a third woman who was divorced, only to discover after a few months that she was periodically going back to her former husband. History repeated itself in one variation or another at every turn.

There is a further aspect to the triangular relationship which therapy or counselling often invokes. There is a type of intimacy between a therapist and client, which others in the client's life may find difficult to understand and to accept. Therapy can be particularly difficult for partners (including sometimes a counsellor's partner). There are some partners, of course, who are content to let the client be identified as the one with the problem, since it lets them off the hook. They may even support the client on the one hand, while undermining progress on the other by refusing to acknowledge any part they themselves play. Other partners may be jealous of the closeness the client feels with the counsellor, and wonder what is being said about them, often feeling that they are being criticized, which of course is sometimes the case. All these are difficult situations for any counsellor who recognizes the realities of the external world, and does not simply concentrate upon the client's inner experience in the session. There is great value in a client having space and time and separateness, all of which is supported by the privacy of the session. At the same time a partner can feel excluded, creating difficulties rather than helping resolve them, and there may be value in some instances in clients sharing some of what they discuss with their partner.

The solution does not necessarily lie in joint sessions, especially if the second partner is brought in after a long spell of the client being seen alone. The partner can feel with some justification that the counsellor has already taken sides. Offering to see the partner for an occasional session is not necessarily any more helpful. The offer might be considered in some situations for the partner to see a second counsellor possibly leading to a 'foursome' involving both counsellors and both clients. Above all, counsellors and therapists need to be sensitive, even more so when clients make significant progress, to the way such changes may mean the need for adjustments in the client's external relationships. Counselling and therapy sometimes leads to the splitting of partnerships; but it is regrettable when therapy so concentrates upon the client that it does not also help the client to recognize the needs of his or her partner. If the partner is given the opportunity to adapt to what is sometimes a new identity emerging in the client, the partner may also change, with the result that genuine intimacy is for the first time discovered by both.

The rejecting parent

The Oedipus complex suggests different facets in the parent–child relationship. The relationship must not become too intense, but at the same time there should be relaxed expression of the affectionate, aim-inhibited love (as Freud would put it) between mother and son, father and daughter, mother and daughter and father and son. Searles expresses it well when he writes of his own children:

> If a little girl cannot feel herself able to win the heart of her father, her own father who has known her so well and for so long . . . how can the young woman who comes later have any deep confidence in the power of her womanliness . . . ?

Then, writing of his son and his wife:

> . . . their deeply fond, openly evidenced mutual attraction is good for my son as well as enriching for my wife.
>
> (1965a: 296)

A child wishes to reach out, and to say, as it were, 'Let me give you, let me love you, let me touch you', with the emphasis here upon 'you', as distinct from the emphasis upon 'me' which has been present in the earlier narcissistic years. Rejection of what a child offers takes place not only through open hostility, but also through passive distancing; and such a rejecting parent so easily becomes translated into difficulties in making accepting relationships in adult life; or fosters fear of rejection, as well as inhibits the expression of love. The child's love and sexuality need to be affirmed as being good; and yet deflected gently away so that love, including sexual desire, can be offered to and accepted by another when the child becomes an adult. Yet in many triangular situations there is as much frustration as there was in the original parent–child relationship. There are some men and women who always seem to be in search of the unobtainable, and who go through a succession of relationships that do not work out for them as they wish.

> Isadora's father was often abroad on construction work during her childhood and adolescence. As a teenager she was not perhaps unusual in developing a crush on one of the male teachers at school, and she tried to show her love by working especially hard for him. She remembered being very disappointed when he did not remark on her special efforts. When Isadora went to university, as a mature student, she again idolized one of her male tutors. Her work again became a way of pursuing him and she felt sure that he also loved her. When, however, her tutor appeared to respond to her (although it seemed from her account only by a friendly gesture, not a sexual move) Isadora became angry with him for wanting to seduce her; and she left university at the end of her first year. She then got a job in an office, where a manager of a different department would come in and flirt with the typists. At first she thought he was 'dishy', but then began to feel he had his eyes on her. Isadora engineered a meeting with him, and confronted him, asking him just what his intentions were.

Taken aback, the man was angry and unfortunately told Isadora she had a screw loose. So she left that job. When she came to the therapist she was experiencing these feelings all over again in another work situation, although by now she had recognized that she was projecting her wishes for a sexual relationship on to an unattainable father figure, and that she needed to look at the reasons for her turning down the genuine interest shown in her by men who were available to her.

This example is a reminder of the possibility that when a child goes to school, he or she may seek in teachers the affirmation not given at home; or may wish equally to please, to give to and to emulate their teachers as much as they do their parents. Some of these feelings encourage the process of learning. Anna Freud suggests that latency relationships will include love, admiration, dislike and rejection of teachers 'not because they are men or women but because they are either helpful, appreciative, inspiring or harsh, intolerant, anxiety-arousing figures' (1973: 159). Difficulties arise where the relationship becomes more than a positive working alliance: where admiration and love become highly charged, and where acceptance or rejection of the child's love becomes inseparable from acceptance or criticism of the child's work, as in this last example. Problems can also arise where teachers (as can happen with those who teach older adolescents and adults in particular) take advantage of their 'parental' role to seduce their students. The damage to some of these students can be as severe as the damage from seduction by actual parents. Teachers and those who work with the young have to master their own sexuality and oedipal wishes in order to relate appropriately to children and adolescents.

Several writers have drawn attention to the significance of the father for the development of a girl, in her growing confidence as a woman, both in close relationships, and in the workplace. Samuels points out the damage when fathers cannot affirm their daughter's attractiveness: 'The father's failure to participate in a mutual attraction and mutual painful renunciation of erotic fulfilment with his daughter deprives her of psychological enhancement . . . In the absence of Eros . . . the daughter loses sight of herself as a sexually viable adult, with disastrous consequences' (1985: 31). The same is also true of the need for a boy to be loved by his mother, although in many cases the problem here is not lack of affection, but over-closeness. Not a few men are still 'mother's boy'. We have to wonder how these situations might work out in single parent families, or in gay and lesbian partnerships, where there is not the presence of two parents of opposite genders. It is of course too early to know whether these dynamics will be any different, since it is only in recent years that such families have been generally accepted as part of the normal range of relationships in Western society. On the other hand there is plenty of experience of families where a father has been absent literally or emotionally, in some of which it is clear that a grandmother in a three-generation household has performed a similar task, acting as the third force that helps to separate mother and child, and reaffirming the child in his or her value. It is possible that the principle of the third person, whether same gender partner, or grandparent, or even sibling, acts in the same way as the father figure to whom psychoanalytic thought has in one way attached so much importance (although in another way has pushed into insignificance in the emphasis given to early mothering!).

Walker provides an interesting example of the absent father, whose place was filled by a grandmother: during the Second World War. Suzanne's early years were spent with mother and mother's mother, with father away in the forces. His return at the end of the war meant that grandmother had to move into a house nearby. 'Suzanne felt ill at ease with her father and missed her grandmother . . . A year later, when Suzanne was six, her sister was born; the baby was adored by her father. Suzanne remembered feeling lonely and isolated, and spending much of her time with her grandmother, who was in considerable conflict with her father' (1990: 1–21).

In this example it is clear that the returning father displaced an important third figure, and came between child and grandmother in a way which was unhelpful for Suzanne's development as a woman. Another client described how her father's particular form of attention to her was similarly unhelpful:

Jane was the third girl in her family, when her father had desperately wanted her to be a boy. As she grew up, her father encouraged her (but not the other girls in the family) to help him around the house; he took her to football matches; he discussed business matters with her. He did much of what some feminist writers have fathers do, that is introduce their daughters to a particular aspect of the wider world. Jane was happy enough to go along with this, and it meant that she was very close to him, but she had never felt close to her father as a woman, but rather as the son he had never had. Her relationship with her father seemed to have resulted in mother devoting herself more to her sisters than to Jane.

As an adult woman, Jane found it difficult to believe in herself as a woman: she was never sure of how genuine friends were when they complimented her on her clothes she wore, on her cooking, and on other sides of her which she thought of as particularly feminine. She was diffident about making love with her husband, who perhaps made it no easier for her, because sex seemed to satisfy his own needs rather than hers. She felt used by him as she had done by her father, to meet his needs.

Many clients struggle with the ambivalence they have towards one or both parents, on the one hand needing them as love objects, and as protective figures especially during a time of emotional turmoil; on the other hand needing to be able to express their resentment towards their parents for what they have not been able to give them. It is perhaps when they have not received what they would have wished for that they become most protective of their parents when speaking of them in therapy or counselling:

Such push–pull ambivalent feelings were clearly present in Kathy, who while at home was always arguing with her father, and pouring scorn on his lack of education and his ignorant and bigoted views; but away from home at college she told her counsellor how much she adored her father, defended him against any criticism, and even wrote letters back home to him telling him what a great father he was. She very much needed the affirmation she did not really get at home – partly she pushed her father away by looking down on him, since he had disappointed her by not matching her intellectual development. She also found it difficult to express those hostile feelings in her counselling.

A counsellor or therapist has a vital role to play in the need for affirmation. Searles's words cited above come from an article (1965a) in which he explores the feelings of oedipal love for the client which he as the therapist has felt towards the conclusion of therapy. Searles believes that counter-transference feelings of the attractiveness of a client are a sign of the value of the therapeutic work, and of the need to work through the final stages of oedipal loss in therapy. The oedipal situation is implicit in all counselling and therapy, especially although not exclusively where therapist and client are of the opposite gender. There is a fine line for the therapist, as there is for a parent, between accepting and affirming a client's attractiveness and sexuality, and being seductive, such as encouraging the expression of sexual feelings to feed the therapist's narcissism. In addition to accepting the expression of strong loving feelings in a client, a therapist must also be prepared to accept the client's disappointment, frustration and anger at the failure of the therapist to allow the active expression of loving feelings. Sometimes a client's expression of inadequacy or unattractiveness arises because the therapist's distance is related by the client to the way his or her attempts to share loving and sexual feelings towards a parent were pushed away. Just as a counsellor or therapist working with dependent clients has to draw out their feelings of the counsellor's failure to be a permanent source of care and nourishment; or with passive clients' needs to tap into their feelings of the therapist's failure to tell them what to do; so the therapist may need to interpret a client's feelings about his or her failure to become a sexual partner or lover, while at the same time sensitively affirming the client's worth.

Some professional relationships involve considerable intimacy: a nurse or doctor is entrusted with a person's body, and often knows the most intimate details about it. Other professionals are trusted with deeply personal material; and some therapists suggest that psychotherapy of any depth or length is on a par with the closest of human relationships. Psychotherapy and counselling in fact involve a curiously one-sided relationship (Lowe 1972: 220–1), and it is important to draw a distinction between the different types of intimacy present in a helping relationship. It is a unique situation, that stems from a client probably being more open to a therapist than he or she is to anyone else. It does not follow that this inevitably involves the wish for an intimate physical relationship, but this can certainly be experienced in the transference and counter-transference feelings of client and counsellor. Although there is something illusory about this desire for the therapist (as Freud defined illusion, as a wish-fulfilment), it represents a deep need, which is difficult to express, and can be difficult to get right.

Lorna was an attractive woman, and her counsellor (a man) was aware of this, as she described her feelings for him. In the first six months of counselling his positive counter-transference feelings appeared to match hers. He was therefore cautious about taking up what she said, lest he should be encouraging her for his own ends. But when Lorna talked of her need to make men admire her and pay her compliments he had a stronger sense of what was happening to him. What he was experiencing with her was not simply his own wish to be found attractive to her, but the sort of flattery which Lorna sought in the compliments she so much needed from others.

The counsellor became less worried about letting her talk about feelings for him; and he helped her begin to realize that she was valued, without having to dress herself up either literally or metaphorically in everything she said; she did not have to put herself in the best light. Lorna found herself relating to the counsellor as a more ordinary man, no longer idealizing; and outside counselling she began a relationship which went better than usual. She did not ruin it by fishing for compliments in a narcissistic way. It was as if the counsellor's ease with issues of mutual attraction had released Lorna to think more highly of herself.

It was a feature of every session that Lorna found it difficult to stay until the end: she wanted to leave about ten minutes before the end, acknowledging that if the counsellor called a halt to the session, it felt like a rejection of her as someone dull and uninteresting. Towards the end of the counselling contract she brought a complex dream, in which a leopard gently got hold of her arm but would not let her go; and in which there was a tussle over a coffin between herself and someone who reminded her of the counsellor. She was in this scene reluctant to let the coffin go. The counsellor interpreted this feature of the dream as a possible indication of her feelings about ending. There was a part of her that wanted to leave and get away, but there was also a part of her that wanted to stay. It was something like the premature end of each session which she had also described as a tussle: she wanted to leave, while he tried to help her to stay.

Lorna agreed that this was a possibility, but said that she did not experience the counsellor as trying to hang on to her. At this point the session had to end, for it was indeed time for her to go. But as she tried to open the door, she found that the latch on the door was down and she could not get out of the room! The counsellor, looking for a hidden meaning to this 'accident', did not believe in sheer coincidence, and wondered whether he had 'inadvertently' slipped the catch when he had closed the door when she first came in. In his counter-transference he seemed to be struggling with the same issues about ending as her.

The critical parent

There is yet another response to children which affects the way in which they negotiate the Oedipus complex, and come to regard themselves later in adult life. It is related to the issues of critical or destructive authority which belong also to the other themes. A parent who cannot trust a child's exploration of his or her sexuality, or who regards anything sexual as messy or dirty, is liable to cause shame or guilt, and so symbolically castrate the child (boy or girl) when it comes to the expression of genital love. When the early 'masturbatory' gestures in the child are smacked down or harshly rebuked, this is likely to lead to inhibition or guilt about more intentional masturbation in adolescence, as well as about the expression of sexual feelings in relationships. Menstruation or wet dreams might similarly become associated with shame, as an uncontrollable bodily emission fantasized as being 'disgusting'. Masturbation may be a matter of choice, but sexual excitement can be spontaneous: erections or vaginal moistening can be embarrassing when involuntary. These are issues of control which are carried over into this theme of competition, where a parent may feel in some way threatened by the developing sexuality of the child.

Where sex has been frowned on in the parental home, such an attitude can be internalized in the adolescent and adult. Sexual games in childhood might similarly be greeted with parental horror, conveying all the wrong messages to the child:

> As a grown man Matthew was terrified by the fantasy (since it had never occurred in reality) that if ever he got close to a child he would want to touch him or her sexually, and that he would then be imprisoned for this. He told an illuminating story of his mother's reaction when she discovered that a slightly older boy had persuaded Matthew to compare the size of their penises. Although Matthew was only five at the time, he remembered his mother threatening to call the police, and himself hiding under the table in fear of their arrival, because he felt he would also be arrested. Mother's concern, perhaps wanting to punish the older boy, led Matthew to think he had himself committed the crime. She did not realize that sexual games and homosexual activity at this age (and even later) is quite a normal precursor to heterosexual development, and does not indicate either perversion or corruption (see A. Freud 1973: 159).

In addition to the rejection and criticism of a boy's or girl's sexuality, therapists notice plenty of examples, illustrative of issues discussed in the earlier section on masculinity and femininity, of clients recalling the scorn poured on them as children at attitudes or behaviour which were not felt to be consonant with 'being a boy' or 'being a girl'. Boys (and men) do cry, and girls and women do like to get muddy, climb trees, etc. Criticism, particularly by the parent of the same gender, may lead in fact to doubts not just about the self, but also about wanting to identify with him or her, pushing the child towards greater identification with the parent of the opposite gender.

The opposite sex as a threat

Any of the reasons indicated in the sections above can damage or threaten the growing sexual identity of the child: rejection, hostility, criticism or seduction may lead to difficulties relating more completely to others, not just in terms of self-esteem, but also in terms of sexuality. One way in which such difficulties are seen is in the splitting up on to different people of the different aspects of a single loving relationship. Love is an elusive concept, involving different aspects in different contexts, but in an intimate relationship love involves sexuality, companionship and mutual caring. Some clients can only relate as long as the parental, the sexual and the companionable aspects of an intimate relationship are split between two or three different people. One defence for anyone who cannot integrate the different aspects of love in a single relationship is to split off friendship and sexuality, or sexuality and care. The partner may therefore become the parent figure who is there to nurture and protect, while a sexual partner is sought outside the relationship. Some can only relate to another person closely as long as there is no obvious sexual attraction; presented with a sexually exciting person they clam up and do not know how to conduct themselves. In these instances it is as if sexuality has to be inhibited before there can be any form of relatedness. Some people can only be sexually active with a person to whom they are otherwise uncommitted. There are other people – less likely to enter counselling unless they begin to experience the shallowness of their relationships – who seem unable to achieve the aim-inhibited development of their sexuality, and who relate to people only in sexual terms, actually or in fantasy assessing them or treating them only as sexual objects. This balance between the ability to integrate sexuality appropriately into some relationships, and the ability to inhibit it appropriately in others, might be taken as one of the signs of maturity as psychoanalytic thought perceives it.

There are other more sinister ways in which the threat presented by the opposite sex is acted out. Freud described variations in normal infantile sexuality as 'polymorphous perversions', defining them as activities which extend beyond the parts of the body most obviously related to sex (such as foot fetishism) or which linger over aspects of relating sexually which normally are only one part of the total sexual act – touching, or looking, or being seen, for example, which can become exaggerated in voyeurism or exhibitionism (1905: 62). Young people in their first love-objects outside the home sometimes fasten upon isolated physical features in the person whom they idealize – their hair, breasts, ankles, eyes, etc. This is of course not unknown in adults too, judging by the Page 3 of some tabloid papers.

Freud later felt that exhibitionism and voyeurism are also related to castration anxiety. I have already suggested that some of these behaviours lie more appropriately within the theme of control and power (pp. 125–7), but since it is mainly men who offend against women we might indeed wonder whether they are threatened by their own castration anxiety, and have in turn to threaten, in fantasy or in fact, the gender which represents genitally for such men the damaged person they feel themselves to be. Attacks on homosexuals would seem to indicate similar fears about their own sexuality in the perpetrators.

It is necessary to distinguish of course between sexual perversions as abusive and intrusive acts towards women and children, and sexual choices in private adult consenting relationships where it is a case of *chacun à son goût*. An abusive act may be more than an extension of sexual pleasure, being more an attempt to exercise power and domination. The women upon whom the voyeur or exhibitionist preys represent the woman such men feel has emasculated them or will damage them. The phallus, symbolic of power (see above, pp. 151–2), as well as the actual penis, and anxiety about castration combine in one abusive act. By interpreting the penis and the vagina symbolically as well as literally, we may relate these acts to the fear of being swallowed up by a woman, not just genitally, but existentially. According to one feminist source it is because 'the hand that rocks the cradle' is female that men

> fear the will of women and the helplessness of infancy, and employ such strategies to avoid facing their fears as the segregation of men and women at work, in religious activities, in legal and social restrictions on women's rights, and the separation of physical and emotional love to avoid the 'melting' experience of intense intimacy.
>
> (Dinnerstein 1978: 236)

Therapy with sex offenders may be a special area of work, but these anxieties may be present less dramatically in other men. Their primitive fears appear to be projected on to their female victims, who are themselves rendered powerless and fearful, not just because of what has actually happened to them, but also because their experience reflects the position women often feel in society. No counsellor or therapist can overlook the reality of this experience. At the same time, especially when these fears are paralysing a woman's capacity to make relationships with men, therapists not only need to give space for past experiences to be talked through, but also to distinguish the symbolic 'man' from men who as individuals do not act offensively and oppressively.

In a paper on feminism Winnicott used the concept of WOMAN to emphasize that every single person 'was *absolutely* dependent on a woman, and then relatively dependent' (1986: 191, his emphasis). Similarly we might therefore need to distinguish MAN from man, so that individual men are not stereotyped. Some women deny the possibility of trusting men at all. In this respect – in their fear of the opposite sex – male perverts, chauvinists and some separatist feminists appear, for different reasons, to have one thing in common: a symbolic and perhaps also an actual perception of the other gender which is filled with hostility and fear.

> Nora's feminism was based on a serious and convincing analysis of sexual politics. Nevertheless it contained a hostility to men in general which led to a wish to humiliate them intellectually and socially. It was not just her political analysis, but also the extreme terror and humiliation which she experienced when she was raped at the age of eighteen, that had led her to this position. Such an event cannot but have made an indelible impression upon her. Nora imagined that every man she passed as she walked along the street had a gun in his pocket. The fantasy was an obvious reference to her horrifying experience. It happened that Nora first saw a male counsellor for her assessment session, and having been able to broach the fear with him, decided to continue seeing him. He tried to help her to talk about the rape, which up to then she had shared with no one, not even her women friends. He helped her too by understanding her wish to exact revenge. Through this therapeutic relationship Nora began to enjoy the company of men, although she remained cautious about getting too close.

She also began to develop a critique of the sexism that she perceived in some of her feminist friends, which she felt was as damaging to good relationships as the sexism present more generally in society.

The gender of the counsellor or therapist

A number of examples and references have illustrated how the gender of the counsellor or therapist may be important. It may be too threatening for a woman to work with a man, or vice versa, when it is a man or a woman who has been seen as responsible for the damage that the client feels has been done to him or her. On the other hand working with a therapist who represents the feared person, and who does not repeat the trauma or abuse, can be a major step towards a new perspective.

It is often expressed in psychoanalytic writing that it matters little what gender the therapist is, since a client will 'transfer' on to the therapist different attitudes, wishes and fears related either to mother or to father. The maternal and paternal transference is equally possible towards therapists of either gender. Furthermore, therapists may adopt a maternal or paternal stance towards a client: Mohamed and Smith make some apposite observations on this in relation to time-limited psychodynamic therapy (1997: 107–9). But on the other side of this argument, Freud doubted whether he as a man received the same transferences as a woman analyst (1931: 373), and I myself wonder whether gender-blindness, as we might call it, is necessarily common. It is true that where there are early issues of trust and dependency, the maternal side of the counsellor and therapist, man or woman, is paramount – but there are trust and dependency issues in relation to actual men in a person's life as much as to mother, which must be taken as gender-specific. Similarly we have already seen in the second theme that to equate authority with the father is a mistaken notion of family patterns. Some clients will fear a woman counsellor more than a man not because she is paternal, but because it is mother who has been the critical force in the family, especially where the father has taken a passive role.

When it comes to matters concerning sex and sexual orientation, the gender of the therapist is more obviously significant. Clients who specifically ask to see a man or a woman counsellor or therapist are making an important choice, which where possible should be respected, even if in making such a choice these clients are already saying something about themselves which it will in time be useful to explore.

If a particular gender match in the therapeutic relationship works well, this can have a ripple effect upon other relationships. There may be some areas in which it is more difficult for a man to empathize with a woman (and vice versa), but this may be compensated for by the experience of working with a therapist of the opposite gender who listens and makes an effort to understand. Some feminist therapists have challenged the separatist position that only women can work with women, although it is interesting that while the separatist argument can also be applied to the trans-cultural counselling, it is rarely expressed that only male counsellors should see men. The following example illustrates how helpful cross-gender pairing might be:

An American woman hospital chaplain was visiting a very weakened man in intensive care. Mario had collapsed after a violent argument with his wife, who had become an active member of a women's group. On one of the chaplain's visits, Mario had unleashed a flood of anger and resentment, pouring out his feelings about his wife. 'He was one of the angriest and most violent personalities I have ever encountered', writes Chaplain Haines. 'We were two enemies with reason to be suspicious and hostile toward one another. I am a liberated woman; Mario is a machismo man. And still we met on common ground. Each of us represented, to the other, someone who had done something unspeakable to us' (Haines 1978).

It is important to bear in mind that clients who have anxieties about closeness to their own gender may need careful allocation if a choice can be offered. The therapeutic relationship is an intimate one, and initial anxieties in clients need to be respected:

Olivia initially saw a woman therapist for an assessment, and the therapist picked up some anxiety in Olivia, although she had nothing upon which to base this sense. Olivia did not ask for a male therapist, but the assessor referred her to a male colleague. Her intuition was confirmed in the first session that her colleague had with Olivia. She told him that there were things she had been unable to tell the woman she had first seen; and that she never went to women doctors. She had once been involved in a lesbian relationship which continued to upset her, and she obviously feared the re-emergence of such feelings if she saw a woman doctor or therapist.

Exhibitionism and being on show

The interplay between the major themes is illustrated in examples of fear of being in the spotlight – a reaction perhaps against a form of exhibitionism; or even in the need to be on show, albeit in a non-sexual way. There is something perhaps narcissistic about this latter desire although it can be socially acceptable narcissism, such as in professional acting. There are other factors involved in being on show, because the stage or screen is a place where different roles can be taken on temporarily and acted out, by actors for themselves, and on the audience's behalf. This type of exhibitionism and narcissism (which I am not portraying as pathological) can be seen in other forms of work and play where people can bask in admiration and applause. Sometimes these people (and this often applies to public figures as well) may also be quite distant in their relationships 'off stage', as if they have a more fragile sense of identity in private. There are therefore plenty of metaphorical stages where people take on roles, and hide behind masks. In this example both aspects are obvious:

Pat had never felt affirmed as a girl by her father, who spent his spare time fishing, away from the home. She was also unable to allow herself any sexual relationship, and was even afraid of being touched. She had been sexually abused by a much older brother. As someone involved in amateur dramatics she not only received some sense of value from the audience's applause, but was also able to play the sexual woman on stage. But if one of her fellow actors ever asked her out, she always refused, even steering clear of post-production parties.

The need to put oneself forward, and to sell oneself, is often a key factor in career and academic success. Ambition involves being comfortable with competitiveness and with showing oneself off. Indeed, it is something which a child needs to feel comfortable with when starting out into the world: success at school depends to some extent on the child's capacity to demonstrate her or his abilities. In a home where there is a repressive attitude to 'showing off', a child may be reluctant to stand out in a class. Certain topics, such as creative writing, require not only imagination, but a certain amount of positive exhibitionism in order to reveal one's ideas, and other sides of oneself. Conversely, it is possible to find examples where clients' shyness and inhibition is linked to a conflict in themselves about their wish to be 'on show' and 'out in front':

Rachel arrived for counselling with a beautiful smile and a striking red beret – these were the first impressions the college counsellor had of her. She had recently started at college as a mature student, but could not go into lectures, because she felt faint in the crowded room. She was able to identify the first occasion of this feeling as the third week of term in one particular lecture.

During the initial session she related how she had once wanted to go to college to study drama, but she had had to go out to work. She had been able to enjoy her interest in drama through amateur societies. She was fine, even now, in crowded rooms, when she felt she was 'the life and soul of the party'. She could not understand what had made her feel so bad in the lecture room. She did not want to faint and 'make an exhibition of myself'.

While she was talking the counsellor registered a number of these phrases, put them together in his thinking, and tested out an interpretation; that though Rachel did not want to make an exhibition of herself, she might also feel frustrated at having to sit still and listen when she liked to be up front entertaining. Her eyes lit up, and she capped his explanation with a forceful condemnation of the lecturer who was teaching at the time when she first felt faint. He was dreadfully boring, he did not allow anyone else the chance to speak, or to ask questions, or make a contribution themselves. It was as if she needed to 'protest' in some way (by fainting or walking out because she felt she might faint) both at the boredom of the lecture, and also at her inability to 'show off' herself, since she could be much more entertaining than him.

Showing ability at certain academic subjects may also be related to the ease with which a child at school or an older student feels comfortable with themself and their body: biology, sport, dance and drama all involve interest and pleasure in the body as well as in the total self; or certain subject areas may be associated with being a stereotypical man or woman, and some subjects may be seen as too 'cissyish' or 'only for boys'. There is greater freedom and opportunity to learn where sexuality and sexual identity are not pressing issues that intrude upon other activities. One of the major problems for learning in adolescence, when so much depends upon being able to secure academic or technical qualifications, is that some of the learning evokes the very emotions to which adolescence is so open. Some young people find it too difficult to hold together their studies of certain areas with their emotional volatility, and either push away their studies, or repress their feelings by using an intellectual defence and becoming over-immersed in their books.

There is a particular form of exhibitionism which is seen in the client who shows off sexually – traditionally called the 'hysteric', although the term has largely become a pejorative label which provides little in the way of understanding of such men and women. These people sometimes flaunt their sexuality, but quickly cut and run if a relationship gets too close. In this example, the counsellor appeared to get beneath the obvious presentation:

> Steve talked for a number of sessions about his relationships with women and his fantasies about them, and led the counsellor to think Steve saw women only as sexual playthings. Eventually the counsellor chanced a remark about all this sexual talk being something of a red herring, and Steve broke down and cried. He began to speak about feeling unloved, unwanted and useless, particularly in relation to his mother. For the first time the counsellor felt she had touched a more genuine side of Steve than the previous bravado had ever allowed her to see.

Although hysterics have commonly been identified as women who taunt and tease, there are plenty of men who do the same, seen perhaps in this last example, and certainly in the Don Juan character. In classical psychoanalytical literature it is difficult to find the term 'hysteric' being used of this type of person. In Fenichel's encyclopaedic work *The Psychoanalytic Theory of Neurosis* (1946), the term does not appear in the comprehensive index. The closest to it is a section on character disorders; and where Fenichel describes the histrionic person and the schizoid character we find parallels to the stereotypical 'hysteric'.

We have in such presentations a further example of the way in which the major themes set out in this book interweave, and how what a client presents may be understood in different ways, depending upon which perspective we take: the theme of trust and dependency, for example, might just as well help us understand this type of presentation of sexuality as the theme of competition and cooperativeness. To be sure, there is a certain metaphorical 'castrating' by such people of those who try to get close to them. But counsellors or therapists trying to work with such clients, if they can help them to stay in therapy, will find problems that run deeper than sexuality, such as a deep hunger for love, and yet a terror of rejection. It is important not be seduced by the excitement of the sexual presentation or to be repelled by distaste of it. It will in time be necessary to interpret deeper levels than the sexual, and counsellors who work short-term may want to refer such clients for longer term work. Fenichel suggests that there are pre-oedipal factors at work in these presentations. Sex is used as a substitute for a more primitive need, such as the wish to be reunited with mother; and the sexual greed which is often apparent is a substitute for infantile needs of love. The flight of such people indicates their ambivalence about closeness.

Jenny was very perceptive about her feelings, and could see what was happening in her regular seduction and dropping of men. She experienced three clear gains for her each time, although she felt some regret afterwards. First, she wanted to give a man such a good time that he was left with a memory of her as someone really special. Second, she chose men who thought they were macho, and she so dominated them in sex that they felt weak and inferior. She compounded this by never speaking to them again, just nodding at them if they met in a condescending way. She admitted she got great pleasure from seeing such 'fine' examples of manhood become so submissive. Third, Jenny enjoyed other women admiring the way she could pick up men and be so disparaging of them afterwards.

There seemed to be a link between her present behaviour and her childhood. For years she had been her father's special favourite, but she was suddenly pushed out of favour when he remarried: his new wife came between them. She hated her father for this. At the same time, while some of this material was obviously linked to oedipal problems, Jenny described her need to treat men the way she did as 'like a drug' – with the possibility that the loss of her mother early in her life had led to this deep hunger for revenge.

Rivalry and competition as a lifelong process

Apart from the rivalry involved in the oedipal triangle, three-person and other competitive situations arise throughout life. This section illustrates some of the ways in which these are seen in the presenting and underlying issues brought by clients to counselling and therapy.

Apart from the parent–child rivalry, there is of course sibling rivalry, with older children having to make way for new members of the family, and younger children born into a shared environment of care. Order in the family, the gap between births, and many other factors need to be taken into account in assessing the impact of new siblings, but when a sibling is born before the older child has become relatively independent of mother, there may be stronger rivalry:

Una was apparently devoted to her younger sister, born when she was eighteen months old. Yet there were signs that beneath the devotion there was much jealousy. Una had been told by her mother that she used to hug her little sister so tightly as a baby that mother thought she was going to strangle her – although Una thought it was because she loved her so much. In her dreams Una would sometimes scratch her sister – even doing this once when sleep-walking. Una was a member of an anti-abortion group, and as a teenager she had sorely tested a close friendship when she told her pregnant girlfriend that she was a whore. Both these factors made the therapist wonder what Una made of her mother's pregnancy when her sister was expected. She was very competitive in nearly everything she did, jealous about anyone else doing well, even when another's success cost her nothing. Over a long period of therapy Una saw how she had felt pushed out by her sister. It may have been significant that she stopped campaigning against abortion, and became much more understanding of the dilemmas facing women. It may have been that her fanaticism was a reaction against her own wish to kill her young rival while still in the womb.

Where there is a miscarriage or still-birth, or the death of a sibling, a child's fantasy of getting rid of the new arrival and rival (often expressed in the apparently innocent phrase 'Can we send baby back now, Mummy?') might cause a child to think their wish has brought this about, in turn leading to a sense of guilt. Rivalry may also be felt in a more obvious way in pregnancy and at the birth of a child by the father, who not only feels pleased, but may also feel excluded. Sex may of course be more difficult during his partner's pregnancy, and the baby may feel like a rival for her care and attention. A few men develop physical symptoms which seem to indicate a sympathetic pregnancy of their own; others turn away from their partner and engage in an affair.

Nursery groups, play groups and school provide for the social development of the child, and for some their first taste of competitive situations. At the same time, children can benefit from learning that they and their peers have varying abilities in different areas. These experiences also encourage co-operative play and learning. 'Mutual play is a keystone in social development', writes Rayner, observing the way in which play requires a child to sympathize with others as having their own needs (1986: 108). In their play children make and break alliances, and forge and forget friendships. Erikson calls this period 'the infantile politics of nursery school, street corner and barnyard' (quoted by Lowe 1972: 91). Children's games and make-believe give them opportunities to fight and make it up, to share power and leadership, as part of the preparation for living as adults in a wider society. Co-operative work in pairs and in groups might be preferable to the subordination of learning to competitive tests and examinations, although this seems far from the spirit of what governments and the inevitably competitive business world wants. What is perhaps frightening, as Erikson writes in *Toys and Reasons* (1978), is not that children should play such games, but that adults (particularly politicians) do not appear to have grown beyond them.

A certain degree of competitiveness is essential for success in life, sometimes in love, often in work. Lack of confidence, low self-esteem or anxiety about losing in competitions may cause all kinds of difficulty. Behind the unwillingness of some people to engage in competitive situations, even those where it really does not matter who wins or loses, we may find shame at lack of success in the past, although there are also some people who appear to react against their unconscious wish to triumph over others.

Other people can become over-competitive, being fanatical over their support for a team, as if the team carries their need to triumph over others. Rivalry with others can become so intense that healthy competition (the wish to achieve what others achieve) disappears, and aggressive competition takes its place. The pressure from some parents for academic success for their child (as if the child is as much a status symbol for them as their car, their house and the latest gadget) may serve a child well in the examination system, but can cause great difficulties later in their education or their career. Alternatively, inhibition of the ability to work may arise from unfavourable comparison with others. A combination of factors is seen in this example:

Victor had lost his father a few months before he was due to go up to university. He initially deferred his place for a year in order to help his mother to cope. University was at first an easy enough place for him, and a relief from the sadness at home. But by his third year Victor explained to a counsellor that some of his difficulty in working academically was because his mother had invested so much hope in his success. He felt he was being asked to work hard to give her the same sort of pleasure she had gained from her husband's success and popularity. Victor felt he had slipped too far into his father's shoes, and not studying was one way of trying to get out of the predicament.

Depending upon the levels of unemployment at a given time in society, seeking work may mean intense competition. Application forms, interviews, and rejections are almost inevitable, for young and old alike; and getting a particularly sought-after job may involve some guilt at succeeding at the cost of others who have not. Professional sportsmen and women often require what is called the 'killer instinct' – the ability to drive the winning stroke home: by contrast some people are concerned at meeting other applicants at interview, because their success will mean another's failure. They find it difficult to present themselves well:

Will (although not a serious sportsman) described his difficulty over winning at tennis. He felt he gave up trying just at the point at which he could win a match, particularly when he was playing his father, even though Will was the better player. This seemed to be the case in interviews too: he felt so bad about out-doing the others waiting with him that he fluffed every interview, until he attended an interview which did not involve meeting the other candidates. This time he was able to secure the position.

The impact of second marriages and of stepfamilies should not be forgotten, as providing occasion for fierce rivalry between step-parent and child, or siblings in a reconstituted family:

Yolande's mother died when she was twelve. Her father remarried a year later. Yolande was very angry, because she thought her mother had been forgotten; but also for herself, since she was pushed out from her special closeness to her father in their shared grief. As soon as she was old enough, she left home to live with a man who was old enough to be her father. She continued to be what she described as 'insanely jealous' of other women, and would not permit her partner to go out for a drink with his friends. She would cause scenes on many mornings when he was leaving for work. To compound the picture, her partner's mother was also very jealous of Yolande, as indeed she had felt about her son's previous girlfriends. Yolande's greatest fear was that her man would look at other women and lose interest in her. Her partner, who came with her for joint counselling, may not have realized how significant the phrase was, when he described her relationship to himself as 'almost incestuous'.

There is a different sort of rivalry which is apparent in adolescence between parents and their growing children. At the same time as young people are finding work and making their first close relationships, their parents may be conscious of imminent or present changes in themselves. A mother may be anticipating the menopause as the daughter has her first periods. A father may be aware of his spreading midriff and lack of muscular tone as his son is reaching the peak of physical fitness. It would be surprising if parents did not in some way feel jealous of their teenage children, aware of their own past youth, and sometimes envious of the freedoms and opportunities which were less openly available to them when they were young. Winnicott describes it well, sympathizing with the problems of being a parent:

> Your rewards come in the richness that may gradually appear in the personal potential of this or that boy or girl. And if you succeed you must be prepared to be jealous of your children who are getting better opportunities for personal development than you had yourselves. You will feel rewarded if one day your daughter asks you to do some baby-sitting for her, indicating thereby that she thinks you may be able to do this satisfactorily; or if your son wants to be like you in some way, or falls in love with a girl you would have liked yourself had you been younger.
>
> (Winnicott 1971: 168)

There may be rivalries as the young adult sets up in a relationship with a partner, obviously someone from outside the family and its values. Conflicts with in-laws may indicate an unwillingness to let go of child and parental roles. A person's parents (in his or her internal world) may intrude upon their own close relationship (Freud once wrote that there are four other people present in the bedroom): in one extreme instance a client told how he found it difficult making love to his wife because he kept thinking she had turned into his mother. The parent–child relationship is inevitably carried over into the husband–wife relationship, with all the positive and negative features of the original relationship enhancing or impeding the present one. In some instances these rivalries will be made more difficult because of living arrangements, such as early in a relationship, where a young couple has of necessity to live for a time with one set of parents; or later in a relationship where a widowed parent is brought into the family home. These are not easy situations, but they are even harder when oedipal ties interfere.

Rivalries can of course exist between the two partners in a couple. Competitive anxieties about gender and role can lead to tensions:

> Adam had always been the major bread-winner in the family. When he was made redundant it was natural that he should have felt depressed. But his depression was made worse through having no income of his own and becoming dependent upon his wife's salary. He became increasingly angry with her and women generally. In his counselling it was a long time before the counsellor (a woman) was able to create a sense of equal partnership,

because Adam also resented her having an occupation. But he was eventually able to tell her that he was also depressed because his situation had made him almost totally sexually impotent.

Winnicott's recognition of the pleasure that accompanies some rivalry, pleasure for the success of the child or another loved person, takes an interesting twist in old age. No doubt the same issues of rivalry can be directed towards the younger generation, but there is a particular pleasure which Hanns Sachs (1948) refers to, that of reading the obituary columns and forgiving old acquaintances for those things in them which have irritated us, because with each death we have triumphed over them by outliving them!

Rivalry and competition is also present in the relationship with the therapist and counsellor. Clients sometimes refer to others the counsellor sees, as if they are wondering how important they are in comparison.

Bob arrived for his session after a three week break. In fact the break had been intended to be two weeks, but the day that he should have met his therapist again, she was ill and had to cancel. When the two of them met, Bob asked her whether she had seen her other clients that week – he imagined he was the only one she didn't want to see.

He went on to say that he felt his mother was more interested in his sister and her children than in him; and how distant he felt from his wife, who was expecting their first child. These references all clearly linked to show the struggle he had with rivalrous situations.

A counsellor's outside relationships may also be the subject of interest, or occasions for jealousy:

Calum had always felt inferior to his brother, and Calum's wife, before he had met her, had been his brother's girlfriend. One night Calum dreamed of anger and jealousy towards a dark-haired man. When he associated to this dream in therapy, he realized that the dream had occurred the night after seeing his therapist at a concert with her dark-haired husband.

There is one further aspect to rivalry, which accords with Winnicott's view of parents and their growing children. Counsellors and therapists need to have come to terms with their own oedipal issues, so that they can rise above issues of rivalry with their client. Hartung (1979) particularly relates this issue to supervision, and the need for teaching to be 'done in order that students finally surpass the teacher'. There are also interesting issues of competition in supervision which Searles (1965b: 601) raises; but in the context of counselling clients, therapists should not cling to their status as authority figures, and should always be working with the aim of clients becoming equal, or better, at the business of understanding themselves. Whatever jealousy and envy may arise in the transference, there is no place for rivalry in a good working alliance (Greenson 1967: 190–216).

Being single

With so much in this theme concerning intimate relationships, we must consider the status of those who do not conform to the norm of being in permanent or serial sexual relationships, at least as understood in psycho-analytic perceptions of adulthood as well as in society at large. It must be remembered that definitions of psychological maturity, whether as an individual person, or in relation to others, are culturally determined, as we see from the way psychoanalytic thought has had to adapt to changing attitudes. Furthermore, although Freud's famous definition of maturity was 'to love and to work', how a society understands love and work at any one time is also a changing concept. People work, even if they are not in employment. People are in loving relationships even if they choose to stay single. Much that can be defined as healthy depends perhaps more upon the inner state of mind than upon external appearances.

We have therefore to be cautious of psychological and societal norms. Erikson (1965), for example, in his scheme of the Eight Ages, believed that before the stage of intimacy a young person must achieve a sense of personal identity; that before coming together with another, there must be a securely based sense of self. Rayner (1986: 192, 196–7) argues that women's comparatively greater discontent with long-term partnerships, which is well documented, might be related partly to their losing much of their identity (characteristically, losing their surname in legal marriage). Nevertheless feminist critics have rightly observed that Erikson's model is male-centred, since it is men who fear losing their identity in closeness more than women. Intimacy and self-identity are issues that run throughout life, not being confined to a particular stage of young adulthood.

Societal expectations for early marriage and childbearing are less obvious in Western society, although they are still prevalent in many other non-white communities even in the West. In addition to these pressures, there are those who find it impossible to contemplate living alone or being alone, and seek for a parent substitute in an early partnership. Some young men look for an immediate replacement for mother, so they never really leave home, particularly in teenage marriage where adolescence is foreshortened. For some young women early pregnancy may also be a way of avoiding being alone, projecting their dependency needs on to their child. Similarly early pregnancy in a new partnership may be a way of avoiding intimacy in just being a couple.

> David's eighteen-month-old relationship had just broken up. He was, of course, very upset, but perhaps as much because he was losing the promise of the home they were going to set up, as because his partner had left him. They had lived together all that time and were creating a secure place in which he enjoyed doing things around the house. He was eighteen. He also spoke in the first session of his parents' separation, when his mother had walked out on him and his father. He went into great detail about the domestic arrangements at that time. The counsellor observed that the present break was all the more painful because he and his partner had been re-creating what he had lost when he was eleven. David agreed, but hastened to add, rather defensively it felt, that his girlfriend was *not* a mother-substitute. A few weeks later he had moved in with an older separated woman.

> Ellen became pregnant when she was seventeen outside the context of a steady relationship. She had been the apple of her family's eye as a baby when she was the only child. When she was two, her brother was born and

her mother told her how her princess-like behaviour changed to constant tantrums. Ellen herself said she had been depressed 'as long as I can remember'. She recalled dreams since early childhood, still occurring now, with images of being locked out, left out, left behind, pushed out, etc. She described herself as 'like a leech' although she also appeared so independent now that it suggested a fear of what might happen if she allowed herself to become attached. Her baby was an attempt to recreate the intense relationship with her mother from which she had experienced her brother's birth as separating her. When her baby was born she put him forward for adoption.

A very high proportion of adults live relatively alone in Western society, some of them single parents with children, some perhaps in community accommodation, such as the elderly. The number of single people appears to be rising, so that despite political sermons about the importance of the family, the traditional nuclear family is nowhere near the norm. Adults living alone are therefore as much part of the counsellor's clientele as those in committed sexual relationships. Some are alone by choice, and others by circumstance, such as the widowed, those whose partners have left, or those who have spent their life looking after parents. Being single may be a problem, but it also may not. There are, for example, distinct advantages in being single, such as the opportunity to withdraw and (as one person put it) 'shut the front door on other people'. A single person need not be without close companions and deep friendships, yet have the bonus of being more free to move, change jobs, make decisions, without the ties of partner and children. Care for others, as well as the generativity and creativity which Erikson associates closely with mid-adulthood, may be expressed in a person's work and interests rather than in partnership and family.

The single status has its own difficulties. Single parents, for example, frequently have to combine two functions, which we might call maternal and paternal, without allocating a specific gender to either role. They generally experience less freedom and greater financial problems than two-parent families. A single parent may have chosen this extra strain instead of the tensions of being in a destructive relationship, but others may have been deserted by their partner:

> Fran described what it had been like bringing up her two children single-handed for five years, contrasting that period with the time since she had remarried. She said how difficult it had been to be both mother and father. It wasn't all sweetness now because 'Daddy is the good guy and I'm seen as the bad guy when he comes home from work, but that is far better than being the bad guy, and having no one to share your feelings with, or to discuss how to handle the kids.'

Single people can experience themselves as being felt to be a threat to couples. A single woman, perhaps divorced or a relatively young widow, can be viewed with suspicion by some women in partnerships. Such feelings of rivalry, although not the single person's issue, can be hard to endure. A single person whose life has been intimately bound up with their work, and has found their principal companions through work, may find retirement or redundancy even harder to manage, although of course some marriages are equally put under enormous strain when in such circumstances the partners are forced too closely together:

Gabby had never married and she had no family responsibilities, so she chose to leave her job when she was offered the opportunity of early retirement. She was able to indulge herself in the reading and thinking which she had always wanted to enjoy. In many respects she seemed to have adjusted well to this way of life; but she had an egocentricity about her which was not the same as the self-contentment often found in an older person. She did not show the same interest which older people often do in those who are younger than themselves. To those who knew her, there seemed a hollow ring to Gabby's constant recommendation: 'You just get out of the rat race. It's the best thing I've ever done.'

In summary, the issues which trouble a single person need be no different from those which concern those in intimate relationships. There are specific areas of concern to each, but being single need not be seen as a failure to relate. Indeed the capacity to be alone has already been seen as a vital developmental achievement, which I discussed as part of the first theme (pp. 81–2). The avoidance of being alone can be understood as a difficulty. Rayner writes that 'to find one's identity it seems centrally important to be *able to be alone . . . alone with one's conscience* (1986: 192, his emphasis). Actual aloneness is also very much part of life: becoming single will be a common experience, as people adjust to being alone at various points such as separation, divorce, the death of a partner, redundancy and retirement. In any relationship too there needs to be an ebb and flow between closeness and solitude. Couples who are too closely bound up in each other appear to be afraid of separating out. Each individual in a partnership needs space to work through his or her particular concerns, alone as well as together.

There are of course instances where a counsellor or therapist wonders whether the single person has difficulties about initiating and maintaining relationships, either of an intimate or a companionable kind. The type of non-sexual relationships, or even the type of sexual relationships (such as the promiscuous) may provide indications as to the apparent psychological health of being single. There may be difficulties breaking the parent–child bond sufficiently to engage freely with others, where the 'child-in-the-adult' cannot leave the actual or internalized parent in order to make other relationships. Living alone may indicate a defence against intimate relationships, which, as long as it works, need not of course be of concern. Fear of closeness may indicate schizoid characteristics (see pp. 60–1), but there are plenty of people with schizoid traits who enter into committed relationships, and are far more lonely in those than single people are in theirs.

Coming together: towards integration

When working on phrases to describe each of the major themes I toyed with others than *cooperation* and competition. Looking for an alliterative ring, I thought of 'coherence' or 'complementarity', but these words indicated too neat a fit, when in fact relationships in the inner world and the external world can work together without having to fit precisely. I thought of 'coexistence', but this was too separate and static a term. Cooperation in the end appeared to express the need to work psychologically towards bringing together parts of oneself, as well as to aspects of relating; although each of the terms I have thought of expresses something of what is involved in the search for contentment and satisfaction.

Freud's original ideas consider the release of tension as our constant aim, without really taking into account the relationships which help this to take place. Later he stresses the need to live by the principle of reality, rather than the principle of pleasure. He also portrays the reality principle as consisting of the need for the central ego to balance the demands of the id, the super-ego and the external world. Klein describes the state of relative equilibrium as the depressive position, one which is able to contain love and hate, and other contradictory emotions, as well as one which shows concern for others as well as self. But the paranoid position is always lurking round the corner, even when things are going relatively well! Erikson elaborates a scheme in which the different strengths of each developmental age come together in the eighth age of ego integrity. Jung wrote of progress, particularly in the second half of life, towards individuation, which is more than a sense of individual identity. It also involves integration of the unconscious, the collective unconscious, and a sense of one's place in the wider scheme of things.

Most of these states of mind describe the inner world, in which different 'parts' or 'objects' need to relate cooperatively. In external relationships cooperation and conflict are seen in the way people relate closely, socially, in work, politically and internationally, as well as how they relate to the environment. The elements that go to make up external and internal relationships have been followed through in the three major themes, described in this chapter and the two that precede it.

Following Winnicott we might also see life as a perpetual adaptation to the environment, or following Erikson as a continuous process of finding identity. Identity achieved at one point probably never stands still for long, even when our basic core of identity is relatively fixed, which is why the early experiences of the child are so vital for later life. What we might hope for is a sufficiently secure sense of self, or ego, or individuality, to meet and work with the inevitable changes that growing up and growing older bring. In the psychological typology of adolescence referred to in the last chapter (p. 137), there is a very different character than the foreclosed adolescent. It is the questioning, identity-seeking adolescent, who, when asked to describe him- or herself, tends to reply, 'I am searching, I am wondering, I am curious' (Marcia 1975). Such a description fits well the adult who is open to development. It also indicates a vital quality in those who best use the help which counselling and psychotherapy have to offer.

The process of change involves introspection, imagination, a capacity to look back as well as look forward, an empathic concern for the impact of personal change upon others, as well as healthy narcissistic concern for oneself. The major points of life for the majority of the population involve having to handle cooperative relationships, with their inevitable conflicts and competitiveness.

Making close relationships normally involves some matching, such as the complementarity of male and female, or of different qualities in a mutually enriching partnership. When working with couples it is helpful to consider the obvious and the unconscious ways in which partners 'fit', what they project on to each other, and how far they identify with each other (see for example Dominian 1980; Skynner and Cleese 1983: 14–18). Complementarity seems to work better when one partner is able to respect the individuality of the other, and can enjoy the other having features and qualities (physical, sexual and personal) which they do not themselves possess. The partner is then not someone to be feared, used or envied. He or she does not become an object upon whom the partner projects, and then criticizes or attacks, what is unacceptable in themselves. Rather the partner is appreciated for providing those qualities one does not have, or some skills in which one is not so proficient. Complementarity is the occasion for positive identification with a partner when it works well; but for jealousies and other negative feelings when it does not.

Relationships also have to adapt to changing circumstances, as a couple do when becoming parents. Rayner emphasizes that:

as a child grows, so it is necessary for a parent to change in sympathetic responsiveness to his/her child. This entails not only being intuitively aware of himself at equivalent ages to the child, but also being aware of his own life and his child's life as separate and with differing present-day problems.
(1986: 203, his italics)

So co-operative relationships do not remain static, and in addition to changes in parent and child, each partner is more or less changing. In the early years of a marital type of partnership there are likely to be changes of home and of jobs. Some career changes bring different identities with them for one or other partner. There may be geographical relocations which involve making new friendships, more easily made when there are children at home, or other social interests that take people outside the home. If in becoming parents a couple changes, this happens just as much when grown children leave home. Some couples take a 'second honeymoon' at such times, but we notice that divorce rates are at their highest at significant points like this: in the first two years (when it is discovered that intimacy does not work); after seven to eleven years (when the children are at their most demanding); after twenty or so years (when the children have left home); and at retirement age.

The work setting provides many opportunities for cooperation and conflict. It is beyond the scope of this book to look at this specific context, although there is a growing literature on the dynamics of the work setting (Obholzer 1994), and on counselling at work (Carroll 1996; Carroll and Watton 1997; Greenwood, in press). Part of the satisfaction of work in the past has been a sense of belonging, of having taught younger people the skills of a job, and upon retirement handing over responsibility, knowing that one has helped others to take over. In a society where jobs are not for life, and where it is rare to work for a single institution or company in one place for more than ten years, the continuity of past employment practices and its attendant psychological rewards have largely passed. Change is frequent in work as well.

Many people at retirement now have ten or twenty years of life ahead of them, with opportunities for them to develop, dependent to some extent upon attitude, as well as upon finance. But one feature of ageing is the way in which the presenting past comes alive in a new way. Ageing provides time for life as a whole to be reviewed. Memory can play tricks, although sometimes memories of the more distant past are clearer than those of more recent events. Perhaps the unconscious need not be feared so much; perhaps the super-ego, those internalized parents, ceases to exert so strong a hold; perhaps what has been repressed comes through in a fine balance of positive and negative experiences – hardship in childhood, for instance, can be remembered for what it was, but its positive qualities are recalled as well. Rayner describes old people as living historians to society (1986: 255), but their history is just as important to themselves. Older people enjoy telling their history, and in this telling of old stories there is a reworking of their life, which Lowe (1972: 225) lists under the Erikson stages: whom one has learned to trust (1); what to hold on to and what to let go (2); initiatives taken (3); practical and social skills (4); confirmation of identity (5); marriage (6); and work (7).

Change, long before old age, means coming to terms with loss, as certain relationships, old patterns, and tangible objects and occupations have to be let go. Involved in all loss, but more obviously following the death of a parent, child or partner, a significant process of change involves the internalization of the person who has gone. C. S. Lewis describes such a process in the diary written after the death of his wife, a story now familiar through the play and film *Shadowland*:

> Something quite unexpected has happened. It came this morning early. For various reasons, not in themselves at all mysterious, my heart was lighter than it had been for many weeks. For one thing I suppose I am recovering from a good deal of mere exhaustion, and after ten days of low hung grey skies and motionless warm dampness, the sun was shining and there was a light breeze. And suddenly, at the very moment when so far, I mourned H. least, I remembered her best. Indeed it was something almost better than memory: an instantaneous unanswerable impression. To say it was like a meeting would go too far. Yet there was that in it which tempts one to use those words. It was as if the lifting of the sorrow removed a barrier. Why has no one told me these things? How easily I might have misjudged another man in the same situation. I might have said, 'He's got over it. He's forgotten his wife', when the truth was, 'He remembers her better because he has partly got over it.'
>
> (Lewis 1971)

The ability to carry on living, with confidence in oneself, after such a loss, depends upon a number of factors. Where a relationship has been brief and only touched the surface, separation is likely to be felt as a simple memory: good, bad or indifferent. Where the relationship has been more extensive and has reached into deeper feelings, the situation is more complex. One which has caused hurt and damage leaves a particular memory, together with pain and caution about relating on the same level again. But most relationships of any depth contain good and bad feelings. Perhaps what is important is how we perceive the feelings towards us of the person we have lost. Yet even that perception may be influenced by our view of ourselves – especially if we have underlying uncertainties about ourselves carried over from early experience. We may feel the other did not care, when in fact he or she did. Any anger we then feel, however unjustified, makes the process of internalization difficult.

Where the relationship has been felt overall to be a good, caring and loving one, then of course that person will be greatly missed; but in time sadness will be combined with the pleasure that comes from recalling positive memories, and from the internalized figure bringing sustenance and strength to the self. There will be no need to cling, no need to rail. Instead there is quiet content-ment, a feeling of good fortune, a deep sense of having been added to; and we can say with conviction, 'I'm glad we knew each other.' Recalling the phrase cited in the list of stages of grief in Chapter 1, 'The loved object is not gone, for now I carry it within myself and can never lose it' (Abraham 1927).

For some people, and in some societies, religious beliefs, images, symbols and rituals assist the process of change, enable coming to terms with loss, and promote psychological integration. A person's faith can be repressive, or can reflect some of their psychological problems, and I have shown ways religion can be so used or misused in both the earlier themes (pp. 67, 89–90, 110–112). Other expressions of faith are much more mature, although I am aware that maturity is a highly subjective concept. I examine these different expressions of faith fully in my book on a psychology of belief, *Living Illusions* (1993a), par-ticularly in the chapters that show how faith can become more integrative, drawing upon different resources in terms of the unconscious as well as poetry, art, and other religions. There can develop a faith position which is essentially cooperative, and coherent, and which in the end proceeds to acknowledge just how much we do not know and do not understand; but in certain respects comes full circle, so that we know old things in new ways.

Full circle? There is certainly a circularity about development, which these three themes have illustrated: a process which is never completed, but is repeated in many forms and at different ages: in forming bonds of trust, in moving from dependency to independence, in becoming more autonomous; in letting go aspirations about relationships with parents, and instead identi-fying with them and leaving them behind; in learning and in training, in work and in play. These patterns recur through adolescence, in first and subsequent relationships outside the family, in becoming a parent and grandparent, at retirement, through bereavement and in approaching death. It is a process not only of relating to others, but of internalizing them in the building up of the self. The continually developing self relates anew to others and becomes, in turn, internalized in part in them. The mirroring of mother and baby in the nursing couple takes place in all kinds of relationships throughout life.

Counselling and therapy have been recognized as legitimate ways of help-ing people deal with crises in this development, by reviewing and reliving the present and the past, and by working out new ways to meet the future. The major themes in these three chapters are just as significant in the therapeutic relationship, where they can be seen being worked out in detail. It is these aspects of trust and dependency, authority and autonomy, and cooperation and competition that the final chapter roots in the interaction of the therapist and client themselves.

MAJOR THEMES IN
THE THERAPEUTIC
RELATIONSHIP

While the core of psychodynamic counselling and therapy is the presenting past, it is certainly not the past alone that is at the centre of the work. It is rather the way the past *presents* itself *currently* in the *here-and-now* of the therapeutic relationship. Such triple emphases on my part here are necessary to correct somewhat forcefully the erroneous impression that those who criticize psychodynamic counselling and therapy have of it. The past is only relevant in as much as it is present, still in the mind of the client. It is also present in that type of 'living laboratory' of therapy, in which counsellors and therapists are presented with opportunities to re-experience with their clients certain aspects of their presenting past; in which the effects of the past can be reviewed; and through which the effects can be to some extent adapted to the new circumstances of the present and the future.

I have already questioned the usefulness of a stage model in relation to personality development, at the same time acknowledging the significance of certain clear events – single events such as birth and death, and continuous events such as childhood, adolescence, and ageing. All of the issues arising in the major themes may be present at any of these occasions or at these periods of time. We similarly need to question whether a stage model can be applied to the process of therapy or counselling, even though there clearly is a beginning, a middle and an end. All of the major themes can be present at any of these points: so that the trust which is so important in the beginning of therapy has also to be present at the end, as the client sets out without any further assistance from the therapist. The trust at that point is in oneself; and that whatever the future holds it can be met without formal therapy. Similarly loss occurs not just upon leaving therapy but, as Wolff's perceptive article describes, upon entering it as well. He cites, for example, the loss to a person's self-image, that they need the help of another (Wolff 1977).

In this chapter I describe the relationship between the sequence of events in therapy, and the major themes set out in earlier chapters. Trust issues are most significant at or towards the beginning of therapy, and issues of letting go are more significant towards its end. Nevertheless the reader will by now be used to the principle that this scheme is one of convenience, and that the major themes may appear at different times. Rarely is anything as clearly sequential as it is in books! The order of the appearance of the themes may then be different from the order set out in this chapter. The different themes may be present at the same time, running alongside each other, so that the emphasis given to one theme rather than to another becomes a matter of careful choice on the part of the therapist in deciding in what way to make an intervention. Furthermore, allowance always has to be made for regression, so that therapist and client may have to rework earlier issues at a point of crisis, when they may be understood more profoundly than they were at the beginning; for example, if one party in the therapeutic relationship lets the other down, the relationship may temporarily go back to issues about trust and dependability.

There is a danger, when a useful model is developed, of forcing everything into particular patterns. My description of the way in which the therapeutic relationship reflects the themes of this book came originally not from a deliberate effort to fit the different stages of the therapeutic process into this thematic model. It was rather that as I analysed more carefully the course of therapy or counselling, I saw how closely the themes in the first edition of this book related to the therapeutic relationship as well. This is, of course, scarcely surprising: a psychodynamic approach suggests that anything to do with past and present relationships is likely to be reflected in the therapeutic relationship. All relationships are different, but it is interesting to see the way the therapeutic relationship, which likewise is different from other types of relationship, can resemble at various points the parent–child, the intimate, the working or the friendship relationship. These various parallels I observe in the sections below.

Preparations

There is some similarity between the initial stages of therapy, and pregnancy and the immediate days after birth. As in a pregnancy, therapy and counselling starts before the client and the therapist meet face to face. It probably starts for a client before it does for the therapist (just as a foetus is developing before a woman knows she is pregnant), since either the client makes a decision to seek help, or another person suggests it, before the therapist can be contacted. This apparently practical business of making arrangements for therapy or counselling involves more than is usually recognized by the therapist, and may indeed influence the start of the therapy itself.

Concentrating for the moment upon what this preparatory period means for a client, there is initially a period of thinking about whether or not to ask for help, and whom to ask. A client may be entering counselling voluntarily, or have had the first meeting arranged for them. In the former case, this involves the client in making enquiries, arranging an appointment and waiting for it. Initial contact, before or after assessment, is often with an intermediary – a receptionist perhaps, or someone else other than the therapist.

This person may be seen as in some way indicative of what to expect from a counsellor or therapist as well. In most agencies clients will have had an assessment with one person, before meeting the actual counsellor with whom they are going to work. Before the first meeting, a client's attitude will probably be ambivalent, with some hope but also with some anxiety. There may be relief at having made an appointment, since it represents taking a first step in a new direction, and to some extent therefore represents trying to take control of the situation. The hope and the anxiety probably include some concern about the counsellor, what he or she will be like, or even look like. There will no doubt be heightened expectations about the therapist's knowledge and expertise.

Much of this can be called 'pre-transference', since it is based on little factual information, and a lot of fantasy and imagination. How the therapist and therapy is anticipated will probably be influenced by past experiences of important figures – whether they could be trusted, what sort of authority they had and how they used it. The setting for the therapy may also enter this imaginary picture: what the place itself will be like. There are also the arrangements that must be made for getting there.

This preparatory phase involves the therapist as well as the client, and if a client needs a therapist, it is just as valid to say that a therapist also needs a client – since this is the therapist's work, and probably her or his means of earning a living. A therapist (albeit relatively passively) may be looking for clients, as much as clients are seeking therapy. Once a client has rung, or the therapist has received a letter of referral, the therapist also has fantasies about the client. There may be previous notes, a referral letter, or information from an assessment, or even the brief conversation making arrangements for the initial session, any of which can provide tentative ideas about the client. A therapist may also wonder what the client will be like, whether he or she will be able to help this client, and how he or she will feel as a therapist when they first meet. There is then a 'pre-counter-transference', that may or may not match the client's pre-transference. There is surely anxiety and hope on this side as well – an ongoing feeling, however experienced the counsellor is. These early feelings may be heightened when the therapist accepts a referral, in that the therapist may also wonder whether he or she can fulfil the expectations of this third party as well.

At this preparatory stage either person may be rejected by the other. A therapist or counsellor may have no spaces; or the initial arrangements may prove abortive, if the client gets cold feet and decides to withdraw. Rejection is less likely on the therapist's side once the initial stages have been satisfactorily negotiated, but for the moment nothing is fixed.

Beginnings

Winnicott uses an interesting phrase in describing the initial relationship between the baby and the breast: he writes about 'the theoretical first feed', as 'also an actual first feed, except that in real experience it is not so much a matter of a single happening as a build-up of memories of events' (1988b: 100). He is describing the phenomenon whereby a baby wishes for the breast, and the breast appears, so that it seems to the baby that she has created the breast (see also pp. 54–5). He suggests that this does not necessarily happen only at the literal first feed, but over a series of early feeding experiences.

A similar phrase might be used of the beginning of counselling or therapy, so that the term 'theoretical first session' might cover what occurs in the actual first session, but probably more accurately includes what may occur over a series of sessions right at the start. This theoretical first session (or series of sessions) is distinct from the first major theme of trust and dependency in therapy, even though it probably runs concurrently with it.

Whether or not the first session is the initial assessment of the client, or the first appointment with a counsellor after another has conducted the assessment, the theoretical first session involves a mutual assessment process on the part of client and therapist. Each will be sussing the other out, trying to get a feel of the other, so that both parties will be wondering whether they want to get to know each other, and whether they will be able to work together. It is something like a job interview, although, like some job interviews, a client may be so desperate for help that the ability to assess the viability of the therapist is hampered by the urgency of the situation.

In a theoretical first session it is possible that a client has much to say and express, but there will also be many facts and feelings that cannot yet be shared. A client will present certain problems, but these may well mask others, which the client does not yet see as relevant. Indeed, this theoretical first session may have a feeling of being predominantly problem-centred, as a client explains his or her difficulties, and the therapist tries to understand their nature and their triggers, making (often silently) some tentative hypotheses. At this stage both the client and the therapist only present their most obvious aspects to the other, although each will also have first impressions of the other. It is an interesting question of whether or not such initial impressions are significant. Many therapists have learned by experience that first impressions turn out to have considerable substance in the light of later events, even if for a time the first impression is temporarily over-ridden by the desire not to prejudge.

On the therapist's part, the theoretical first session consists of building up an initial picture of the client, mainly through receiving the preliminary information the client wants to share, with perhaps some judicious questioning. Taking a full history of the client is rare in counselling, although it is a little more common in some forms of psychotherapy – in psychodynamic as well as other approaches. Given the significance attached to the past, it is scarcely surprising that a psychodynamic therapist begins the task of piecing the client's history together from the start, although the pieces are like those in a jigsaw, falling into place throughout the therapy, but always with some, even many, missing. A therapist or counsellor is particularly looking for pointers that might link presenting issues with past experience. In the first session, he or she may ask about earlier occurrences in order to get a wider picture – find the edge pieces of the jigsaw perhaps. A psychodynamic approach also involves testing a client's capacity to make or see such links, because for this approach to work well, a client needs to relate his or her history, both as narrative, and as a connection to the present. Where they are very distressed, clients may not yet be in a position to engage in this type of thinking, and building a history may come later, as a client begins to see the significance of their past.

I think it is also possible that in this theoretical first session clients are interested in the therapist's history. I mean by this not simply their wish to know about a therapist's own past or their connections outside therapy – because much of this interest is likely to come later. I mean rather that there may be some concern for their history as a therapist: where they have trained, how long they have been working as a counsellor, what their orientation is, etc. Where this information is important to a client, and where it concerns professional background, it should be shared. Good therapists have no reason to hide their training or their way of working. They want clients to find the best person for them.

Just as when other relationships are first formed, they often include finding out enough about the other to identify whether they have enough about them that might encourage the relationship to develop, I suggest that this happens through a mixture of explicit information and implicit clues in the early meeting of client and counsellor. At the same time there is much that is not known and not shared. On the client's part, this includes the greater part of their history, and the client's perception of the therapist; on the therapist's part this includes preliminary ideas about the client and the presenting issues.

This initial exploration, being to some extent a mutual one, also involves finding a common language. The client is the one who provides the impetus for this; the therapist follows, trying to understand her or his images, metaphors and symbols, as well as the actual way in which the client uses words. Clients vary in the way they use the first session: sometimes they wish to offload, and they care little whether they are being understood – they simply need to spill it out. The therapist may experience this as being 'dumped on', but this is an important part of the start of the therapeutic process. The therapist receives what is said, holds it and contains it, so that later in therapy, or towards its conclusion, much of it can be handed back in a reprocessed form. Therapeutic listening is not waste-disposal, but the first stage of recycling.

> George brought a box of live cartridges to the second session. He had a shot-gun, and he was afraid that he might use it against his former wife who had walked out on him. He asked the therapist whether he could look after the cartridges for him. The therapist took them from him, and in front of George he put them into the bottom of his filing cabinet, under his client files, so that the box was hidden but safely contained. They stayed there throughout a year's therapy, and when the rage and the suicidal feelings had passed, and George felt more secure within himself, at the last session he asked for return of the cartridges. In this symbolic act the therapist had contained the rage until such time as it was safe for George to receive it back.

If some clients at the start just want to let it all out, and dump it on the therapist, others are desperate to know whether what they are saying has been understood. This is especially important when they have not been believed in the past – a devastating experience, all too common in survivors of abuse. On her or his part too, a therapist or counsellor is also keen to know whether the therapeutic language, suitably put across in words that make sense to the client, can be understood and worked with. This capacity to communicate is essential for the working alliance. One question which both parties will be pondering, although it is more likely to be at the forefront of the counsellor's mind, is whether they *can* work together. This is not the same question as whether I *want* to work with this client or this therapist. There may be features of the other which I like, but I still consider that therapy will not work. There may be aspects of the other that I dislike, but do not believe will prevent us working relatively well together.

Both parties are therefore looking for ways to make sufficient contact at this early stage to know that they have been heard. It may be a passing glimpse of something at a deeper level, but enough to signify for both the hope of going on. On the part of the therapist or counsellor this is often found in the client's response to a 'trial interpretation', a rather grand term for an attempt on the therapist's part to make a link between what the client is describing, and what may be happening to the two of them in the session. If a client responds to this – either with a flash of recognition, or at least thoughtfully – this is a good sign for the use of a psychodynamic approach.

There is another important aspect to the first session which sets the tone for much that follows, and that may arise again as it is tested out at a later stage. This consists of the practicalities, such as the contract, fee, time and frequency of meetings, and boundary issues which need to be clarified; for example, whether contact can be made outside the times of sessions. While these are in one way technical matters, each of these aspects involves setting up a boundary, which gives an indication as to the type of relationship being offered. The practical arrangements suggest how far this relationship can go; for example, contact is limited to sessions, or making contact in emergency situations is clearly fenced. It is not the same as a friendship. Arrangements about time and fees create a working contract, entered into by the two parties as adults – however much a client at other points may regress and behave in more childlike ways. Similarly the frequency of sessions sets a marker for the likely intensity of this relationship. Once-monthly meetings create a fairly distant relationship; twice-weekly sessions suggest the willingness to permit or even encourage dependency, which in turn leads to a very intimate relationship – more continuous attention to the client than anyone else in her or his adult life is likely to give them. It is interesting that once-weekly sessions in therapy and counselling appear to have become the norm (even for psychotherapists trained in greater frequency), as though this arrangement provides the right balance between intimacy and separateness, and between dependency and independence.

The psychodynamic approach is also interested in how a client responds to these practical issues, and the way boundaries are treated as the therapy or counselling progresses. I discuss this more fully below and in my chapter in Sills (1997).

Arrangements for times, frequency and places of meeting give a clear indication of the limits of the therapeutic relationship. It is interesting to note, in an article by Schwartz (1989), that research into psychiatrist–patient sexual abuse suggests that the use of first names, the extension of the length of sessions, and flexible appointment times are the first three steps on the path to full sexual relations. This does not mean that use of first names inevitably leads in that direction. It is common practice (although certainly not universal) for first names to be used when addressing clients, and when clients address therapists and counsellors. This may be indicative of a general loosening of formalities of Western culture, although it is interesting to note that GPs are encouraged *not* to use first names, as well as colloquial terms like 'dear'. Flexibility with appointment times is less common, and extending session times generally not acceptable in psychodynamic work. Such variations in the original contract alter the frame of the therapy or counselling, often to the detriment of the therapy as well as the therapeutic relationship. There is a particularly strong concern for 'the frame' in the work of Langs and his followers: e.g. Smith (1991); Sullivan (in press).

Before the first session it is clients who hold most of the information, and therefore most of the power in the therapeutic relationship. During the assessment session or the theoretical first session, sharing this information, and perhaps exposing strong feelings, puts the client in a very vulnerable position, a position which is reinforced by the therapist having a much clearer sense of what therapy is about and what may happen in therapy. Since it is also the therapist's 'territory' upon which they are meeting, and the therapist calls the tune over most of the practical arrangements, the therapist at this point will probably be seen as, and indeed have become, a very powerful figure.

Trust and dependency – the early sessions

Early sessions are not like the theoretical first session. There is not the same clear agenda, not necessarily the same 'excitement' that there was in the first, when there was so much to say and so much to hear. At a first meeting a client usually has a mental list, or a diary of events which he or she wishes to relate. Therapy now needs to move away from a person's 'problems' to the less tangible aspects which up to now have not been in the forefront of the client's mind: other significant people, other events, what a client thinks, how they relate to themself, and how they relate with the counsellor or therapist. The relevance of the therapeutic relationship may at first seem bewildering to a client, who is used to contact with other professionals being about problems 'out there', and not what is passing between them 'in here'. The trial interpretation in the theoretical first session may have given a clue to the client's willingness to shift from the immediate issue to underlying factors, and from outside relationships to the relationship in therapy itself.

Building up trust is a lifelong and a therapy-long process, but initial trust is vital. In time that trust is probably going to be tested more fully, but at this stage the client is looking for initial trust in the therapist and in the process. The therapist is looking for a sense of commitment to the process on the part of the client. This usually becomes clear after four or five sessions, which is why some counsellors like to offer an initial period and a review, before deciding upon a longer or open-ended contract.

Clients place enormous hope in their therapist, and sometimes even ask for confirmation that therapy will work. This is not an easy question to answer, because at this early point a client probably has little knowledge of what is involved. They know that it may take time, and (given the greater public knowledge about counselling) they probably think they will be encouraged to find their own answers. Underneath these rational attitudes, clients are often desperate for much more, expecting the therapist or counsellor to be both omniscient and omnipotent, and wanting therapy to be immediately effective. How might a therapist handle these expectations and this idealization?

Winnicott is helpful here with his concept of illusion, and his description of a mother as enabling her baby to have the illusion that the baby has created and governs the breast (1965b: 180; 1975: 240). He prefers the term illusion to that of 'magical thinking'. At the beginning a mother allows her baby to hold this illusion of the baby's omnipotence; later she gradually allows the baby to experience disillusion, coming to terms with the reality that mother is also independent, outside the baby's control. I suggest that where a client wishes it, a therapist or counsellor may also allow the illusion that therapy or the therapist has this omnipotence, that therapy *works*, and that the therapist *knows*.

Therapists know, of course, that therapy does not always work, or that its results are not always as profound or extensive as the client wishes. Counsellors and therapists are only too aware that while they know something, they never know enough; and that it is just as much a struggle for them to understand the client, as it is for the client to achieve self-knowledge. Openness about the nature of the therapeutic task and the limits of the therapist is not necessarily desirable at this early point. I am not here in any way supporting deception or false promises. It would be wrong for a therapist to make inflated statements about the efficacy of therapy. But it is possible to keep quiet, and to permit the illusion, when a client speaks of what they are expecting of therapy and therapist. The time for disillusion will come sooner or later, and that will need to be handled well.

Another interesting parallel to the early mother–baby relationship is seen in the way clients begin to see the therapist. This is sometimes shown as clients for the first time notice pictures, or other aspects of the surroundings of the consulting room. I once had a room in which a large poster of the Victoria Falls covered a particularly ugly feature opposite the door. It was significant how many clients, at about the third or fourth session, would enter the room and comment on 'your new poster' – although it had been there all the time. This focus on the more immediate surroundings is a reflection of the client's relationship with the therapist too: it is a sign that he or she has become a significant figure, and that clients are turning outward from their preoccupation with their initial concerns to what is happening within the session. This might also be called the first sign of attachment – the realization that the therapist matters, and that (for the time being at least) 'I need him/her'. Indeed for some clients therapy becomes a literal lifeline, and the therapist's room a haven, a place they long to return to almost as soon as they leave the session. A therapist probably feels this close attachment too, although it is frequently masked because they immediately turn their attention to the next client and the next session. Beginning counsellors, who have only one or two clients, know how much they invest in them, and how much they too look forward to their client's return. Similarly, when clients do not turn up, the counsellor's disappointment is a sign of this early attachment.

Coming together and being apart become significant – depending to some extent on the neediness of the client and the degree of dependency fostered by the frequency of meetings. The setting of boundaries in the assessment session, as stated above, is likely to mean that infrequent meetings deter the development of intense need for a close relationship with the therapist, which more frequent sessions often encourage. For some clients being apart in the time between sessions will be very difficult, and it is through these reactions that a therapist or counsellor may predict how a client will face breaks and holidays. Although these reactions may also suggest a difficult ending, this intense need early in therapy (or a return of such intense need when in crisis later in therapy and counselling) may make the absence of the therapist much worse, and more painful than it will be if therapy is able to end both successfully and at the right time.

It is perhaps an indication that this early period of therapy or counselling has passed – even if issues of trust and dependency continue – when the therapeutic relationship itself is seen as having developed its own history and acquired a life of its own. Client or therapist begin to recall things that have been said or experienced a few weeks or months ago: 'Do you remember two weeks ago, when you said . . .?' There is a sense of continuity, that this will go on, without the ending at this stage being in focus, except in short-term work where the ending is a constant factor in a counsellor's interventions. A client begins to share more thoughts and feelings, which were perhaps initially too dangerous to express. There are also memories and feelings, and thoughts about the therapeutic relationship itself that are not yet ready to be shared. The therapeutic relationship may still be idealized, although as the first signs of frustration and the hint of negative feelings appear, this may be a sign that therapy is settling down, and that issues related to the next theme are ready to come into focus.

Authority and autonomy – testing the therapeutic relationship

The middle phase of therapy and counselling is usually the longest, often consisting of working and reworking particular themes that make their appearance time and again in different guises and various situations. It is also a time of testing – testing out how much can be said, what feelings can be allowed, trying out different ideas, daring to think the unthinkable, and in some cases testing the authority of the therapist, or the validity of the initial boundaries. Clients who feel secure enough can therefore ask the question, 'How far can I go?' of themselves and of their therapist:

• in honesty to myself, to the therapist, and to others outside therapy or counselling;

- in dependence upon and trust of the therapist;
- in the expression of negative feelings of all kinds (bearing in mind that for some clients even love is a negative feeling);
- in using the therapist, by putting feelings and object-relationships on to her or him, that partly belong towards others (through transference and projection);
- in challenging the therapist on points where I detect he or she is weak, perhaps by pushing at boundaries (such as the arrangements made in the theoretical first session).

At the same time therapists are also faced with the question of how far they can go in honesty with their client, and in putting back to the client some of the projections and transferences that the client has placed on to them. Both client and therapist may also test out how far they can go in entering and staying with the 'chaos' of the inner world. For a client this may mean facing terrifying feelings from the past, or even the void within; for the therapist or counsellor it may mean pushing at personal frontiers of knowledge, thought and experience. To do this means assessing how much the client can take, and how much the client can be allowed to express, as well as how well fitted and supported the therapist is for this task. The descent into chaos may involve regression (and all the issues of trust and dependency again), although counsellors and therapists need to remember that the deliberate encouragement of regression is only for the most experienced. Winnicott, for example, experienced and highly skilled though he was, would apparently only allow one of his patients at a time to enter a deeply regressive phase. Little describes how 'he spoke of patients having to "queue up" sometimes to go into such a state [full regression], one waiting until another had worked through it and no longer needed him in that way' (1990: 47–8).

Essentially what the client needs to test out is what kind of relationship the therapeutic one is, and whether the therapist can accept, and even withstand, the expression of strong negative and positive feelings. In the case of boundaries the client may also be testing out what the therapist is prepared to tolerate, and where the therapist draws the line. We are reminded of Winnicott again, and his description of the need for parents to be responsible, while their adolescent children are permitted in their immaturity to test out aspects of relationships for themselves (see pp. 122–3, 138). But while clients may push at boundaries to test the therapist, we have to remember that rejection of the therapist's interventions, for example, is not always defensive. It is sometimes because the client is now strong enough to tell the therapist that he or she has got it wrong.

Involved in this testing is the almost inevitable occurrence that a counsellor or therapist will from time to time let a client down. If nothing else he or she will fail to understand, or will make wrong interpretations. But there are other ways in which failure can be experienced. There will be breaks, times when the therapist is late, or ill. The therapist or counsellor has to fail the client who is looking for the therapist to become the parent, lover, friend, the magician, or even the authority that he or she so much desires. Without the client therefore pushing at boundaries, the relationship is bound to be tested in another way. The experience of such failures may be seen as equivalent to Winnicott's concept of disillusion, whereby a mother gradually lets the baby down, as far as the baby is able to take it, allowing more and more of the reality of the external world to impinge upon the baby. Some of what I am describing here about therapy is not necessarily such a gradual process. Therapeutic failure may be unplanned, accidental or the result of a mistake. Yet working through the experience of the therapist's failure, the negative feelings in the client, and the disillusionment with the therapist and the process, is of equal importance to therapy as is the whole psychological 'weaning' process in infancy. Kohut similarly emphasizes the need to work with empathic failure, so that with narcissistic clients, even if empathy is the principal intervention, failure to be empathic, or failing the narcissistic needs of the client, is a second major intervention (Kohut 1971, 1977; Siegel 1996).

Where this testing does not break the therapeutic relationship, and where both client and therapist survive these experiences, this leads the client to a realization of the 'permanence' of the relationship: that whatever happens and whatever is said, it will stay secure within the boundaries initially stated and negotiated. I am of course describing a process which may have been repeated many times before it reaches this stage. Things may go wrong on either side, but they can (eventually) be overcome, as long as both parties stick with their commitment to the process. The client knows the therapist will still be there; the therapist knows that even if the client misses one week in anger, he or she will still turn up to the following session. Disappointments and failure no doubt continue, but they can now be overcome without disastrous consequences for the therapeutic relationship. Disillusionment proves creative.

Although there is this strong sense of permanence, and confidence in the survival of the relationship, this is yet another illusion: therapy or counselling must end, and when it does the actual relationship will finish. For the present moment, however, even if the impermanence is head knowledge, it is not the way it feels; and it need not feel otherwise. Attachment deepens as a result; and therapist and client now deeply value the reliability, rock-like, staying qualities of the other as a foundation for all the other turbulent material that in many cases continues to emerge. At this stage there may be no thought of the therapy or counselling ever ending. It has yet to reach a point where the client is confident that 'I will survive even though these sessions have to end.'

The process of working through involves recognizing patterns, some of which are rather too tightly fixed in place, and which need to be loosened up so that change and new development can take place. This happens within the context of the therapeutic relationship where those patterns can be repeated, and where there can be a sense (as in other relationships) of being 'stuck'. Defences have to be worked through, not attacked. These may prove to be points of potential breakthrough, to new material, to things that have never been said before, nor even been realized before.

Where it works well therapy and counselling begins to model how therapeutic other relationships might also be. While it is obvious that this particular relationship is perceived as unique by the client, who has probably not had a relationship quite like this one before, this is also true on the therapist's side. The client's emerging history and the particular relationship which is forged with this client makes her or him different from everyone else the therapist has seen, however much there are inevitably memories evoked of similar patterns and experiences with former clients.

Towards ending: internalization and oedipal love

I do not wish to force the theme of cooperation and competition into this model of the therapeutic process, but there are aspects of it, particularly those to do with the negotiation of the Oedipus complex, which have particular relevance for the penultimate phase, towards ending. Rivalry and competition issues, like the other major themes, emerge in the material and in the context of the therapeutic relationship itself long before this closing phase, as illustrated for example in the section on 'Rivalry and competition as a lifelong process' in Chapter 5 (pp. 181–5). So while these themes and stages of therapy are sure to overlap and merge, the next distinctive development for the client is the internalization of the therapist or counsellor. I am sure that therapists and counsellors also internalize the clients with whom they work most intensely, in a way that is different from memory. It would be interesting to know how this affects the process of ending.

Signs of this process are seen, for example, in the way a client describes how 'I caught myself talking to myself, and then I thought "That's what you might say"!' This is a different internal process from talking more directly in fantasy with the therapist, as may happen earlier in therapy, where the client imagines what the therapist would say; it is rather that the client's ideas seem to match those of the therapist. This more developed internalization is far less conscious, and shows how both the therapist and the therapeutic method have become more part of the 'me' of the client. In time even the thought that 'this is what my therapist might have said' gives way to an unconscious internalized process in the client, joining the other internalized objects past and present. On a more obvious level the therapy or counselling has become a joint venture, in which a client becomes confident of her or his own autonomy and separateness. All this resembles the way a child resolves the Oedipus complex, internalizing the parental figures, and moving forward on her or his own.

In this phase there are likely to be other signs of progress: the further withdrawal of projections and transferences; a growing realization that 'I' (i.e. the client, and not just, as in the early phase, the therapeutic relationship) am able to survive the breaks, which in turn gives hope for the ending of therapy or counselling itself. On the therapist's part there may be experienced that phenomenon which Searles describes as 'oedipal love in the counter-transference' (1965a). By this Searles means the therapist's strong feeling of the desire to be married with the client (of whatever gender), which Searles relates to the pride and pleasure that a parent has in their growing child, and their fantasy of wishing to continue in such an intimate relationship (see p. 169). Another parallel is the Pygmalion myth, where the sculptor falls in love with the statue into which he has breathed life. Searles believes this is an indication of the successful outcome of therapy, that therapists should regard 'their' client so, although he stresses that these counter-transference feelings are a sign that the ending has to be faced, with pain and grief on both sides, because the therapist cannot hang on to the client, any more than the client can go on depending upon the therapist.

This may be one explanation for such feelings. It is true that it is sometimes at such a point that a therapist begins to like a client in a deeper way, making them realize just how far the client has come. But it is important not to confuse Searles's explanation with another different phenomenon, more sinister than Searles's obvious message about the need to let the client go. A therapist or counsellor may see himself as the omnipotent white knight, who will rescue the beleaguered princess and carry her off to his castle in the sunset. Such fantasies may only be those of male therapists in relation to some vulnerable female clients, and certainly it is male therapists who are more likely to err by acting them out. The female therapist's fantasy may be a different one – of over-protectiveness and smothering, rather than sexualized.

In any event, these latter fantasies are different from Searles's experience, and often appear early, rather than late, in the therapy or counselling. Searles is making a particular point about counter-transference feelings long into therapy, which are accompanied by pain and not simply by pleasure; and indicate the possibility that therapists can sense the approach of the ending by the way they feel about the prevalence of an adult-to-adult relationship with the client. Searles first saw the significance of such feelings when one of his patients rebuked him for continuing to see her as a child, and not as a grown woman. He realized how much he was resisting the therapy entering its final oedipal phase.

> It seems to me clear enough, then, what this former child, now a neurotic or psychotic adult, requires from us for the successful resolution of his unresolved Oedipus complex: not such a repression of desire, acted-out seductiveness, and denial of his own worth as he met in the relationship with his parent, but rather a maximal awareness on our part of the reciprocal feelings which we develop in response to his oedipal strivings.
>
> (1965a: 303)

Endings

The setting of the end of therapy or counselling is a sign of the need to work upon the ending in the sessions that follow. In the case of short-term contracts this is recognized as something that takes place from the start. In mid-term contracts the ending may have been set at the beginning, but its advent is now imminent. One rule of thumb is to allow a further quarter of the time already spent in therapy for working through its finish. The end will be linked in its significance to earlier endings, both in therapy in respect of earlier breaks, and outside therapy to the client's experiences of separation and loss.

Inevitably there are occasions for ending which have to be more rapid than had been anticipated, because therapy (and particularly counselling) cannot always finish at the right time for both parties. The client, or even the therapist, may move, or other outside factors intervene that are beyond the control of either party. In these instances there is more unfinished business than would otherwise be the case – remembering that even long-term therapy never finishes, prompting from his own experience of his patient, the Wolf Man, Freud's famous paper on *Analysis Terminable and Interminable* (1937a). At the same time there are rather sudden endings that occur because the counselling or therapy has been successful, when the client's readiness to take advantage of new opportunities does not permit a neat termination.

Once it is announced or arranged, making sense of the experience of ending becomes the key feature of therapy or counselling. The process that anticipates the end has obvious parallels with many of the stages of grief (described more fully on p. 4). There may be disbelief ('surely the time hasn't passed that quickly?'); anger ('you said that you would see me as long as I wished'); sadness ('I already feel how much I shall miss you'); relief ('thank goodness I've come through this terrible period of my life'); and the recognition of unfinished business. Although ending sometimes (as in Samuel Johnson's phrase about hanging) 'concentrates the mind wonderfully', what has not yet been achieved or understood can be acknowledged.

Ending includes evaluating what has taken place during the therapy or counselling, separating what belongs to the client from what belongs to the therapy and the therapist. Some therapists suggest that it is important to be more self-disclosing towards the end to assist this separation to happen, and so that the transference can be dissolved in favour of a more realistic perception of the therapist or counsellor. I am not myself sure that transferences are that readily dissolved, certainly not through deliberate effort.

The process of internalization of the therapist and the therapy continues through the ending phase, with the added impetus that the client has some sense of what he or she wishes to go working on within him- or herself. We are however compelled to recognize that where therapy has really failed, especially if it has been abusive of the client, a more persecutory internalization takes place.

And then there is the finality of ending, which cannot, like the theoretical first session, be seen as an extended period. There is no theoretical last session. The end is the end. Where the relationship has been a long one, or where real contact has been made between the counsellor or therapist and the client, there will no doubt be *real* sadness on both sides – such feelings cannot be projected on to the transference or counter-transference alone. In most cases, the ending is a kind of death, because counsellor and client will probably never see each other again. Certainly a counsellor or therapist must assume that this is the case, so that even if it is possible that at a future date the client may seek out the therapist again, the ending is worked with absolutely, as if there will be no further meeting. Of course, however final the ending, where the therapeutic relationship has come through these different phases and faced the issues raised by these three major themes well enough, in both parties something very deep and valued lives on.

APPENDIX

Summary of the three major themes and their presentation in psychodynamic therapy and counselling

For each of the three themes the summary is divided into four parts:

(a) How difficulties relating to that theme might be presented in terms of a client's character, relationships and inner world.
(b) How such difficulties may be seen in relation to the therapist and counsellor – 'in the transference'.
(c) How the therapist or counsellor might relate to and work with the client in order to help the client to change or progress developmentally.
(d) Ways in which more mature development might show itself in relation to the major theme – this section also indicates possible aims in therapy and counselling.

The definition of difficulties (a) and of more mature development (d) is of course historically, culturally and socially variable – as has been emphasized throughout this book. It is hoped that these working ideas are useful not because they are definitive, but as pointers to what may be particular norms in a particular culture at a particular time.

By identifying an issue under section (a) or (b) in one or other of the major themes, a therapist may also find it helpful to look through the other issues in the same section, as a pointer to what the therapist may not yet have identified.

Trust and dependency

(a) Difficulties associated with trust and dependency

The development of a protective false self, which is more extensive than the front most people find useful in some work or social situations.

Klein's 'paranoid–schizoid' position – experiencing the outer world, or external pressures or internalized 'objects' as persecutory, without this necessarily being as extreme as the mental disturbance known as 'paranoia'.

The narcissistic personality: over-inflated concern for the self, drawing attention to self, no apparent interest in how others feel.

Idealization of significant others (including the therapist/counsellor).

Splitting: idealizing some, denigrating others, problems with coping with ambivalence.

Destructive anger, especially where it is acted out, or fear of showing anger lest it proves destructive.

Anxiety or guilt over destructive wishes having severely damaged others.

Envy, perhaps with destructive wishes attached.

Over-dependent, clinging, possessive, demanding person.

Anxiety about the reliability of others.

Fears of being abandoned, rejected, being left alone.

Fear of being engulfed or overwhelmed by the other in intimate and sexual relationships.

Deep lack of trust and fear over invasion of personal boundaries – arising from experience of childhood (perhaps even very early) sexual or physical abuse: this may sometimes also be seen in being boundary-less in relationships.

The withdrawn person, schizoid personality; unable to trust, afraid of being swallowed up by others or of draining them with demands.

Addictions: drugs, drink, food; overeating or reaction against food in anorexia (although bulimia and anorexia are also about control, related to the next theme).

Acting as if limitless supplies available: including over-spending.

Problems with deferring gratification: must have it now.

Intense anger, hate, or rage as a reaction to frustration: the rage is felt as, or seen in action as very destructive: tearing apart, killing, ripping open, etc.

Difficulties accepting limits.

Guilt about making demands upon others for fear of damaging them, or of being rejected.

Ongoing anger (years on) following bereavement or loss.

A temporary loss of the sense of self or identity, particularly following a major change, or loss.

The feeling of being 'in pieces' or 'chaotic' – although note below the extreme form of this in psychotic illness.

The failure of the environment (e.g. the workplace and redundancy) to provide, awakening feelings associated to earlier failures of care.

Magical beliefs and thinking, grandiose or omnipotent beliefs about oneself.

The search for unitive experiences – perhaps through drugs.

The perennial search for a partner who will bring 'completeness', and rejection of each one as faults are found in them.

Making relationships in order to meet own needs, with little or no concern for others: narcissistic rather than altruistic.

The projection on to others (e.g. a baby, children, clients) of one's own needs, caring for the needy side of the self through caring for others, not allowing them to be (or become) separate.

Some pregnancies (especially in adolescence) as ways of avoiding breaking dependent ties.

The self-denigrating person, unable to accept the self as having any worth.

Sense of shame about the basic sense of self.

Chronic hopelessness, despair and pessimism.

Lack of faith; inability to believe *anything*; absence of a value-system; hopeless cynicism.

Hypochondriacal (narcissistic) symptoms.

Learning difficulties arising from lack of trust.

Problems with ageing and loss of physical strength or appearance where related to narcissistic concerns.

Dependency issues relating to care of ageing parents.

Bitterness and demandingness in illness and old age – ingratitude to those who show their care.

Dissociation – psychologically absent while in the presence of the therapist: often linked with severe trauma or abuse – a defence indicating inability to trust their own ability to handle memories of trauma or feelings associated with these memories.

Manic-depressive swings from omnipotent feelings to self-loathing and worthlessness.

The borderline personality – on the border between reality and psychotic signs below.

Take particular care of the following signs. They may well indicate a level of psychotic disturbance beyond the capabilities of most counsellors and even many psychotherapists:

Confusion of self and not-self; confused time and spatial boundaries.

Confusion of body and mind.

Confused speech and imagery, thoughts or perceptions.

Cognitive disturbance, bizarre thoughts or behaviour.

Long-standing feelings of chaos, or being 'in pieces'.

Delusions or hallucinations.

Paranoid feelings from extreme self-hate to paranoid schizophrenia.

Intense prejudice, or feelings of being discriminated against without basis in reality.

Living in a fantasy-world which is out of touch with reality.

Absence of 'as if' thinking: it is all too real.

(b) Trust and dependency issues in the therapeutic relationship

Demanding, sometimes explicitly, but sometimes through incessant talking; counter-transference feelings of being drained, 'sucked dry'.

Requests for more time, or greater frequency of sessions.

Reliance on the therapist – as a lifeline (rather than as advice-giver in the authority/autonomy theme).

Swallowing everything the therapist says, although not always pausing to 'taste' it.

Inability to accept anything the therapist says, as if it is poisonous, or dangerous – not in the argumentative way seen more in the authority theme.

Use of an intellectual defence to avoid closeness.

Difficulty in forming and sustaining the relationship.

Fear of dependency on the therapist or therapy.

Suspicious, not trusting the therapist.

Fear that the therapist will reject or turn hostile.

Extreme difficulties about breaks and ends of sessions.

Idealizing or worshipping the therapist, perhaps denigrating the self as well, or running down other helpers.

The eroticized transference – may be expressed in sexual terms, but indicating early oral needs.

Demanding more time and attention, perhaps also physical affection (the need to be held rather than sex).

The need to be special – perhaps to be the only one in the therapist's life, or the only client – and . . .

. . . the opposite: unable to accept the time and attention offered by the therapist.

Little regard for the feelings of the therapist, who exists purely for the client.

The therapist (woman or man) is treated as a maternal figure – 'hold me', 'feed me', 'touch me' – conveyed in tone and manner even if not in words.

The client's language and images have an 'oral' quality to them: images of feeding, biting, comfort, etc.

Magical expectations of the therapist, together with difficulty accepting own responsibility for change.

Intolerance of the frustration of therapy being a long process – wanting solutions now.

Hostility to the therapist when he or she appears uncaring by setting limits, or not obviously helping.

Unable to relate to the therapist because too caught up in inner fantasy world – bizarre thoughts and associations which are hardly responsive to the therapist's interventions (this probably indicates serious disturbance and the need for supervision and/or referral to specialist resources).

(c) The therapist's task, as related to trust and dependency issues

Containing and holding what the client presents, until such time as it is safe enough for the client to begin to look at it, or take it back.

Providing a protective and facilitating environment, which may sometimes involve managing, or helping the client to manage, external pressures and demands.

Being reliable, dependable, and consistent; keeping to time; not acceding to demands for more except in special circumstances.

Showing care and sensitivity when setting limits.

Constant empathy when working with narcissistic clients.

Holding in mind, whatever the client says or does, the depth of helplessness, emptiness or sense weakness in the client, even when the client does not recognize this.

Receiving the client's projections until such time as it is safe to put them back.

Permitting an illusion about therapy until such time as it is possible to be discerning about its weaknesses; fostering disillusion.

Monitoring counter-transference, particularly to assess how far the therapist is picking up the client's 'unwanted' feelings.

Using silence carefully, discerning a client who is learning to be alone, from a client for whom the silence is a void, leaving them deserted and lonely.

Containing one's own anxiety: not showing panic even when the therapist and/or the client feels overwhelmed.

Surviving attacks by the client (even when they hurt).

Allowing oneself to feel hate of the client, without taking it out on the client.

Setting limits upon acting out of anger and rage in the session.

Accepting as positive, tokens, gestures or words of reparation – remembering that this is sometimes after, but sometimes *before* an attack.

Encouraging expressions of concern towards others, especially those whom the client may have damaged; and of appropriate guilt.

Creating a climate of trust, where the client does not fear rejection for what they feel or say; where client does not have to fear damaging counsellor by being open about his or her demands, their love or their anger.

Helping clients distinguish what lies in them and what lies in others – observing projections on the one side, and negative introjections on the other.

Helping distinguish between appropriate feelings of being 'got at', or the victim of prejudice (which does occur, and has a basis in reality), and persecutory feelings involving the projection of hostility on to others.

Not colluding with the client splitting helpers – not allowing oneself to be set up as the 'good parent', while others seen as bad: or the opposite, although at times it may be important to take on the negative feelings temporarily.

Encouraging the client's ability to experience positive and negative feelings towards the same 'object'.

Encouraging the positive signs of independence – although be careful about premature independence for fear of intimacy, or fear of rejection.

Enabling clients to find self-esteem.

Linking where possible previous difficulties of trust and dependency to obvious examples of this in the therapeutic relationship.

Using failures on the part of the therapist (to understand, absences, etc.) to allow the client to express frustration and anger; linking in with other failures of care which the client has experienced.

With clients showing signs of serious disturbance:

- attempting to find out about any psychiatric history, suicide attempts, and previous episodes of similar disturbance – all this will assist a supervisor to assess the risk, and plan appropriate help
- supporting the client's positive thinking, constructive wishes or actions, and supporting all realistic perceptions of situations
- avoiding deep interpretations, or confronting defences, unless experienced in working with this client group, and well supervised
- short, more frequent sessions may be more appropriate than longer weekly sessions, especially at the height of a crisis
- trying to remain a good enough figure, to help referral elsewhere to be seen as caring, not rejecting
- encouraging a client's own wish for more specialist help.

(d) Indications of more mature development and possible aims in therapy and counselling in relation to trust and dependency

Basic sense of trust and faith in others, the environment and the self; basic sense of the 'world' as good.

Healthy mistrust, discrimination about who or what can be trusted.

Klein's 'depressive position', with feeling of more well-being, recognition of ambivalence, and concern for others.

Recognition of positive and negative feelings towards the same person(s) without the negative destroying the positive.

Containing and working through bad experiences and feelings, without being overwhelmed by them in the long term.

Healthy self-respect and self-regard, while still able to accept one's shortcomings, own mortality, and weaknesses.

Recognition of the boundaries between self and others, self and the world.

Presence of and distinction between subjective and objective thinking and experience.

A separate identity: able to own thoughts and feelings, without continuous use of projection or introjection.

Identifying through empathy and concern for and with others.

Trust of others when learning from them, chewing over ideas, and digesting them, but also (authority theme) questioning them.

Trusting and depending appropriately upon others.

Being intimately involved with another while still retaining a core sense of self.

Caring for others and receiving care from others.

Capacity to be alone – inner harmony and self-esteem.

Putting experiences in perspective, retaining a sense of hope even in adversity.

Tolerance of frustration; ability to defer immediate gratification when necessary, or to be able to make appropriate substitutions.

Expressing appropriate anger or assertiveness when frustrated or discontented, without (fear of) being destructive.

Creative use of fantasy and imagination, and of identification, without it becoming a substitute for real relationships or achievements.

The internalization of the positive features of others, in the course of relating to them, particularly as part of the grief process after loss or bereavement.

Authority and autonomy

(a) Difficulties associated with authority and autonomy

Perfectionism: over-tidy and over-organized.

Wanting to over-order and over-control the self, events and others.

Messy or disorganized person (i.e. in terms of the way they manage things, rather than the internal disintegration more typical of trust and dependency issues).

Holding back feelings, inhibition, emotional 'constipation'.

Rigid self-control, or rigid control of others.

'Law-and-order' type (as the answer to everything!), sometimes with strict religious moralizing.

Inability to exercise legitimate authority.

Dependent upon authority figures to take decisions.

Unable to be critical of others, especially authorities.

Over-reliance upon rules and orders from others.

Unthinking conformity to the peer group, society or authority figures.

Foreclosed adolescent type, unable to use adolescence to challenge conventions or to experiment with alternative ways of thinking and acting.

Unable to take acceptable risks.

Unable to resolve anything unless everything is crystal clear.

Difficulty adapting to new circumstances, because they disturb the old 'order' too much.

Cautious and over-protective of self and others.

The 'yes . . . but' person; 'on the one hand . . . on the other hand', without being able to make up his or her mind, or come down on one side or the other.

Lack of spontaneity.

Resentful and often passive submission to authority figures.

Passive-aggressive (making others angry, rather than being able to express hostility directly – often towards an authority figure).

Rejection of authority just because it is authority.

Highly critical internal 'voice' – often that of internalized parent(s); an over-active conscience (punitive super-ego or 'internal saboteur').

Sense of shame or low-esteem over what he or she can or cannot *do* (more han over who they *are* at a core level, more typical of trust and dependency theme).

Compulsive behaviour – checking; or unnecessary repetition of actions, or words: obsessional rituals; guilt or anxiety, if things are not done 'properly'.

Obsessional thoughts (although the latter may indicate greater disturbance, such as paranoid thoughts – see trust and dependency theme).

Intellectualization as a way of avoiding feelings, or as a way of trying to order areas of conflict without engaging in the conflict.

Afraid of getting hands dirty (literally or metaphorically).

Over-anxious need to achieve to satisfy one's own demands or what others are imagined to require.

The constant use of words like 'ought', 'should', 'must'; 'the hardening of the oughteries'.

The workaholic – inability to play, or even to relax in playing.

Inability to relax at times usually set aside for leisure; or following retirement, having to work as hard as before.

Inability to engage in work because it is seen as too conformist.

Inability to produce work (e.g. studying, or creative expression) through fear of other's criticism and consequent loss of self-esteem; or through own over-ambitious standards.

Difficulties in learning associated with perfectionism, fear of criticism, authority problems.

Parents who push their children to achieve, who over-value children for their achievements, and critical of any failure, perhaps using their children as signals to others of their own worth.

Having to be a perfect parent (perhaps using books as providing 'rules' of child-rearing).

Experiencing love only as conditional love – having to please others to gain their love or approval.

Fear that expression of feelings will lead to lack of control, to disorder, or to spoiling or soiling situations, relationships or the self.

Explosive anger as a result of bottling it up and letting go too forcefully.

Fear of expressing anger because, having been held back, it may be explosive.

Need to 'confess' in order to feel 'clean', without any desire to look at underlying difficulties.

Uncontrolled, impulsive expression of feelings (although in some cases, especially where this is inappropriate to the situation, or where the feelings do not match the situation, this may be evidence of deeper disturbance, as summarized in the trust and dependency theme).

Domination of another through sex or pain, sadistic behaviour, sadistic attitudes and fantasies.

Satisfaction and relief through being the recipient of pain and domination (which may of course be pleasurable participation in sado-masochistic sex, but may be the only way of being able to achieve a sense of relief from guilt).

Sex seen as dirty, or soiling.

Sexual *performance* seen as more important than sexual *enjoyment*.

Shame at lack of bodily control (e.g. in illness or ageing).

Turning the tables on ageing parents by becoming authoritarian and dominating of them.

(b) Authority and autonomy issues in the therapeutic relationship

Attitudes to the therapist or counsellor as an authority figure:

- fear of therapist's imagined demands or criticism
- expectation of therapist being controlling, or taking control
- looking to therapist to provide guidance or answers
- unable to accept what therapist says 'on principle'
- being very critical of the therapist.

The client's need to 'get it right' when telling his or her story – having to get the right word, or the correct explanation.

Holding back or holding in feelings – tears, anger, affectionate feelings, even not showing anxiety.

Difficulty revealing thoughts and feelings through shame.

Intellectualizing, being vague, or introducing a lot of detail and trivia, being very precise.

Boring and monotonous talk and delivery.

Difficulty acting upon insights, listening but unable to make decisions for fear of getting them wrong.

Shame may be seen in the bowed head, or lack of eye contact.

Shifting blame at times on to others, denying own responsibility.

'Yes . . . but' responses, that might be accompanied by sullenness, or complaints about no-one helping.

Hesitancy about, or fear of, the therapist taking control; not wishing to feel tied down.

A sense in the therapist that he or she and the client are getting into 'rational' arguments, each struggling to control other.

Splitting different helpers so that one 'authority' figure is set against another, or one played off against the other.

Treating the therapist like the dominant authority figure in the family of origin: 'make me', 'tell me', 'do it for me', 'approve of my actions', etc.

(c) The therapist's task, as related to authority and autonomy issues

Developing the working alliance in which the client is encouraged to take as much responsibility as the therapist for thinking and reflecting upon him- or herself.

Encouraging therapy to be a place where work can be done, but also where therapist and client can 'play' with ideas, with words, with free associations.

Developing a working partnership where the therapist's expertise becomes an aid to the client not an authoritative influence over the client.

Not acting as an authority figure – e.g. avoiding laying down rules or giving advice (unless a person is very disturbed in which case such management is appropriate).

Observing the client's wish to make the therapist more authoritative or expert than he or she can be.

Observing when the client appears to be giving away own authority to the counsellor.

Monitoring the client's fear of the therapist being critical, making it more difficult for some thoughts and feelings to be expressed.

Fostering spontaneity in the client (as well as being spontaneous oneself!).

While adhering to boundaries, not practising therapy or counselling in a rigid, rule-dominated way.

Being able to develop one's own way of being a therapist, not hide-bound by tradition or training.

Linking the wish for, or fear of, therapist as authority figure to the way client felt about parental authority, and the authority of quasi-parental figures in childhood and later life.

Locating client's fear of judgement or criticism, where it seems to be projected on to others as being the only critical ones, as in fact in the client's inner world.

Working to help lower defences against expression of feelings when the client is becoming monotonous and boring, or engaging only in distant intellectual talk – remembering that the client is afraid to own such feelings, and probably feels ashamed of or guilty about them.

Distinguishing between appropriate and inappropriate guilt, enabling client to express concern in cases of appropriate guilt, but looking for possible reasons for inappropriate guilt.

Where shame is expressed, showing obvious acceptance of the client, over and above the thing(s) that have gone wrong; questioning where such shame comes from (e.g. over-critical parents in childhood, cultural determinants).

Helping the client to leave therapy at the right time, as a true expression of their new found, or newly affirmed independence.

(d) Indications of more mature development and possible aims in therapy and counselling in relation to authority and autonomy

Self-esteem and sense of competence in one's abilities: what a person can do or perform, rather than the more basic self-esteem of the trust and dependency theme.

A sense of order, justice and fairness – that the 'world' is felt to be basically fair.

Ability to be self-controlled without being over-controlled.

Sense of personal autonomy without arrogance.

Confidence in the ability to make things happen.

Adaptable to new situations; able to create new order out of fluid situations.

Industriousness and creativity.

Ability to let go feelings in appropriate ways.

Confidence to take initiatives, including measuring any risks.

Acting independently when required to do so.

Making judgements of right and wrong, using information or even advice, but taking decisions for oneself.

Ability to challenge authority figures when necessary in a manner which encourages dialogue.

Acceptance of personal responsibility.

Balance between work, play and relaxation.

Enjoyment of physical activity and expression.

Learning from the authority of others while at the same time being able to question them.

Sense of inner order, but also capable of adaptation and change.

Tolerance of temporary disorder or uncertainty.

Acceptance and enjoyment of the whole body – especially those parts commonly seen as 'nasty' or 'dirty'.

Able to make mistakes and learn from mistakes.

Sense of coordination – being able to do things without fearing mistakes.

Ability to exercise authority fairly.

Sharing authority and decision-making (e.g. in working relationships or in intimate partnerships, parenting, etc.).

Ability to relinquish authority over children as they mature (without relinquishing offer of guidance and sharing of experience).

Ability to let go of positions of power and responsibility with increasing age, encouraging and enabling others to take over.

Cooperation and competition

(a) Difficulties associated with cooperation and competition

Problems in three-person or triangular situations:

- splitting of sex/affection/care on to two or more persons
- parent using a child as an ally against the other parent, or as a replacement for his or her partner
- children coming between parents
- 'the eternal triangle': one person, two partners
- feeling left out when in threesome.

Sexual difficulties, and difficulties within sexual relationships.

Sexualizing non-sexual relationships.

Sexual inhibition.

Sexual provocativeness.

The Don Juan, tease character: although also look for trust and dependency issues.

Gender anxieties: particularly over being 'masculine' or 'feminine' – personal qualities and gender expectations.

Under-valued as a boy or a girl by parents who wanted a different gender child.

Problems accepting sexual and genital differences (although there may also be legitimate difficulties caused by society's treatment of men and women).

Destructive or aggressive envy of women or men.

Anxieties about sexual orientation or sexual preferences.

Castration anxiety whether in actual or, more likely, in symbolic form.

Shame or guilt about sexuality.

Lack of confidence as an adult man or woman due to rejection or distancing by parents of the client's love and sexuality as a child.

Inhibition of sexuality through guilt or fear of rejection.

Rivalry, often as feelings of inferiority in relation to other members of own gender.

Sex experienced or contemplated as threatening because too associated with oedipal ties.

Incestuous relationships or experiences in childhood (or adult life), acted out sexually or emotionally.

Over-attachment to parents, inability to leave them psychologically in adult life.

Difficulties identifying with parent of same sex – internalizing their negative rather than their positive qualities.

Guilt about having broken parents' relationship, if they separate and/or divorce.

Rivalry or jealousy of siblings: birth of siblings; achievements of siblings; parents' relationship to siblings.

Rivalry in step-family relationships.

Rivalry in a couple relationship, over role, earnings, abilities, etc.

Guilt over the death of a sibling, or perhaps of a feared or hated parent.

Jealousy, or feelings of exclusion, upon the birth of a child (particularly experienced by the father).

Over-competitive: seeing situations as competitive when they are not.

Unable to engage in competitive games or sports (may be due to anxiety about displaying or using the body, may be to do with winning or losing).

Difficulty being 'on show', or in the limelight.

Unproductive rivalry and competitiveness in working situations, in working in a team, in measuring oneself against colleagues.

Jealousy in all types of relationship.

Inaction or lack of initiative through fear of rivalry or competition, which can take the form either of anxiety about losing or about winning.

Inhibition of curiosity, initiative and adventure, perhaps taking its cue from sexual inhibition, but seen in other areas too.

Exhibitionism or furtive sexuality (voyeurism) and implied doubts about potency and sexuality in such behaviour.

Only able to relate to opposite gender as long as they are 'safe' and unattainable – that is not sexually arousing, 'safely' married or engaged, untouchable, distant figures.

Perceiving the opposite gender generally as a personal threat.

Feelings of inadequacy as a man or woman.

Sexual relations which show need for a sexual object who is 'inferior' or submissive, who does not present too great a threat, for example paedophilia (attraction to children), or attacks on women because they represent a threat to potency.

Denigration of the opposite sex.

Denigration of the younger generation due to feelings of inadequacy and competitiveness, or envy of their opportunities.

Anxieties about own homosexual fantasies and desires, or fear of gay men and lesbians (homophobia).

Learning difficulties associated with inhibitions or competitiveness.

Learning difficulties due to sexual or loving desires towards teachers.

Difficulties with the intimate physical examinations in the medical context.

(b) Cooperation and competition issues in the therapeutic relationship

Difficulty talking about sex, not as in authority and autonomy theme because it is disgusting or dirty, but because it is too stimulating or exciting.

Using stimulating intimate talk to excite or interest the therapist: seductive behaviour, or using sex to denigrate therapist (may be used by male client towards female therapist).

Counter-transference feelings of sexual excitement in the therapist – although be sure to trace where these come from – these may be the therapist's issue.

Implicit or explicit wish for therapist to be a friend or partner or lover.

Attempts to make an 'alliance' with one therapist against another helper, or against client's partner.

Jealousy of, interest in, or comparison to other clients seen by the therapist, or of other persons in the therapist's life outside work.

Wanting to be a special client: *primus inter pares* (first amongst equals), not the only one as in the trust and dependency theme.

The gender of the therapist or counsellor may be particularly important:

- fear of the opposite gender, perhaps because of the experience of abuse (although occasionally the therapist of the same gender may also be feared for the same reason)
- the client feels only a therapist of the same gender would understand the gender issues
- homosexual anxiety.

(c) The therapist's task, as related to cooperation and competition issues

Respecting and where possible honouring client's wish for male or female therapist or counsellor; or working with these difficulties where client has no choice yet wishes to continue.

Watching for rivalry between client and therapist, especially where both of same gender.

Using the gender of the therapist as a model of good relating when working with a client who sees the gender the therapist represents as threatening.

Linking current triangular situations, or problems in sexual and other relationships, with what is known of the relationship between the parents, or the parents and client.

Avoiding being caught up in splitting, becoming an ally for the client against another helper or member of the family.

Helping clients talk naturally about their sexuality, their sexual fantasies and their feelings towards others without being inhibited, and without titillation.

Accepting sexual or loving feelings in the therapeutic relationship (in the client or in the therapist), without deliberately encouraging them, or playing on them.

Avoiding being seductive; avoiding being unduly interested, voyeuristic or prying into the client's life; creating instead an atmosphere of trust which enables a client to show the more intimate details of their memories, thoughts and feeling when they are ready.

Looking for previous experiences in the client's life which might have led to doubt about themselves in terms of their gender, and their sexuality.

Affirming the gender, the sexuality and the sexual orientation of the client when this is appropriate, where it is genuinely felt, and where it seems helpful to the client's self-image, while not holding out the promise of a special relationship.

Observing and accepting the anger and frustration that may be expressed that the therapist cannot be a friend or a special person; linking in perhaps with the distant, unattainable or rejecting parent figure.

Remembering the partner of a client: encouraging signs of concern for the partner's difficulties, or adjustments to the relationship where the client makes significant progress through the therapy.

Considering the possibility of a client working with a therapist or counsellor of the opposite gender after working with the present therapist, especially where this may help provide a corrective experience for a client now strong enough to tolerate the anxiety of the feared gender.

(d) Indications of more mature development and possible aims in therapy and counselling in relation to cooperation and competition

Growing sense of integration, within the self, with others including people who are different, and with the external environment.

Friendships and other relationships free from sexual anxieties (aim-inhibited love).

Detachment from parents to be able to make independent choice of an intimate partner, not too influenced by the relationship with parents (especially by negative factors).

Internalization of positive qualities of parents and significant others, including the therapist.

Firm foundation for sexual identity, both in respect of predominant sexual orientation, but also the ability to accept bisexual aspects of the self.

Acceptance of physical and genital differences without fear or envy.

Comfortable with both (supposed) masculine and feminine traits within the self.

Ability, where the client wishes it, to make an intimate relationship with a partner, to bring sexual, affectionate, caring and other feelings together.

Where a client wishes to be single, to feel confident with this status, finding appropriate expression for different feelings, perhaps in sublimated form.

As parents, to be able to accept and respond appropriately to a child's sexuality and love, not crushing it, not colluding with the child against the partner.

Sharing and cooperating with others, in the family, peer group, in mixed gender groups, etc.

Valuing the complementarity of the other in a relationship, as extending the capabilities of the self.

Engagement in teams or small groups at work, recognizing own and others' particular strengths and abilities.

Ability to compete in genuinely competitive situations, without guilt at succeeding or undue anger/shame/depression at not succeeding.

Growing sense of being able to integrate different experiences.

BIBLIOGRAPHY

Abraham, K. (1927) *Selected Papers*. London: Hogarth Press.

Adler, S. (1922) *Understanding Human Nature*. Oxford: One World.

Alexander, F. and French, T. M. (1946) *Psychoanalytic Therapy*. New York: Ronald Press.

Anzieu, D. (1984) *The Group and the Unconscious*. London: Routledge and Kegan Paul.

Auden, W. H. (1976) *Collected Poems* (ed. E. Mendelson). London: Faber & Faber.

Balint, M. (1968) *The Basic Fault*. London: Tavistock Publications.

Bancroft, J. (1983) *Human Sexuality and Its Problems*. Edinburgh: Churchill Livingstone.

Becker, E. (1972) *The Birth and Death of Meaning*. London: Penguin Books.

Belotti, E. (1975) *Little Girls*. London: Writers and Readers Publishing Co-operative.

Berne, E. (1968) *Games People Play*. London: Penguin.

Bettelheim, B. (1978) *The Uses of Enchantment: the Meaning and Importance of Fairy Tales*. London: Penguin Books.

Bettelheim, B. (1983) *Freud and Man's Soul*. London: Chatto and Windus/Hogarth Press.

Bowlby, J. (1947) *Child Care and the Growth of Love*. London: Penguin.

Bowlby, J. (1969, 1973, 1980) *Attachment and Loss*, vols I, II and III. London: Hogarth Press.

Breen, D. (1989) *Talking with Mothers*. London: Free Association Books.

Broucek, F. J. (1982) Shame and its relationship to early narcissistic developments. *International Journal of Psycho-Analysis*, 63: 369.

Burck, C. and Speed, B. (eds) (1995) *Gender, Power and Relationships*. London: Routledge.

Burman, E. (1994) *Deconstructing Developmental Psychology*. London: Routledge.

Byatt, A. S. (1990) *Possession*. London: Chatto and Windus.

Carroll, M. (1996) *Workplace Counselling*. London: Sage Publications.

Carroll, M. and Watton, M. (1997) *Handbook of Counselling in Organisations*. London: Sage Publications.

Case, R. (1978) When birth is also a funeral. *Journal of Pastoral Care* (USA), 32: 1.

Casement, P. (1985) *On Learning from the Patient*. London: Tavistock.

Chessick, R. D. (1983) Mental health and the care of the soul in mid-life. *Journal of Pastoral Care* (USA), 37: 5–12.

Chodorow, N. (1978) *The Reproduction of Mothering.* London: University of California Press.

Chodorow, N. (1989) *Feminism and Psychoanalytic Theory.* New Haven and London: Yale University Press.

Chodorow, N. (1994) *Masculinities, Feminities, Sexualities.* London: Free Association Books.

Clulow, C. (ed.) (1996) *Women, Men and Marriage.* New York: Jason Aronson.

Collick, E. (1986) *Through Grief: Bereavement Journey.* London: Darton, Longman and Todd.

Davies, D. and Neal, C. (eds) (1996) *Pink Therapy.* Buckingham: Open University Press.

Davies, D. and Neal, C. (eds) (in press) *Theoretical Issues in Pink Therapy* (working title). Buckingham: Open University Press.

Davies, J. M. and Frawley, M. G. (1994) *Treating the Adult Survivor of Childhood Sexual Abuse.* New York: Basic Books.

Dinnerstein, D. (1978) *The Rocking of the Cradle and the Ruling of the World.* London: Souvenir Press.

Dominian, J. (1980) *Marital Pathology.* London: Darton, Longman and Todd.

Dunne, J. S. (1979) *Time and Myth.* London: SCM Press.

Erikson, E. (1965) *Childhood and Society.* London: Penguin Books.

Erikson, E. (1968) *Identity, Youth and Crisis.* London: Faber.

Erikson, E. (1978) *Toys and Reasons.* London: Marion Boyars.

Fairbairn, W. R. D. (1952) *Psychoanalytic Studies of the Personality.* London: Tavistock/Routledge.

Fenichel, O. (1946) *The Psychoanalytical Theory of Neurosis.* London: Routledge and Kegan Paul.

Flanders, S. (1993) *The Dream Discourse Today.* London: Routledge.

Fowler, J. W. (1981) *Stages of Faith: the Psychology of Human Development and the Quest for Meaning.* New York: Harper and Row.

Freud, A. (1973) *Normality and Pathology in Childhood.* London: Penguin Books.

Freud, S. (1900) *The Interpretation of Dreams.* Penguin Freud Library, volume 4. London: Penguin Books.

Freud, S. (1901) *The Psychopathology of Everyday Life.* Penguin Freud Library, volume 5. London: Penguin Books.

Freud, S. (1905) *Three Essays on the Theory of Sexuality.* Penguin Freud Library, volume 7. London: Penguin Books.

Freud, S. (1907) *Obsessive Actions and Religious Practices.* Penguin Freud Library, volume 13. London: Penguin Books.

Freud, S. (1908) *'Civilized' Sexual Morality and Modern Nervous Illness.* Penguin Freud Library, volume 12. London: Penguin Books.

Freud, S. (1913) *On Beginning the Treatment.* Standard Edition, volume XII. London: Hogarth Press.

Freud, S. (1917) *Mourning and Melancholia.* Penguin Freud Library, volume 11. London: Penguin Books.

Freud, S. (1923) *The Ego and the Id.* Penguin Freud Library, volume 11. London: Penguin Books.

Freud, S. (1925a) *An Autobiographical Study.* Penguin Freud Library, volume 15. London: Penguin Books.

Freud, S. (1925b) *Some Psychical Consequences of the Anatomical Distinction between the Sexes.* Penguin Freud Library, volume 7. London: Penguin Books.

Freud, S. (1927) *The Future of an Illusion.* Penguin Freud Library, volume 12. London: Penguin Books.

Freud, S. (1931) *Female Sexuality.* Penguin Freud Library, volume 7. London: Penguin Books.

Freud, S. (1933) *New Introductory Lectures on Psychoanalysis.* Penguin Freud Library, volume 2. London: Penguin Books.

Freud, S. (1937a) *Analysis Terminable and Interminable.* Standard Edition, volume XXIII. London: Hogarth Press.

Freud, S. (1937b) *Constructions in Analysis.* Standard Edition, volume XXIII. London: Hogarth Press.

Freud, S. and Breuer, J. (1895) *Studies on Hysteria.* Penguin Freud Library, volume 3. London: Penguin Books.

Gilligan, C. (1982) *In a Different Voice.* Cambridge, MA: Harvard University Press.

Golan, N. (1981) *Passing Through Transitions.* London: Collier Macmillan.

Greenson, R. R. (1967) *The Technique and Practice of Psychoanalysis.* London: Hogarth Press.

Greenwood, A. (in press) *Workplace Counselling.* Buckingham: Open University Press.

Guntrip, H. (1961) *Personality Structure and Human Interaction.* London: Hogarth Press.

Guntrip, H. (1968) *Schizoid Phenomena, Object Relations and the Self.* London: Hogarth Press.

Haines, D. G. (1978) Paths and companions. *Journal of Pastoral Care* (USA), 31:1.

Hartung, B. (1979) The capacity to enter latency in learning pastoral psychotherapy. *Journal of Supervision and Training in Ministry* (USA), 2: 46–59.

Heimann, P. and Valenstein, A. (1972) The psychoanalytical concept of aggression: an integrated summary. *International Journal of Psycho-Analysis*, 53: 31.

Hunter, M. (1983) Personal communication.

Jacobs, J. L. (1994) *Victimized Daughters: Incest and the Development of the Female Self.* London: Routledge.

Jacobs, M. (1976) Naming and labelling. *Contact: Interdisciplinary Journal of Pastoral Studies*, 1976: 2–8.

Jacobs, M. (1982) *Still Small Voice.* London: SPCK.

Jacobs, M. (1988) *Psychodynamic Counselling in Action.* London: Sage Publications.

Jacobs, M. (1991) The therapist's revenge: the law of talion as a motive for caring. *Contact: Interdisciplinary Journal of Pastoral Studies*, 105: 2–11.

Jacobs, M. (1992) *Sigmund Freud.* London: Sage Publications.

Jacobs, M. (1993a) *Living Illusions.* London: SPCK.

Jacobs, M. (1993b) *Still Small Voice* (2nd edition). London: SPCK.

Joffe, W. G. (1969) A critical review of the status of the envy concept. *International Journal of Psycho-Analysis*, 50: 533.

Jung, C. G. (1953) *Two Essays on Analytical Psychology.* London: Routledge and Kegan Paul.

Kirkley-Best, E. *et al.* (1982) On stillbirth: an open letter to the clergy. *Journal of Pastoral Care* (USA), 36: 1.

Klein, J. (1987) *Our Need for Others and Its Roots in Infancy.* London: Tavistock/Routledge.

Klein, M. (1957) *Envy and Gratitude.* London: Tavistock.

Klein, M. (1963) On the sense of loneliness. In M. Klein (1975) *Envy and Gratitude and Other Works 1946–1963.* London: Hogarth Press.

Klein, M. (1975) *Envy and Gratitude and Other Works 1946–1963.* London: Hogarth Press.

Kohlberg, L. (1981) *The Philosophy of Moral Development*. San Francisco: Harper and Row.

Kohut, H. (1971) *The Analysis of the Self*. London: Hogarth Press.

Kohut, H. (1977) *The Restoration of the Self*. International Universities Press.

Kubler-Ross, E. (1969) *On Death and Dying*. London: Tavistock Publications.

Lago, C. (1996) *Race, Culture and Counselling*. Buckingham: Open University Press.

Laing, R. D. (1967) *The Politics of Experience and the Bird of Paradise*. London: Penguin.

Laufer, M. (1974) *Adolescent Disturbance and Breakdown*. London: Penguin Books.

Le Carré, J. (1974) *Tinker, Tailor, Soldier, Spy*. London: Hodder and Stoughton.

Lechte, J. (1994) *Fifty Key Contemporary Thinkers*. London: Routledge.

Le Guin, U. (1971) *A Wizard of Earthsea*. London: Penguin Books.

Lendrum, S. and Syme, G. (1992) *Gift of Tears*. London: Routledge.

Levinson, D. J., Darrow, D. N., Klein, E. B., Levinson, M. H. and McKee, B. (1978) *The Seasons of a Man's Life*. New York: A. Knopf.

Lewes, K. (1988) *The Psychoanalytic Theory of Male Homosexuality*. New York: Simon and Schuster.

Lewis, C. S. (1971) *A Grief Observed*. London: Faber Paperbacks.

Lieblum, S. and Rosen, R. (1989) *Principles and Practice of Sex Therapy*. New York: Guilford Press.

Little, M. (1990) *Psychotic Anxieties and Containment: A Personal Record of an Analysis with Winnicott*. Northvale, NJ: Jason Aronson.

Lowe, G. (1972) *The Growth of Personality*. London: Penguin Books.

Macquarrie, J. (1966) *Principles of Christian Theology*. London: SCM Press.

Maguire, M. (1995) *Men, Women, Passion and Power*. London: Routledge.

Malan, D. H. (1979) *Individual Psychotherapy and the Science of Psychodynamics*. London: Butterworth.

Marcia, J. E. (1975) Development and validation of ego-identity status. In R.W. Muuss (ed.) *Adolescent Behavior and Society*. New York: Random House.

Masson, J. M. (1984) *The Assault on Truth: Freud's Suppression of the Seduction Theory*. London: Faber and Faber.

Masson, J. M. (ed.) (1985) *The Complete Letters of Sigmund Freud to Wilhelm Fliess*. Cambridge, MA: Belknap Press of Harvard University Press.

Miller, A. (1979) Depression and grandiosity as related forms of narcissistic disturbance. *International Review of Psychoanalysis*, 6: 72.

Mitchell, K. (1982) A death and a community. *Journal of Pastoral Care* (USA), 36: 1.

Mohamed, C. and Smith, R. (1997) Time-limited psychotherapy. In M. Lawrence and M. Maguire (eds) *Psychotherapy with Women: Feminist Perspectives*. London: Routledge.

Mollon, P. (1996) *Multiple Selves, Multiple Voices: Working with Trauma, Violation and Dissociation*. Chichester: John Wiley.

Munroe, R. L. and Munroe, R. H. (1975) *Cross-Cultural Human Development*. New York: Jason Aronson.

Mussen, P., Conger, J. and Kagan, J. (1969) *Child Development and Personality* (2nd edition). New York: Harper and Row.

Neal, C. and Davies, D. (eds) (in press) *Further Client Issues in Pink Therapy* (working title). Buckingham: Open University Press.

Neubauer, P. B. (ed.) (1965) *Children in Collectives: Child-rearing Aims and Practices in the Kibbutz*. Springfield, IL: Charles C. Thomas.

Obholzer, A. (ed.) (1994) *The Unconscious at Work: Individual and Organizational Stress in the Human*. London: Routledge.

O'Connor, N. and Ryan, J. (1993) *Wild Desires and Mistaken Identities: Lesbianism and Psychoanalysis*. London: Virago Press.

Parkes, C. Murray (1986) *Bereavement* (2nd edition). London: Tavistock.

Parkes, C. Murray, Stevenson-Hinde, J. and Marris, P. (eds) (1991) *Attachment Across the Life Cycle*. London: Routledge.

Pedersen, P. B. (1994) *A Handbook for Developing Multicultural Awareness*. Alexandria, VA: American Counseling Association.

Piaget, J. (1950) *The Psychology of Intelligence*. London: Routledge and Kegan Paul.

Prins, H. A. (1975) A danger to themselves and others (social workers and potentially dangerous clients). *British Journal of Social Work*, 5: 297–309.

Prins, H. A. (1995) *Offenders, Deviants or Patients?* (2nd edition). London: Routledge.

Prodgers, A. (1991) On hating the patient. *British Journal of Psychotherapy*, 8: 144–54.

Quinodoz, J.-M. (1993) *The Taming of Solitude*. London: Routledge.

Raphael, B. (1984) *The Anatomy of Bereavement*. London: Hutchinson.

Ratigan, B. (1996) Working with older gay men. In D. Davies and C. Neal (eds) *Pink Therapy*. Buckingham: Open University Press.

Rayner, E. (1978) *Human Development* (2nd edition). London: George Allen and Unwin.

Rayner, E. (1986) *Human Development* (3rd edition). London: Allen and Unwin.

Rey, J. H. (1988) Schizoid phenomena in the borderline. In E. Bott Spillius (ed.) *Melanie Klein Today. Volume 1: Mainly Theory*. London: Routledge.

Rosen, I. (1979) *Sexual Deviation*. Oxford: Oxford University Press.

Rubins, J. L. (1978) *Karen Horney*. London: Weidenfeld and Nicolson.

Rudnytsky, P. L. (1991) *The Psychoanalytic Vocation: Rank, Winnicott and the Legacy of Freud*. London: Yale University Press.

Rushdie, S. (1990) *Haroun and the Sea of Stories*. London: Granta Books.

Rycroft, C. (1972) *A Critical Dictionary of Psychoanalysis*. London: Penguin.

Ryle, A. (1973) *Student Casualties*. London: Penguin.

Sachs, H. (1948) *Masks of Love and Life*. Cambridge, MA: Sci-Art Publishers.

Samuels, A. (ed.) (1985) *The Father: Contemporary Jungian Perspectives*. London: Free Association Books.

Samuels, A. (1993) *The Political Psyche*. London: Routledge.

Scharff, D. and Scharff, J. (1994) *Object Relations Therapy of Physical and Sexual Trauma*. London: Jason Aronson.

Scharff, D. E. (1988) *The Sexual Relationship: an Object Relations View of Sex and the Family*. London: Routledge.

Schwartz, R. S. (1989) A psychiatrist's view of transference and countertransference in the pastoral relationship. *Journal of Pastoral Care* (USA), 43: 41–6.

Searles, H. (1965a) Oedipal love in the countertransference. In H. Searles, *Collected Papers on Schizophrenia and Related Subjects*. London: Hogarth Press.

Searles, H. (1965b) Problems of psycho-analytic supervision. In H. Searles, *Collected Papers on Schizophrenia and Related Subjects*. London: Karnac Books.

Segal, H. (1973) *Introduction to the Work of Melanie Klein*. London: Hogarth Press.

Segal, J. (1992) *Melanie Klein*. London: Sage Publications.

Seidler, V. (1991) *Recreating Sexual Politics*. London: Routledge.

Sendak, M. (1970) *Where the Wild Things Are*. London: Penguin Books.

Siegel, A. M. (1996) *Heinz Kohut and the Psychology of the Self*. London: Routledge.

Sills, C. (ed.) (1997) *Contracts in Counselling*. London: Sage Publications.

Simon, G. (1996) Working with people in relationships. In D. Davies and C. Neal (eds) *Pink Therapy*. Buckingham: Open University Press.

Skynner, R. and Cleese, J. (1983) *Families: and How to Survive Them*. London: Methuen.

Smith, D. L. (1991) *Hidden Conversations – an Introduction to Communicative Psychoanalysis.* London: Routledge.

Speck, P. (1978) *Loss and Grief in Medicine.* London: Balliere Tindall.

Stern, D. (1985) *The Interpersonal World of the Infant: a View from Psychoanalysis and Development Psychology.* New York: Basic Books.

Storr, A. (1979) *The Art of Psychotherapy.* London: Secker and Warburg.

Storr, A. (1989) *Solitude.* Glasgow: Fontana Paperbacks.

Sugarman, L. (1986) *Life-Span Development: Concepts, Theories and Interventions.* London: Routledge.

Sullivan, E. M. (in press) *Unconscious Communication in Practice.* Buckingham: Open University Press.

Thomas, D. M. (1981) *The White Hotel.* London: Gollancz.

Thompson, F. (1973) *Lark Rise to Candleford.* London: Penguin Books.

Thurber, J. (1962) *The Thirteen Clocks.* London: Penguin Books.

Walker, M. (1990) *Women in Therapy and Counselling.* Buckingham: Open University Press.

Walker, M. (1992) *Surviving Secrets: the Experience of Abuse for the Child, the Adult and the Helper.* Buckingham: Open University Press.

Walker, M. and Antony-Black, J. (eds) (in press) *Hidden Selves: an Exploration of Multiple Personality.* Buckingham: Open University Press.

Weatherhead, L. (1963) *Psychology, Religion and Healing* (2nd edition). London: Hodder and Stoughton.

Winnicott, D. W. (1964) *The Child, the Family and the Outside World.* London: Penguin Books.

Winnicott, D. W. (1965a) *The Family and Individual Development.* London: Tavistock Publications.

Winnicott, D. W. (1965b) *The Maturational Processes and the Facilitating Environment.* London: Hogarth Press.

Winnicott, D. W. (1971) *Playing and Reality.* London: Routledge.

Winnicott, D. W. (1975) *Collected Papers: Through Paediatrics to Psychoanalysis.* London: Tavistock Publications.

Winnicott, D. W. (1986) *Home Is Where We Start From.* London: Penguin Books.

Winnicott, D. W. (1988a) *Babies and Their Mothers.* London: Free Association Books.

Winnicott, D. W. (1988b) *Human Nature.* London: Free Association Books.

Winnicott, D.W (1989) *Holding and Interpretation: Fragment of an Analysis.* London: Karnac Books.

Wolff, H. (1977) Loss: a central theme in psychotherapy. *British Journal of Psychology,* 50: 11–19.

Worden, J. W. (1983) *Grief Counselling and Grief Therapy.* London: Tavistock.

Worden, J. W. (1991) *Grief Counselling and Grief Therapy* (2nd edition). London: Tavistock.

Zohar, D. (1991) *The Quantum Self.* London: Harper Collins.

INDEX